Disputable Decisions in Special Education

Disputable Decisions in Special Education

William M. Cruickshank

The University of Michigan Press
Ann Arbor

Copyright © by the University of Michigan 1986
All rights reserved
Published in the United States of America by
The University of Michigan Press and simultaneously
in Rexdale, Canada, by John Wiley & Sons Canada, Limited
Manufactured in the United States of America

1989   1988   1987   1986   4   3   2   1

Library of Congress Cataloging-in-Publication Data

Cruickshank, William M.
  Disputable decisions in special education.

  Bibliography: p.
  Includes index.
  1. Exceptional children—Education—United States.
I. Title.
LC3981.C78   1986   371.9'0973   86-4371
ISBN 0-472-10077-7 (alk. paper)

Hopefully, Jason, aged 17; Jon, aged 13; Jill, aged 13; Emily, aged 11; Naomi, aged 5; and Devin, aged 1, will not have to dispute inappropriate decisions as they reach their majority.

Preface

Why did I write this book? Probably more than one person will ask this question. For a number of years I have felt a need to speak out on certain matters relating to the field of special education on which I hold strong feelings. There has been for me a growing need to speak out as an individual on those things in which I believe, not as a member of a committee nor as a representative of an organization (e.g., chaps. 9, 10, 11, and 12), but for myself.

Second, I see some pressing problems in work with physically and mentally disabled individuals that must be addressed in a manner not currently in vogue in the United States, and I have devoted chapters 6, 7, and 8 to this end. Obviously there is some overlapping among the reasons for my writing here, but the primary purposes related to various chapters are being indicated.

Advocacy and greater understanding of the nature and needs of exceptional individuals constitute a third reason for writing these disparate pieces, and this issue is reflected in chapters 2, 3, and 4.

Fourth is intelligent anger as a motivational issue. I am angry with such concepts as noncategorical education (chap. 7), and I am angry that psychologists do such a poor job in assessing children with little or no reflection of their observations and data to classroom teachers (chap. 6). ⚹ p 84

Fifth, I am concerned that not all of the life needs of handicapped persons are being met, even though special education in the United States is about two hundred years old. These feelings are reflected in chapter 9 and particularly in chapter 12, but these thoughts appear at times throughout the entire script.

Finally, I have a deep respect and love for my former students. Many of them are close to me and to my family, and over the years our feelings have become solid and mutual—a two-way street. Their children are often almost our children; their families, our families. I hope this feeling tone is apparent in chapter 13 and elsewhere as the reader explores the volume.

Since I am writing alone in this volume, I do not have to protect the feelings of coauthors. As a result I have come down hard on those things that I feel are inequities and that constitute hurdles to good adjustment for exceptional children and youth (Cruickshank 1985). I know in advance that not all will agree with me, but if a small percentage of what I say here were placed in operation immediately, life for handicapped persons would in reflections be better at once. Reviewers will have a heyday with this volume unless they are serious and realize the essential honesty of what I have written. Reviews mean little to me, however, unless they are truly constructive. One person's point of view is no greater or lesser than that of the author's own. But, readers, take note. Special education for what it is, is the essential responsibility of those of us in the profession. If it is good, we can take credit for it; if mediocre, it is our responsibility also.

The chapters do not necessarily hang together. This was not my intention. They are not sequential but topical. They were written as individual essays on individual topics with which I was concerned at the time of writing. I have suggested that not all will agree with what I write, but that is not news or unusual in my experience. I am not embarrassed by controversy, nor have I ever avoided it. I also do not necessarily advocate differences of opinion for the mere sake of dispute, for often these can be a mechanism to weaken a program. I am determined that quality and standards so high as to be painful in their maintenance be achieved in special education. We do not have this now. To the end of quality and high standards this book is dedicated, and to this end students of mine and of others are challenged.

Different than with other books of which I have been a part, there is no foreword to this volume. I want the book to stand on its own as "my beliefs." I want no one to have to defend points of view I have expressed or feel he must disagree with opinions in opposition to his own. I have come down hard on some things that are going on in special education, and with which I thoroughly disagree. There will be criticism of what I have written. Fortunately in a scholarly democracy as is represented in the United States, personal opinions differing from those of others are permitted. If argument results from what is written here, I welcome that, for in honest dialogue advances in understanding and concepts are achieved. Thousands of students and an equal number of disabled children and youth with whom I have had almost daily intimate contact—a privilege not given to many—have helped to form the warp and woof of the essays contained here. I am grateful to every one of them; the long lines of both continue to march to me and with me. Almost every day brings another student with a problem to solve, a parent's telephone call to seek aid for his child, or a handicapped child or youth or adult hoping in some manner for the alleviation of his or her problem. How can being a professor under these circumstances be a dull existence? The latest in this procession was a graduate student in one of my classes who at the close of the first session stopped me as I was leaving the room, and quietly told me she had epilepsy that was not fully controlled. Here is a new challenge between the professor, the student, and the balance of those in the class.

I feel lucky to have been and to continue to be a professor. It is a tremendous responsibility and often a tiring one. But it is rewarding. To those students to whom as I say in chapter 13, "this is what it's all about," I hope the book repays their contributions to my life and that of my family.

There is some humor in connection with the writing of this book. My students know that much of my writing has been done between planes in airport terminals! This set of essays has had a more varied history. They have been created in numerous places. Delta and Republic airlines between Detroit and New Orleans during one year were the settings for several. An elderly lady sitting next to me on one trip said, "Are you writing a book?" When I replied affirmatively, she said, "Oh, I never knew anyone who wrote a book. How do you do it?" My room in the University of Michigan Hospital was the birthplace of another chapter while I was convalescing from a heart attack; this, the writing, somewhat to the consternation of the physicians. The SS *Stattendam* cruising up the inside passage to Glacier Bay in Alaska saw another chapter take form. The Canadian VIA Trains No. 1 and No. 2 between Toronto and Vancouver provided the writing setting for two more chapters. My Ann Arbor university and home offices produced others, and a typewriter on my lap on planes between Detroit and New York City finished off the job. Does this sound like the traditional ivory tower in which professors are accused of isolating themselves? No, it is an allocentric life, the kind I wish for all my students, for as such it is a major way to approach and confront the realities of our profession.

Reference

Cruickshank, W. M. "Learning Disabilities: A Series of Challenges." *Learning Disabilities: Focus* 1, no. 1 (1985): 5–8.

Acknowledgments

Regardless of authorship, the preparation and publication of a book is a team effort. To three young people, Marc, Jon, and Donna, in the chapter on gifted youth, I owe much for their honest and forthright replies to my often personal questions. Maureen Fleming, then an undergraduate student at the University of Michigan with extraordinary editing talents and experience on the *Michigan Daily,* gave me much assistance in editing the initial manuscripts. My secretary, Madeline Groshans, practically married the word processing computer as original manuscripts and revision after revision flowed in and out of those machines. I am in the debt of these two persons.

Permission from publishers and individuals to quote from materials is gratefully acknowledged. The Associated Press Newsfeatures allowed me to reprint the article that appears at the beginning of chapter 1 and originally appeared, among other places, in the *Denver Post,* July 5, 1982.

Prentice-Hall, Inc., permitted the reprinting of the figure (used in chap. 12) from *Psychology of Exceptional Children and Youth,* 4th ed., edited by me. Copyright © 1980, pp. 346–47. Reprinted by permission.

Random House, Inc., allowed me to reprint numerous selections from *The Basic Works of Cicero,* edited by Moses Hadas, Copyright © 1951. Isolated words and phrases from the original basic works are translations by me.

I also thank Dr. Steven Russell for his permission to quote material pertaining to single-subject research found in chapter 6, from his study entitled *The Syntactic and Pragmatic Oral Language Production of Normal and Learning Disabled Children: A Single-Subject Approach.* Ph.D. dissertation, University of Michigan, 1984.

The quotes from Aristotle are taken from *The Pocket Aristotle,* J. D. Kaplan, editor. New York: Pocket Library, Pocket Books, 1958.

Contents

Arizona Quadriplegic Denied Marriage in Catholic Church

Associated Press

PHOENIX, Ariz.—The Roman Catholic Diocese of Phoenix has refused to marry a couple because the man is a quadriplegic unable to consummate the union, the church says.

Jose Sosa, 28, and his fiancee, Barbara Albillar, 23, both of Mesa, are Catholics who want a church wedding. Sosa said the diocese's decision was a shock to both of them.

Sosa said he didn't understand the church's decision and "I never thought there would be this sort of trouble."

"But just before we went to the priest about our marriage, I saw an article about a similar case. Then I began to think that something might come up about my disability."

Larry Bonvallet of Kankakee, Ill., after initial rebuffs in a publicized case, won approval for a Catholic wedding and was married in May. Church officials said they believed he might eventually be able to consummate the marriage.

Sosa injured his spine in a diving accident four years ago. He retains some use of his arms and hands, but is paralyzed from the chest down.

"I thought marriage was a unity of two people in love, respect and understanding," he said in an interview last week. "I guess from the church's perspective, marriage is just sex. I think they have love and lust confused."

The couple met with the Rev. John Giandelone at St. Mary's Church in Chandler, a suburb near Mesa. When the priest learned of Sosa's disability, he referred the case to the diocese's marriage tribunal, which turned down the couple's request.

Sosa and Miss Albillar plan to be married in October in a civil ceremony if they are denied a church wedding.

"Basically the church law is that in order for the Roman Catholic Church to recognize a sacramental marriage, it must be consummated," said the Rev. John Spaulding, chancellor of the diocese.

"As the canon law stands, a sacramental marriage cannot exclude children, is indissoluble and must be kept with total fidelity to the marriage partner," Spaulding said. "If one of these conditions is completely and utterly lacking, the church can't allow it. There is no sacramental marriage.

"This is really a sad situation and we want to do what we can, but a statement of the church is a statement of the church and it must be obeyed," he added.

Spaulding said there is no appeal beyond the tribunal and that Bishop Thomas O'Brien is aware of the case and has reviewed it.

Reprinted by permission: The *Denver Post,* July 5, 1982, p. 3A; permission from AP Newsfeatures, Associated Press, New York, New York.

Chapter 1

Introduction

Brown v. *Board of Education* (1954) brought to a head the rights of minority groups for an equal education in the schools of the United States. Since that time, and to a certain extent before 1954, the courts have been full of cases demanding equal rights for the handicapped. Some of these have been class action suits in federal district courts; others, cases brought initially before state courts. Concepts of minority rights, affirmative action, and respect for the disabled have become an integral part of the legal thought of Americans. The Equal Rights Amendment came close to passage and undoubtedly will pass in the reasonable future. Although it may not be implemented everywhere in the United States, minority groups have obtained the legal basis for equality and for accessibility to American life generally.

The action taken by a marriage tribunal against the legal rights of two people who desired to enter into marriage was a step backward, and was undoubtedly illegal if the matter had been carried into the civil courts. The omnipotent attitude expressed in this action as reported in the newspaper is one that thoughtful people cannot tolerate. It is characteristic of medieval thinking long since not in vogue in the United States. It is a shocking story of discrimination upon first reading, and it becomes more so as one thinks about its implications. That one person or a small committee of individuals has the presumption to act in the manner reported is contrary to everything we have been teaching regarding the rights of the handicapped for the past several decades. No wonder young people are leaving the churches in droves. The type of leadership reported herein is sufficient cause for many persons rightfully to mistrust the religious leadership of the church in question and to provoke a fear that such an attitude might be contagious and involve other sects as well. It does not express the point of view of this book, nor the philosophy of this author. The latter is more clearly stated and is more in harmony with current legal thought and attitudes toward rights of the handicapped in the area of human sexuality. At least a two-hundred-year gap exists between the quoted article and chapter 12 of this book.

There will be many who will not agree with the contents of this book. Certainly those who are members of the aforementioned marriage tribunal will have difficulties in accepting what I have written, as will some of my very close friends. The total field of education and life adjustment of the physically and mentally handicapped individuals has changed radically since World War II.

Regardless of one's personal attitudes toward two issues, deinstitutionalization, first, has literally closed some institutions for the individuals with retarded mental development and others who are emotionally ill. For still others, concepts of group homes in the communities, while not always accepted with favor by future neighbors, have returned thousands of institutionalized residents to community living. The November, 1985, decision of the U.S. Supreme Court undoubtedly settled this issue in favor of handicapped persons. Schools for the blind and for the deaf children—both public and private—have been radically changed insofar as their clientele is concerned. Instead of being schools for their original clinical populations, they are now more likely to be sheltered institutions for the severely and multiply handicapped children or adults. Children and youth pronounced educable have been placed in community-based—often neighborhood-placed—schools, often not even in self-contained classrooms. Literally hundreds of thousands of children and adults, formerly in residential schools and hospitals, have been returned to function at some level in their communities. Such is not to indicate that I as the author of this book necessarily agree with this position. This issue will be discussed more fully in later chapters. It is to state a major change in the direction of service provision, and it reflects to a very large degree on the contents of the newspaper article.

In general, one can state that no longer are the handicapped people of this nation hidden and sheltered from public view. The goal is the integration of this population of people into the prevailing current of American society. To accomplish this goal, as we shall see, has not always been easy, nor has it always been successful. Except for the questionable assurance that the public schools of the nation are providing fully equal programs of education to these children and youth, the plan has certainly swept the nation and is being implemented, ready or not. This book, second, is not solely about the pros and cons of mainstreaming. To a certain extent this issue will be treated.

There are numerous issues regarding handicapped children and youth about which the profession struggles, and it is to some of these I wish to turn my attention. My first contact with handicapped children took place in 1933. That is more than fifty years ago. While in no manner was I directly involved with these children at that early date, I did have contact with them, secondhand, through the person of a professor, Dr. F. E. Lord, with whom I worked as an undergraduate student. By 1938, five years later, I had made a career commitment and began, with a great deal of energy, to prepare myself for a career in this field. The opportunity of looking back over a half-century is a privilege, and it is with this advantage that I desire in this book to examine some of the conflicts and decisions that exist or have been made that in turn affect the lives of handicapped children and youth and their families.

I do not wish to make this book completely autobiographical, but in a sense self-references are bound to enter into some of the discussions. There will be statements and concepts with which many in the field will not agree. I have always espoused some unpopular ideas about special education, and I certainly retain that privilege now. I have no tolerance for less than quality; I do not believe that handicapped youth and their families deserve less. The ineffective programs of teacher preparation, research, and legislation that I have seen put into place I have not hesitated to criticize, and I will do so here when the occasion arises and when I believe that criticism may have the advantage of pushing the field into a more wholesome position professionally. There have been tragic experiences in special education over the decades I am considering, four of them in active participation in the field. We have some history about which the profession cannot be proud, and some of this extends into contemporary activities. We have, as perhaps in all fields where human beings are involved, some who have climbed over others to achieve their goals and in doing so have left a hurtful impression not only on individuals, but on the profession itself. Unfortunately, since many of these situations are the reflection of people who live, I will not personalize. The facts of the matters exist, however, and those involved must be aware of their roles, and probably are.

While there have been tragic experiences to which I will allude in this book, there have been good things happen too. Not all of these have been the result of special education. Indeed special education as a professional field cannot take credit for many if any of them. The field has been affected by those things that have gone on in related disciplines. For example the Salk vaccine has reduced poliomyelitis to negligible proportions. With the vaccine developed by Jonas Salk and verified by Salk's mentor, the world-famous epidemiologist of the University of Michigan School of Public Health, Dr. Thomas Francis, Jr., poliomyelitis, which used to be the dread and fear of almost every parent in the civilized world, is rarely spoken of as I write.

With the advent of the sulfa drugs and penicillin, osteomyelitis succumbed almost completely to the former and congenital lues to the latter. Both of these diseases were those that were represented in classes for orthopedically handicapped children as late as 1950. The great variety of medications developed in laboratories of many countries has reduced epilepsy, or at least placed it in a position of control, for many many children and youth. It still exists, but no way in the frequency of a few decades ago. Diabetes, still a dreaded disease, is less feared than it was due to the availability of insulin. This is not a generalization that can be made across the total disease entity, for infantile diabetes is still a factor in early mortality. But many youths live comfortable lives because of the available supply of insulin.

Not as great strides have been made in the field of mental retardation. Some issues have been curtailed, but these have usually been relatively esoteric diseases affecting only a small percentage of subjects. Kernicterus, with all of its potential severe neurological symptoms, can be controlled if discovered early enough, but the percentage of these children among those with mental retardation is miniscule. The great problems of genetic types of mental retardation (disrelated to environmental deprivation) have not yet been touched from the point of view of magnitude. Exogenous types of mental retardation resulting in perceptual processing deficits and severe learning problems seemingly have increased, although there are no adequate epidemiological studies to verify this. The presence of increasing numbers of these children throughout the civilized world leads professional people to this conclusion. The increased use of hard drugs among women who are pregnant has increased the incidence of a variety of birth-related injuries and diseases, e.g., mental retardation, cerebral palsy, deafness, blindness, and others. Caffeine, alcohol, and food additives, while conclusive data is not always available, may be related to certain of these factors. Soft drugs available without prescriptions may also play a significant role (Brackbill, McManus, and Woodward 1985). Whatever the cause or cure of some of the physical and mental conditions mentioned here, special education and its ancillary professions are the recipients of the children for long-term periods for training and education. Change in the demography of childhood illness, however, has been observed, and undoubtedly this will continue, hopefully for the better.

While some aspects of medicine have been active, particularly those related to public health and prevention, the fields of epidemiology, chemistry, and bioengineering have also been significant contributors to better lives for the handicapped. Likewise, the professions related to psychology, particularly neuropsychology, have made great strides in understanding the issues of perception, learning, sensation, memory, and biological intelligence. While these learnings have not become universally accepted by the profession, more and more young psychologists are aware and are in a position to be of major assistance to special educators as appropriate educational regimens are developed for children and youth with neurophysiological impairments. There are sufficient data available at the present time so that if trained personnel were available a corrective educational program for all cerebral-palsied children, for all those with learning disabilities, and for all those with other forms of neurophysiological dysfunctions could be established within twenty-four hours. This would assume not only the availability of personnel, but also unanimous agreement among the leadership in special education as to the most effective methods to use to accomplish the task. We have sufficient clinical information to be able to accomplish this job; it takes only persons of goodwill to put it to work in appropriate and effective ways.

Special education is not a new concept historically. Recently I was speaking in a midwestern state. Following the meeting a person came up to me and, thanking me for a presentation, said, "Isn't it wonderful to be in such a new and active field." When I commented, "Yes, it is wonderful, and has been so since about 1830, if not before," she turned away bewildered to say the least. It is not a new field and has not been so for more than a century and a half in the United States. There is a problem much more significant than mere history, however, that needs to be expressed. This is the issue of individuals who, some with data and most without, take opposing positions on significant problems to the end that children are not provided with first-class education. What are some of these crucial issues that have plagued the field since its inception?

1. The issue of the manual method of education of deaf children versus the oral method occupied the attention of educators for many many years, often in violent arguments in professional meetings and in print. Today this situation raises itself again in some-

thing called the "total method," which combines both the oral and the manual methods. I shall take no stand here on this matter. My position has been known for many years. The chaos that has been created for children and for parents in the inability of professional people to solve this issue has been great and tragic.

2. The definition of learning disabilities, or the lack of one, has grown in proportions that have become ludicrous. Canada is an exception to this statement as recently as 1982. The failure of sensible persons to look at the problem historically, to visualize the nature of learning disabilities as it is, and to match problems with educational techniques is beyond the capacity of many to understand. There has been a definition of learning disabilities since the mid-1930s, yet in the 1980s the problem is still argued. It is hard to withdraw from this scene and to remain patient when the outcome is so obvious and of such long-standing.

3. Related to the definitional issue in learning disabilities is the staggering fact related to the inability of some professional persons to set personality problems aside and to cooperate one with the other. In 1986 and for at least a decade preceding that date, there has been controversy in this professional field seemingly essentially motivated by power hunger and personal gain that has split the profession and has negated effective service to children. What in the name of conscience has been gained by this infantile behavior is hard to conceptualize. Nevertheless, it has existed and continues to exist today to the disadvantage of everyone who comes into contact with this contagion.

4. The controversy over the issues of special classes versus mainstreaming is among the more recent issues that have affected both teacher education in special education and the education of children in the public schools of the nation. I have written on this topic many times and have been misunderstood in so doing. I shall try again in one of the chapters that follows. The failure to reach solutions to the problem, however, has ripped apart good special education programs at both the college and the public school levels.

5. Later we shall speak to the problem of categorical versus noncategorical education and teacher education in special education, a conflict that currently characterizes the profession.

6. A further issue that may or may not be as important as some of the others, but has characterized this field for years, is whether or not teacher education should be based on the education of normal children and whether it should be centered at the graduate or undergraduate levels in colleges and universities.

7. A problem that is definitely outside of special education and psychology pertains to the dietary control of learning disabilities. The Feingold diet is undoubtedly the program that has caused the greatest amount of discussion, and in fact controversy. Dr. Feingold, a fine gentleman, died in 1981 with his advocacy of his diet still a matter of suspicion and question. His opinions rested essentially on clinical observations. Dr. C. Keith Connor's volume indicates the negative value of this diet for most learning disabilities children, but still additional laboratory experimentation is required. While educators are constantly bombarded by parents with questions regarding the validity of this approach to their children's problems, this issue is not within the province of special educators. Research from nutritionists, psychopharmacologists, and other noneducational disciplinary representatives must be undertaken to settle this issue.

8. Along with the Feingold diet other unproven approaches to the solution of dyslexia and other similar childhood problems have appeared on the professional scene. A technique advanced by Dr. Harold Levinson utilizes drops of motion sickness drugs in the ear as a technique of modifying the vestibular action and thus correcting the symptoms of dyslexia. It has not been demonstrated to be valid, but teachers are constantly asked for their opinions, and often give them without adequate data being available. Until rigorous research models are applied to Levinson's suggestions, I, among others, am approaching this panacea with extreme caution.

9. Of long-standing is the controversy surrounding the Doman-Delacato method of "patterning" and supposed resultant "neurological reorganization." This issue, while still alive and without independent research corroboration, has become a somewhat lesser issue in the past few years. It is still controversial, however, and still needs to be subjected to careful and independent research. This approach would need study by an interdisciplinary team to be certain that all aspects of child development were fully covered, special education included.

10. There are those who see a one-to-one relationship between perceptual-motor training and acquisition of reading skills. At times I have been accused of this. Those who believe I support this notion are in error. It is a point of view, however, that exists within the professions, and it is one that needs careful research within the limitations discussed elsewhere in this volume.

11. Historically, although not such a great problem as this volume is being written, is the controversy that has existed for

many years regarding the efficacy of the residential school versus the community special education programs. This controversy has been settled essentially via the avenue of deinstitutionalization, but it still appears as significant to many special educators.

12. As I will later write, there is a continuing concern regarding the best manner in which to educate gifted children and youth, i.e., integration or mainstreaming versus a fully or partially established special class or special school.

13. Because so many unsolved issues swirl around and within the field of education of exceptional children, another bearing on those already mentioned also exists, namely, the issue of certification and preparation of teachers of these children. No university does an adequate job of preparing general educators to work with exceptional children, and now that mainstreaming has become a way of life in public schools the issue is much more serious. What special educators need in order adequately to instruct one or another type of exceptional child is controversial. This issue needs swift attention before more generations of these children are harmed. The concept of noncategorical education accentuates this problem and makes its solution even more pressing than in the past.

A baker's dozen of pressing problems, each impinging on the effective education of children with handicaps, has been listed. More could be added, including the occasional rash of persons who believe that mental retardation can be "cured" through hypnosis, or learning disabilities through the application of tinted lenses in glasses! The fact, however, that after such a long history these problems, or many of them, still continue to plague the field is tragic and detrimental to the best efforts of the best teachers to bring exceptional children to the maximum of their capacities.

Special education is all too frequently seen as a frill in public education. Parental vigilante committees must continually be active to see that programs for their children are not subject to the whims of budget officers attempting to pay for football instead of education for these children. With the advent of the Reagan administration, the United States has seen this become a national problem in a most dastardly manner. On whatsoever basis one compares educational efforts for the handicapped population of this nation, i.e., with the Department of Defense expenditures, a single battleship or submarine, with capitalistic expenditures involving the changing ecology of the nation, with highway construction, or at the local level with the school's athletic program, special education, often for deep-seated nonverbalized reasons, has rarely been given the same status as education for so-called normal children. Special education is not the only program to feel the edge of the axe, but in comparison with music programs, art, or some others that could be listed, special education is an absolute in the lives of a large percentage of children in any community. The conservative leadership of the Republican party in the United States, along with that of conservative foundations, is grossly in error, both in thought and action, when funds to reduce the effectiveness of education in any form are cut back or eliminated entirely.

Historical Overview

I have earlier made reference to a conversation I had with a member of an audience who believed that special education was a "new" field. This myth is completely false, although we must admit that since World War II, with the advent of new medications and operative and diagnostic procedures, the general community has become more aware of the educational programs available for these children. With the return of thousands of men from the wars who left home normal and returned handicapped, the concepts of physical disability and normalcy were tied together much more closely. "If John was normal when he went to war, he must still be now even though he has lost a leg," thought the members of the community who knew and still know him. He is no less a man. He is a physically disabled normal person. The alignment of disability with normalcy has been an important step forward in the acceptance by the total community of disabled persons in the United States. However, the war was not the beginning of work for the handicapped people of this nation or elsewhere. It was a significant implementer of additional efforts and more favorable attitudes toward them.

Educational activities for disabled persons in a very restricted sense of that term began more than one hundred fifty years ago in the United States. Albeit primitive and essentially custodial, residential schools for the blind, the mentally retarded, and the deaf were visible early in the history of this country. The earliest law on this subject affecting the midwestern states of the nation was passed in 1790 by the governor and judges of the Northwest Territory meeting in Cincinnati (specifically on November 7, 1790). This was an act that authorized the courts of the territory to divide the lands, reserving a portion of each governmental division for the future care and education of those with "any misfortune or inability." Facilities sponsored by the newly created states and by some religious organizations began to appear following this date.

The period for the next hundred years was one of founding, refinement, and agitation for the development of additional programs for varying types of physically and mentally disabled children and adults. This continued until about 1920 when the growth of cities was sufficient to permit local school boards upon pressure from parents to create their own special schools and classes, and thus to retain handicapped children within the home. It is interesting with the concept of deinstitutionalization that began in the mid-1960s, the issue has again come full circle. Immense institutions, particularly for the mentally handicapped, grew up in the period 1900–1965, some housing as many as six thousand residents. These institutions generally had very poor programs, and parents began agitation with the aid of the federal district courts to restrict their growth or to abolish them entirely. But this is getting ahead of chronology.

After 1920 a dual system for the care and education of the handicapped persons within the states was observable, namely, the state system of residential schools and the community special schools and classes. It is interesting that, save for hospital schools that were essentially private institutions, few special schools for crippled children were developed and practically no state residential schools. There were exceptions to this statement, i.e., the Widener School in Philadelphia, the Spaulding and Christopher schools in Chicago, Percy Hughes School in Syracuse, and others. For the most part, however, crippled children received a different type of educational approach than other forms of disability in children. This was the educational plan adopted by almost every state between 1920 and 1965.

As the concept of deinstitutionalization from residential schools began to take hold, a parallel concept of mainstreaming likewise began to be developed by the special education educators of the nation. Neither program had research on which to base its development, but a strong feeling tone was present. In large measure, these were reflections of the civil rights movement stimulated and reaching into most aspects of American life, by the Selma, Alabama, march led by the Reverend Martin Luther King and the spirit of Rosa Parks. The push was on to "normalize" education for handicapped children in America. This was soon followed by similar programs in many other countries of the world, often with the presumption that the program in the United States was based on proven research. None in reality existed—and still doesn't.

Thus, as this book is written one can see a variety of programs in effect throughout the country each in its own way attempting to solve the life needs of handicapped children and youth, namely, (1) the remnants of the residential school programs now essentially for multihandicapped and severely retarded residents, (2) some few special schools and classes in the community public schools, (3) programs of mainstreaming with disabled children integrated into the regular grades of the neighborhood schools, and (4) private schools in small numbers—both day schools and boarding schools—often serving only those with learning disabilities. Examples of these include the Pathway School, Jeffersonville, Pennsylvania; the Havern Center, Littleton, Colorado; the Pine Ridge School, Williston, Vermont; the Landmark School of Massachusetts; and a very small number of additional facilities that are deemed good.

Special education is not new, either in the public or the private domains. The New York Institution for the Education of the Blind is over one hundred fifty years old as this volume is written; Perkins School for the Blind of similar age. Public school programs are newer, but these go back for more than fifty years in the United States. A variety of educational programs has been tried, and undoubtedly others will be tried in the future or old ones reestablished. A single positive course has never been agreed upon.

This Book

I have listed numerous problems existing in special education. In preparing this volume, I have chosen to ignore some and expand on several. I have not made an attempt to be inclusive, nor to solve all of the problems of the special education world. I have selected those that in my estimation deserve immediate attention by the profession. I have also not attempted to give each problem on which I have written equal space. One, such as the issue of the growth process, has been mentioned, but has not been treated fully in the face of whole books that have been devoted to this problem. Another, namely, that of gifted and talented children and youth, has been accorded a significant amount of space, because it is such a neglected aspect of education in the schools of the whole nation. I have tried to make the discussion of each topic complete in that it contains the essential issues and is rounded out to a conclusion. Each could be expanded into book length. I have not attempted to be delicate in my comments, nor have I avoided statements I know will bring on criticism. If handled adequately, criticism is healthy, and I welcome impersonal, but constructive opposing comments. It appears to me that my positions on various issues raised in this book are logical and professionally accurate. It is with this position in mind that I have approached the writing of this book.

References and Related Readings

Adamson, W. C., and Adamson, K. K. *A Handbook for Specific Learning Disabilities*. New York: Gardner Press, 1979.

Brackbill, Y., McManus, K., and Woodward, L. *Medication in Maternity*. Ann Arbor: University of Michigan Press, 1985.

Connors, C. K. *Food Additives and Hyperactive Children*. New York: Plenum Press, 1980.

Cruickshank, W. M., ed. *Cerebral Palsy: A Developmental Disability*. 3d. ed. Syracuse: Syracuse University Press, 1979.

Keogh, B. K., Major-Kingsley, S., Omori-Gordon, H., and Reid, H. P. *A System of Marker Variables for the Field of Learning Disabilities*. Syracuse: Syracuse University Press, 1981.

Ochroch, R., ed. *The Diagnosis and Treatment of Minimal Brain Dysfunction in Children*. New York: Human Science Press, 1981.

Springer, N. S. *Nutrition Casebook on Developmental Disabilities*. Syracuse: Syracuse University Press, 1980.

Chapter 2

The Exceptional as a Minority Group

Minorities exist in many forms throughout the world. Save in certain very unusual situations—mostly of those connected with mythology—minority groups are viewed among the lower classes of society. As individuals or as a group, they almost universally possess differences that are unique to themselves. They are different from the majority. The differences may be of a physical nature (i.e., skin color, physical size, or body structure) or more subtle but equally as forceful and of a psychological, religious, economic, or political nature. In any case, those differences are shunned. In this chapter, I shall discuss physical or intellectual differences for the most part, but it is important to consider minorities of other dimensions by way of comparison.

Because of the historical relationship that has existed between white and black people in the United States and, more recently, in England, the problem of racial differences first comes to mind when the minority issue is raised. One need not repeat history in detail to recall slavery, the Civil War, and the terrible struggle in American courts to decree over the years a semblance of equality between the two races. More than a century after the Civil War, rather than seeing any resolution to the race problem, there is an increase in the numbers of minority groups demanding equality. The Hispanics have become active, as well as the Native Americans, Vietnamese, Haitians, Cubans, Hmong, Cambodians, and others.

But it must not be assumed that racial strife existed first between blacks and whites. When explorers landed in the Americas, native-born North and South Americans were labeled erroneously as Indians and were looked upon as a minority on the basis of their skin color, despite the fact that they far outnumbered the new arrivals. Again, in the early history of the United States and Canada, the Acadians were a minority that had to migrate in order to find social peace. The Cajuns of Louisiana are low in the social ladder except when their differences are exploited commercially as part of tourism. The Canadian Inuits form still another racial minority, although they antedate the English and the French settlers.

In some ways the argument of majority versus minority is logically inconsistent. For example, take the Native Americans. They far outnumbered the European settlers yet were conquered by them. If a majority is powerful, then Africans never would have allowed European traders to steal from them. Which comes to the point that there are two types of majority—physical and economic. Eastern Asia has the largest population in the world, yet these countries, with the exception of Japan and Taiwan, are characterized by starvation and poverty. Caucasian is a minority group but controls the wealth of the world. Europeans conquered because they had guns. It seems as if physical numbers do not matter. What matters is the quantity and quality of power, and that is controlled by wealth. The one consistency among those who rule is their wealth, whether in private economy or in governments. Consider the power of the United States in the United Nations and be reminded how powerful the defense industry is, as well as the multinational oil companies.

Majorities have always responded to minority infiltration with cruel and inappropriate stereotyping. A good example of this was the tension that existed when the Irish emigrated to America. The majority responded by discriminating against the émigrés in jobs, housing, in almost any form of human services. The result was violence.

To strengthen its position of superiority, white society, at best, invents cruel and often despicable terms to apply to minority groups (e.g., "spic," "kike," "nigger," "Jap," "Chink," among many others). At worst, it runs around in white sheets, lynching and burning, or it brings shotguns to "watch" a peaceful march for human rights. The Republic of South Africa in this regard belies its name "Republic."

There are two different kinds of majorities—population majority and economic majority. Unfortunately, the economic majority (those who control the money) comprise a population minority. But one thing we learn early, if nothing else, is which of these two groups wields the power—the economic majority. There is another element to this, but since I am not an anthropologist I discuss it superficially. However, consider the Native Americans and the early American settlers. The natives were a population majority, yet, were virtually obliterated by aggressive transplanted Europeans who had superior firepower. It seems that whoever has the gun is the majority, regardless of population percentages. That is a basic premise of imperialism. That is why the poor continue to be poor, and the learning disabled continue to be persecuted and shunned. This chapter will be better if this premise is integrated into it. Otherwise, there are too many paradoxical situations—how could Africans become slaves; why were native Americans obliterated; why are Orientals discriminated against?

Ultimately, minority groups take various forms of positive or protective action to subvert their suppression. Emotions reach a boiling point. Terrorism is a result, as in the case of the Palestinian Liberation Organization. Consider the horrors of minority struggle in Northern Ireland as this book is written. Closer to home, it is easy to recall the race riots of 1967 in Detroit, Michigan, when twelve hundred fires burned at one time in the city, when snipers shot from the freeway overpasses, looting took place, when blacks ruled for a few hours, and white Detroit was cowed.

Youth as a minority broke with the majority adult establishment in the late 1960s and early 1970s, and became identified as flower children, hippies, yippies—again with labels applied by the sacred majority. In India, the caste system is minority regimentation to the greatest degree—political and religious in combination—with the Untouchables at the bottom. This continues true even when legislation was passed elevating the Untouchable class. Often laws are many years ahead of the ingrained prejudices of a social structure that is based on the minority-majority principle.

In America, the Declaration of Independence states that all men are created equal. If the document were to be considered accurate today, though, it would have to be amended to state that all *white* men are created equal. Minorities still are discriminated against, as are women. In the 1950s, President Eisenhower ordered the military to accompany nine black youths up the steps of Central High School in Little Rock, Arkansas, so that those black students could receive a semblance of equality in education. It took the presence of the military to keep white men from physically blocking black adolescents from entering the school. That seemed unreal in America at the time, but the action was a political and social necessity.

The labor movement is a bloody history as worker, viewed as a minority, fought with owner, vis-à-vis, the beatings of Walter Reuther and his coworkers on the bridges of the Ford Motor Company property by bullies employed by Mr. Floyd Bennett. The majority conflict does exist between worker and employee, although employers can be defined as a majority only economically.

It is possible to carry the issue of minority conflict through an almost endless list of tragic situations and remembrances. Six million Jews were slaughtered by the Axis powers during World War II, the same war that saw Japanese-Americans put into concentration camps by the United States government. The controversies surrounding the busing of black and white children and youth outside their neighborhoods to establish racial equality were and continue to be a sociological farce in the face of "equality" of all humans.

If constitutional protections had been accepted by the majority of Americans, there would have been absolutely no reason for the lawsuits of the 1960s and 1970s (i.e., *Brown* v. *Board of Education* [1954], *Diana* v. *State Board of Education* [1970], *Covarrubias* v. *San Diego Board of Education* [1971], and *Arreola* v. *Board of Education* [1968] among dozens of others) that were required to try to enforce the constitutional guarantee of equality of opportunity. We in the United States and elsewhere still make a burlesque of the concept of equality. Minorities are with us still and unfortunately probably will bear the brunt of discrimination for decades.

My friends and I were cautioned, as children, against playing with Brian. "He's Catholic," whispered one child to another without knowing the meaning of Catholic. The incident leads one to suspect that prejudices are passed down from parent to child. Catholics and Jews were not permitted to join certain golf clubs and yacht clubs in the communities of my boyhood. The first black pupil to enter my high school was both an object of curiosity and hostility and did not remain there long as a pupil.

The Puritans of England, the Huguenots of France, the Lutherans of Germany, and other minority religious groups were the objects of violence by the Holy See representatives, the very persons who preached tolerance or, at least, should have. In modern day, the Hutterites of Saskatchewan have suffered. The Amish still must often sacrifice religious beliefs for the narrow interpretation of state educational laws and regulations. Look at the minority comprised of homosexuals and the rantings of Anita Bryant and bigoted religious spokespersons, which can cause otherwise significant human beings much psychological disturbance and distress.

There is a poignant and pathetic bumper sticker that appeared frequently in the early 1980s that said, "The Moral Majority Is Neither." A conservative religious conglomeration—the moral majority, a paradoxical minority in the United States—attempted to upset the majority, using techniques of threat, control of the media, political attack based on public religious themes, and other ignoble means. The 1980 congressional elections were characterized by upset victories of conservative Republicans, endorsed by the moral majority, over liberal, humanitarian incumbents. The methods used were ones that the majority, or even some thoughtful members of the minority groups, did not accept for very long. Hence, the appearance of the bumper stickers. Sarcasm, too, is an effective method of social control.

In the United States, the peculiarity of the electoral college system sometimes results in the fact that a minority government administers. The Republican party is a minority party, and often, this results in a minority government not representative of the majority of the citizens. The fact that only about one-third of U.S. citizens vote in elections is another indication of minority rule.

Minorities then represent a wide variety of different types of groups: religious, racial, political, economic, educational, and social, among others. In a democracy, political minorities can and do provide a vital force assuring openness in government. But social, economic, and racial minorities, although protected by fundamental laws of the land, remain oppressed and often must resort to the courts for protection. Even decisions in their favor by the Supreme Court do not necessarily result in acceptance or in the correction of wrongs on the part of the majority.

The Minority of Handicapped Persons

I come now to the issue of the handicapped, or disabled, as a minority group. Someone said to me once that there was only one minority group in which he could become an immediate member—the disabled. An accident or illness could change one's entire life. It happened to me. In a matter of a second, there was a loss of an eye, and I was thereafter known as a partially sighted individual! Fortunately, through prosthetics, the handicap is minimized and really is not very noticeable. Further, laws regarding this type of disability are liberal to the extent that I could pilot an airplane, if I so choose. But the disability, nevertheless, must be reported on some legal documents (i.e., a driver's license in some states), and this is discriminatory. It has been suggested that handicapped individuals comprise the largest minority group in the world. It is a unique minority in that it crosses all other minority groups—religious, economic, social, racial, etc.—and respects no single group.

For most people, handicapping conditions are also related negatively to other factors, such as fear, the end result of which is a greater isolation from society in general. For example, when poliomyelitis was at its height, it was feared as an ultracontagious disease. Thus polio victims became outcasts. Encephalitis is feared because of the brain damage it produces. Cerebral palsy often produces disfigurement, which repulses well-intended people. Amputations, visual defects such as "cross-eyedness" and prosthetic arms and legs result in curiosity, rejection, revulsion, or a variety of other emotions. A daughter faints when she visits her father in a hospital and sees the bandage over one eye, knowing that the eye no longer exists. Fear of what the father might subsequently look like, as well as empathy regarding the supposed pain, motivates the fainting behavior.

Multiminority status is a significant factor that has not received attention by sociologists or psychologists. Black people, for example, are often feared by whites because of color. Throughout history and in many religions, the color black has been conceptualized in a negative manner. Dark, evil nights, black witches, black cats, black comedy, the Black Death, are common in literature, music, and art. Negative connotations are doubly significant where race is combined with a disability. Multihandicapped white individuals, such as Helen Keller, are immortalized. However, black cerebral-palsied children have far greater difficulty in receiving equality of service than does the white child similarly handicapped. More black children than white are placed in classes for the mentally retarded via the technique of the supposedly impartial Individual Educational Planning Committees (IEPC), required under Public Law 92-142. White children of comparable characteristics are labeled "learning disabled" (Cruickshank, Morse, and Grant, ms.).

Black blind youth (except those with exceptional talent), black deaf children, black epileptic children, and others doubly handicapped all represent a minority within a minority, an issue that needs much attention in terms of the provision of necessary services and the development of positive social attitudes. One wonders, for example, how much support white America gives to research on sickle-cell anemia—a disease of the blacks. In some South American countries, there exists a high percentage of *mestizos*—people with mixed native and European parentage. Families may consist of a large number of children, all with different skin colors, ranging from very light to very dark. Unfortunately, the dark-skinned children frequently are less favored by their parents. A light-skinned second son often may take precedence in the eyes of his parents and relatives over a darker-skinned firstborn son. One day in a school for crippled children in Lima, Peru, I sat and talked with a twelve-year-old boy, who looked particularly sad. "Raul, what is the matter?" I asked. "Yo estoy negro," he responded. Indeed, he was very dark skinned, the darkest child in a family of seven. Rejection by Raul's parents complicated his acceptance as a crippled boy—a multihandicapped minority representative.

These two issues combined—racial color and disability—make the position of the minority member more difficult in almost all respects, a double-indemnity minority. Minorities, in general, and this multiminority group, in particular, represent the extremes of differences between individuals and illustrate how isolated people can be from the center of society, through no fault of their own.

Reasons for handicapping conditions are generally unknown to the population as a whole, and then, when a reason is given, it is often untrue. As such, handicaps are frequently associated, consciously or unconsciously, with disease, decay, disfigurement, and even death. These penetrating and unresolved emotions are causes for the psychological and social isolation of handicapped persons from the center of social thought and behavior. Even some educators of the handicapped, who have entered the profession of special education, express negative attitudes toward exceptional children based on the stereotype of the majority. "I couldn't work with the mentally retarded," says one. "That's true," says another, "but I couldn't possibly teach the cerebral-palsied either. They revolt me." Even the well-educated teacher is not ever powerful enough to effect change in social prejudice and in personal negative attitudes or emotions.

In contrast to many other minority groups, the handicapped is composed of a variety of subminorities, each often working in isolation and sometimes in opposition to others (e.g., the subgroups of the mentally retarded, the gifted, the learning disabled, the orthopedically handicapped, the visually, aurally, or emotionally impaired, ad infinitum). Organizations representing these subminority groups often fail to cooperate with one another. There are many mentally retarded, learning disabled children, for example. Yet because of an erroneous definition, there have been many instances where parents of mentally retarded, learning disabled children are not welcomed in parent associations for learning disabled children.

There are multiple organizations in the United States even within a single subminority group. For example, there exists the National Association for Retarded Citizens, the American Association on Mental Deficiency, the American Academy on Mental Retardation. Individuals often hold memberships in all three. The national Council for Exceptional Children also has its large division for mental retardation, as does the American Psychological Association. This proliferation of minority interest groups reduces the effectiveness of each in terms of social, economic, and political power. "Divide and conquer" is a reality in these cases. So-called charitable organizations that are dependent on public conscience represent almost every disability from cerebral palsy, learning disabilities, epilepsy, dyslexia, Reye's syndrome (all with neurological implications and dysfunction) to autism, childhood schizophrenia, delinquency, child abuse, and emotional disturbances (all related to mental health). Long-lasting social progress cannot be achieved in this fragmented manner. More than fifty different appeals for funds arrived in my mail prior to Christmas of 1985, some for the most esoteric of diseases. While all of these problems undoubtedly need attention, their multiplicity and appeal for the same available dollar means that most requests go directly into a wastebasket and contribute to extraordinary overhead costs, which are usually hidden from public view. Years ago, a man in red livery greeted all arrivals off the elevator of the then National Foundation for Infantile Paralysis and accompanied them to their desired office, located in expensive Wall Street real estate. It takes a large number of "dimes" to finance such irrelevant and unnecessary administrative frills. This is all a fundamental part of the problem of the extremely competitive subminority groups within a larger minority. Worse yet, even to get professional disciplinary groups together to deal with a basic definition of what is a learning disability is a gargantuan task. The results are frequently futile. Professional jealousies get in the way of helping those whom these groups profess to help.

When fears, unresolved emotions, and fallacious attitudes exist in the majority of society regarding the handicapped, overt hostility is often the result. We see this most clearly in terms of racial and political minorities and in large measure in human service priorities of the Nixon and Reagan presidential administrations and appointments. A Republican political minority makes decisions that affect all other minorities. This is an almost unreal situation. At the least, it is difficult to understand insofar as its motivation is concerned. Worse yet, the minority of handicapped persons bears the unfortunate brunt of thoughtless political decisions, which are rationalized on an economic basis. I see handicapped children and youth denied life-needed services as a result. I see college and university students deprived of scholarships and training grants that would make it possible for them to become experts in any one of many disciplines needed by handicapped persons. I see a diminution of all types of research basic to the alleviation or eradication of handicapping conditions. Political decisions are central to the further isolation of a minority from the core of modern society. Exceptional children are different from normal children. Costs to educate and repair damaged bodies are enormous. Decision makers cannot ignore these facts. Unfortunately, political, economic, and social majorities rationalize their thoughtless decisions by surface pretentions and public appeals to private altruism.

I have previously mentioned appeals for altruism and their concomitant duplicative overhead costs and dollar competition. But appeals to altruism at least hit up the rich rather than further burdening the poor. If the government bears the burden of the handicapped, then the lower classes of society will pay. Why can't the government tax corporations and the rich for this purpose? It seems that this latter "minority group" is the one that always escapes from paying for public guilt.

The issue of minorities and, particularly, the minority of handicapped persons is a difficult one to solve because of the human equation. In making judgments about others, human beings use "self" as the focal point for formulating ideas and opinions. People are fundamentally egocentric, and thus, the protection of self is an essential human characteristic. "I am right because I am I," is an unreasonable, but nevertheless virile, human dynamic. We form attitudes in terms of our personal self-concepts and body images. As such, humans strive for conformity within their ranks. Unfortunately, groups of people are thrown out of society when they cannot conform, either because of physical, mental, or philosophical differences. For example, religious persecution caused the Puritans to move to America. In turn, these victims became the majority in the New World and threw out those who were different from them. The outcasts often were called demons or witches (or Indians), and some were burned to death. While handicapped people are not burned to death, they are victims of this same type of persecution because they cannot fit in with the norm. Thus, society today is little different in attitudes than its seventeenth- and eighteenth-century ancestors. Our civilized society is too often a farce.

Attitudes toward handicapped individuals are not limited to the uneducated. The quantity of misinformation and, in reality, ignorance of the total field of handicapping conditions always astounds me. College professors, for example—perhaps the intellectual elite of a nation—do not know much about the subject. Some years ago I was considering moving, as I eventually did, to a new university position. I requested the interviewing dean to arrange for me to visit a number of agencies in the community that served handicapped children. Among these agencies was a school for physically handicapped children. The dean and I arrived there at lunchtime and visited the children's lunchroom. Shortly thereafter, I realized that the dean was no longer with me. I found him weeping in an adjacent hallway—a man of national reputation and long experience as an administrator in higher education, weeping. While he was undoubtedly the best dean with whom I have ever been associated, this strong and active emotion did not enhance his work in that university in the preparation of young administrators, all of whom would have some future relationship with handicapped children. Teaching future administrators to weep, or passing on images of the pathos of handicapped people, does nothing to enhance the status of this minority.

Undoubtedly, there are other strong forces that could be discussed in relationship to disabled persons as a minority, but only prejudice will be singled out here. Prejudice, with its related prejudgment and intolerance, plays a significant role in attitudes toward some subminority groups of handicapped persons. As state after state attempts to implement a policy of deinstitutionalization, with its corollary of community living centers for retarded adults, emotionally disturbed adults, and in some places halfway houses for former prisoners, communities have reacted with hostility. Unsubtle citizens have bombed and torched these centers in order to keep the neighborhood "pure" and "safe." Other, more sophisticated ways to keep the unwanted out have involved illegal zoning ordinances, houses taken off the market, and many other pseudolegal methods. The above examples are reminiscent of the attitudes toward racial minorities who sought to improve their quality of living by purchasing homes in "white neighborhoods."

Some years ago, the members of my family and I decided to sell our home and move to another part of the city where a larger home could accommodate our needs. As this decision was reached, the home next to ours was sold to a black family, the husband with a recidivist criminal record, a similar record for an adolescent son, and the wife employed as a social worker. A conservative neighborhood group expected me, a university professor, to lead in blocking this sale. The liberal university community, on the other hand, vocally assumed that I would lead the drive for integration. Unbeknownst to my wife and children, threats of bombing and of harm to my children were received at my office. I finally had to ask for police protection when I was out of the city. Also, we did not move for two years. Criticism poured into the university because of my apparent passive behavior—or any behavior I demonstrated, for that matter. The university chancellor took action to demonstrate to the community that his administration stood behind me. He publicly invited me to sponsor Supreme Court Justice Thurgood Marshall for an honorary degree. This calmed the storm. One wonders if these cycles of intolerance and irrationality will ever end.

H. Wayne Morgan makes an interesting observation that couples minority issues with racial imagery and drug usage (Morgan 1981, x).

> The racial imagery that was so common at peaks of concern about drug use is complex. Every such image represented profound conflicts and fears. The Near Easterners who figured in the early concern about cannabis use symbolized passivity and backwardness that seemed diametrically opposed to the developing American nation. Opium use appeared to be a major factor in China's apparent stagnation and inability to become modern. The black who figured in the sharp debate over cocaine represented violence and irrationality, as did the Mexican in the later debate about marijuana. And the hippie flower child, the most analogous stereotype, was supposedly passive, unproductive, and hostile to the basic values of thrift, productivity, rationality, and realism.
>
> These images were powerful foci of debate, but in each case the adverse public reaction grew not only from fear of these groups or the need to control them. It also represented the desire to isolate the effects of their actions from the larger society. . . .

Morgan sees a direct relationship that couples minority status with personality characteristics, which works to the disadvantage of the minority group. His point of view is an accurate one, I think, and can also be seen in the characterizations of those with handicaps. The majority act and think and feel without any accurate understanding. It is easy, although inaccurate and illegal, for an employer (representing a majority point of view) to refuse employment to a handicapped person because to do so would increase his insurance liability. The employer makes an incorrect generalization from a single case to the total population of the minority of handicapped individuals.

The Vietnamese boat people and other groups of refugees represent the latest minority groups to enter the United States. These people have been accepted or rejected in direct relationship to their command of English, their personality characteristics, their cosmetic differences, and their skills.

There are exceptions to this bleak picture. Recently, my wife and I were in a large, chain supermarket in New Orleans. I was aware of a great number of "foreign looking" employees and, at first, assumed these were longtime Chicano citizens of the city. Later, I realized my mistake and made an inquiry as to who these employees were. I found that the owner of the chain of grocery stores had announced a public policy of employing as many refugees as he could, most of whom were Vietnamese. The owner assisted them in learning English and taught them appropriate skills. Hence, stock boys, cashiers, baggers, clerks at various specialty counters, and classifications of background employees were working in large numbers in each of these stores. Their presence provided not only an international flavor to the experience of shopping, but an interest to many customers, who noticed the rapidity with which English language was being assimilated and "Americanization" was occurring. A minority was being assisted to become a part of the majority without losing the significant characteristics that made it a valuable part of the melting pot. There is a difference here, however, with this minority group and that of the handicapped. Society senses a significant empathy with the Vietnamese refugees because of the tragedies they have experienced and, also, because of the guilt Americans have regarding the Vietnam war itself. Handicapped persons are not victims of the "domino theory," of napalm, or of war in general. Cosmetically, the Vietnamese are often described as "cute," a label rarely, if ever, applied to a group of handicapped persons.

Adolescents with visible physical disabilities tell us that it is the adults in society, not their chronological-aged peers, who impress on them the limitations of their handicaps. Adults impose the limitations of minority status on the handicapped and turn this status into so many negative qualities for disabled youth and adults alike.

Morgan continues by pointing out that public reaction to the various minority groups and their use of drugs ". . . also represented the desire to isolate the effects of their actions (in the use of drugs) from the larger society" (Morgan 1981, 142). In the case of the handicapped the analogy to drugs may be analogous to the visible physical appearance of the handicap and the related desire on the part of society in general to isolate. Morgan goes on to state that "Control, education, or prohibition were thus in order. This attitude was also clear in social disapproval of marginal groups such as bohemian intellectuals and artists, itinerant musicians, and petty criminals who seemed uninterested in accepting society's central values. Critics saw drug use as an aspect or cause of this rejection" (143). The analogy here to the handicapped is not fully appropriate. In the case of the latter minority group "control" and "prohibition" are not in order, and education while appropriate should be directed to the majority not the minority. Likewise the heterogeneous minority groups that Morgan lists are different from the handicapped minority, since the latter *want to be* a part of the central values of society and to be seen as such. Regardless, the insight Morgan provides regarding the minority problem per se is appropriate and germane.

It is inevitable that minorities and majorities exist, and probably always will, human nature being what it is. From Palestinians to Inuits, from hobos to corporate executives, from the physically normal to the physically and intellectually handicapped, each is a minority or a majority in an economic, social, or physical sense. Utopian concepts, hopes for a World Federation, implementation of the Judeo-Christian ethic, or just the acceptance of every individual as an individual for what he is and what he can or cannot contribute to society—these high-sounding dreams of cooperation and personal worth, in the light of the history of man, may never be accomplished. If this be the case, then human beings must be impressed with the fact at least of the worth of people, and in this case the worth of a minority whose physical or mental status is not within their powers to control. Acceptance of people as they are must be a dynamic substitute for fear.

Society fears the unknown. Fears are applied to those with a disability and are allowed to characterize all the individuals within the minority group. These accurate or inaccurate characterizations permit the majority to reject the minority. Rejection is essentially synonymous to societal rebuff and unacceptablity. Fear of disability and its concomitants will be the topic of the following chapter.

References and Related Readings

Clyne, P. *The Disadvantaged Adult: Educational and Social Needs of Minority Groups.* London: Longman, 1972.

Coles, R. *Children in Crisis: A Study of Courage and Fear.* Boston: Little, Brown, 1967.

Conference on Exceptional Children. *Cultural Diversity and the Exceptional Child.* Las Vegas, Nevada, 1973. Reston, Va.: Council for Exceptional Children, 1973–.

Cruickshank, W. M., Morse, W. C., and Grant, J. D. "The IEPC Meeting: A Step in the History of Special Education." Ms.

The Developmental Disabilities Movement: A National Study of Minority Participation. San Francisco: New Dimensions in Community Services, 1979.

Eleven Programs for Strengthening Navajo Education. Window Rock, Ariz.: Navajo Division of Education, 1973.

Hensel, A. *The Forgotten Ones: A Sociological Study of Anglo and Chicano Retardates.* Austin: University of Texas Press, 1972.

Morgan, H. W. *Drugs in America: A Social History, 1800–1980.* Syracuse: Syracuse University Press, 1981.

Oakland, T., ed. *Psychological and Educational Assessment of Minority Children.* New York: Bruner and Mazel, 1977.

Passow, A. H., Goldberg, M., and Tannenbaum, A. J. *Education of the Disadvantaged.* New York: Holt, Rinehart, and Winston, 1967.

Towards Quality Education for Mexican Americans. Mexican American Education Study, Report 6. Washington, D.C.: U.S. Commission on Civil Rights, 1974.

Wright, B. J., and Esenstein, V. R. *Psychological Tests and Minorities.* Rockville, Md.: National Institute of Mental Health, 1977.

Chapter 3

Fear, Guilt, and Rejection

If one were to believe all the newspaper reports pertaining to "good causes," one would believe that a Utopian-like society existed for the handicapped person. Such is not so. In chapter 2, I discussed the exceptional child as a minority representative, as well as addressed some factors intimately related to the issue of minority status that are significant in the adjustment of these children and youth to society. In the present chapter, I will examine three factors that relate to minority positions: fear, guilt, and rejection.

Fear

People generally are fearful of those things unknown to them. Aristotle, in his *Nichomachean Ethics* (Kaplan 1958, 160–209), writes,

> . . . each man judges well the things he knows, and of these he is a good judge. And so the man who has been educated in a subject is a good judge, and the man who has received an all-around education is a good judge in general. (P. 162)

The converse of this may well be true: if each man judges well the things he knows, each man may be a poor judge, even fearful, of those things he does not know.

So it is with individuals who represent external, visible characteristics different from those we ourselves possess. We accept human forms similar to our own, but those that are different are often rejected by the viewer. Rejection is often based upon fear and guilt—fear of the unknown and guilt over this fear.

Fear is an illusive human characteristic, for it is often hidden by intellectualization. The fearful person usually is not aware of the underlying emotion because it has been sublimated by the intellect. Referring again to Aristotle,

> For to such persons . . . knowledge brings no profit, but to those who desire and act in accordance with rational principle knowledge about such matters will be of great benefit. (P. 162)

27

But when fear undergirds rational principle, "knowledge brings no profit." Fear as an active personality ingredient lies, not dormant, but actively inactive, under the cover of intellectualization and self-acceptance.

Another factor contributes to social and personal sublimation of fear of the handicapped person. Intellectually normal, emotionally and socially healthy human beings are taught not to fear those things smaller than themselves. Witness the extent to which adults go in order to avoid the unpleasant—fear of snakes or moving reptiles, blood. A response of "blood" to one of the color cards in the Rorschach Test may be viewed as an intellectually uncontrolled response to environmental stimuli, and, except in persons of very superior intellect where a great capacity alone may assimilate some abnormal responses, these "pure C (color)" responses are seen as negative, other things being equal. These responses may be substitutes for the unconscious, but nevertheless are dynamic fears. In another instance, the fear of germs may be an almost psychotic response on the part of some individuals. Fear is a dynamic and controlling emotional entity that sometimes produces irrational behavior and attitudes. Attitudes toward disabilities follow from this line of reasoning.

In our society, the macho concept is, to some degree, the mode for both men and women. Being fearful is a sign of weakness and social unacceptability. While I am certain to misjudge the motivation of many persons, I find it difficult to accept a number of annual "events" that are thrust upon handicapped children in terms other than as group reactions to fear of the distasteful and, to a large degree, of the unknown.

On one hand, compliments can be extended to the Shrine fraternal organization, for example, for the efforts its membership puts forth in the support of hospitals for burn patients. On the other hand, one could question the basic motivating factor behind the endless series of newspaper photographs of a "Shriner"—head complete with fez—holding a crippled child on his lap at a Shrine circus. Who is enjoying the situation more: the child who might have attended the circus anyway with his family, or the fraternal member whose face and name that will appear in newspapers give evidence of "charitable intentions"?

Further, these actions often serve to cover up personal distaste for the handicapped and, in turn, obscure the subtle rejection of the handicapped child or youth. Why are not equally public projects undertaken with the handicapped adult or the older person? Perhaps the little child, always cute and photogenic, compensates for the unpleasantness of a drooling quadriplegic cerebral-palsied man or woman. The child can at least be held on one's lap; the adult handicapped person does not lend himself to photogenic displays that are self-serving to others.

How many turkey dinners have been served to crippled or to blind children by service club members when the majority of these children do not need such annual food supplements? Who truly benefits from the public displays, each equipped with newspaper photographers and all the other accoutrements necessary for the full impact of community approval? Did any service club ever invite the late Franklin D. Roosevelt to an annual turkey dinner, to a circus, or to other public events where his crippledness and his braces were exploited for the benefit of the sponsoring group? Is this a subtle, but socially acceptable, form of child abuse? Does the community itself experience feelings of relief from its own fears by viewing photographs of community leaders feeding a child with upper extremity congenital deformities or that of a blind child sitting on the lap of a "Lion"?

It can be debated what motivates the membership of these organizations. In some communities, the biggest reason for joining the service groups is to socialize or to use the organization as a stepping-stone for politics. The men remember what the purpose of their club is only a few times a year—when they sell white canes or candy, etc. I don't think these men join because of fear; they couldn't care less about the disabled.

Recently, I was invited to undertake an in-depth study of an historically significant institution for the education of handicapped children. The institution, like many of its kind due to the impact of Public Law 94-142, no longer was "educational" in nature, but was essentially a training center for profoundly retarded, multiple handicapped children and youth. One of the members of the board of directors told me that the last place he wished to visit was the building housing the most severe "patients." The chairman, reaching into rhetorical history, redundantly referred to the institution as "charitable and eleemosynary," although for its first one hundred years it had served as a school and a fine educational center with a worldwide reputation. Did fear motivate the board members? Did the chairman receive his recognition from the community for his perennial leadership of a "charitable agency" now serving a population of residents with whom he and his board colleagues would think twice before sharing a meal and about whom they knew little?

It was stated earlier that fear is often clouded by intellectualization. In the example I have just cited, it was impossible during the study to recall the number of times I was reminded of the difficulties of raising funds, of his excuses concerning the time spent in planning for the repair of roofs. "I must spend so much time that I have no time left for staff or pupils," the chairperson reported to me on one of the few occasions we talked. Fear probably clouds his actions. He is knowledgeable of his business, but as Aristotle wrote centuries ago, his "knowledge brings no profit" to the community of the handicapped. No board member ever gets his or her hands dirty with direct efforts for the handicapped children being served by a splendid staff. The board gains its satisfaction by holding infrequent board meetings in the institution. Some board members rarely see the children being served. Fear might be the motivation for this type of adult behavior.

In *Ethics,* Aristotle reminds us that, ". . . we feel anger and fear without choice . . . the man who feels fear . . . is not praised, nor is the man who feels anger blamed" (p. 188). Aristotle sees a close relationship between fear and anger, the latter, of necessity, is under control, but as a subtle emotion that shields fear.

I recently met a community leader coming off an elevator during a visit to a hospital school situated in a university hospital. I greeted him and asked him what he was doing there. His response ignored the question and belied his own basic feelings.

> I had to come here for the club. I'm chairman of the equipment needs of this place. You'd think that the state or the lousy parents themselves would give this place enough money to buy what it needs. But now our club has decided to buy the frills and things that most of these kids would never have at home.

A modern-day Scrooge is dressed in sheep's clothing, to mix some metaphors. In parting, the committee chairman was honest enough to admit his own emotions: "Some of these sights actually make me ill, but I have to go there once in a while for the club."

After working for many years with handicapped children and youth and their families, I could cite hundreds of examples that express the hidden but vital attitudes of the community toward a large segment of our twentieth-century society. But there are also many professionals who either work with the handicapped or function in general education who also reflect similar negative attitudes. Their attitudes are seldom verbalized, for they are not condoned by the community even though they may represent the thinking of a large portion of it.

For instance, I once encountered a situation where a third grade teacher refused to hold Joey, a three-year-old blind boy "because I have never touched a blind person before." What is the basic motivation here? It could not be anything else but fear of the unknown on the part of a professionally trained educator. What of a fourth grade teacher who cannot accept a deaf child in her class "because I have been told hearing aids explode"? Reality or fear?

Once, a sixth grade teacher could only whisper the word *epilepsy* to me. When pushed as to the reason why she could not audibly verbalize the word, she said it was too embarrassing. "Why?" I asked. "Because it is immoral," she replied. "Everyone knows that epilepsy is caused in a child when the baby is sleeping in the same room with his or her parents while they are having sexual intercourse." Ancient myths have contemporary impacts and serve to cloud fears. Perhaps these few examples could be termed extreme, but they are not. They represent hundreds of similar feelings in others, but are without any foundation of reality.

It is interesting to note facial grimaces by some when they visit a school for physically handicapped children. The annual visit of society leaders is marred by head turning and a supposedly unheard remark to a friend, "How awful!" The group photograph causes a rush to the back rows so their presence can be noted but direct encounters with crippled children are neatly avoided.

It may not be as prevalent today, but in past years, society avoided the presence of handicapped children and youth by placing them in residential institutions located in rural communities. As a result, parents either could, and often did, forget their children or found visitations difficult, and competent professional staffs were difficult to assemble. Where is Wahjamega, Michigan; Malone, New York; Lapeer, Mt. Pleasant, Newberry, or Gaylord, Michigan; Orient, Ohio; Dixon, Illinois; and Fort Meyer, Florida? Every state is so characterized. In each of these communities, a large residential facility houses (or formerly housed) one or another type of handicapped group of people. Politics and economics are partial reasons for the locations. Fear and guilt are unstated but are magnifying factors in placing many, if not most, of the facilities where they cannot be seen and, therefore, where they can be forgotten.

As public school programs began to be established in large cities, schools for handicapped children were separated from neighborhood schools. In addition, they were often named after a community leader or were given names that embodied emotional overtones salving the conscience of the community (i.e., the Sunshine School of Cleveland, Ohio; the Florence Nightingale School [for mentally retarded children!] in Binghamton, New York; or a dozen schools throughout the United States called "Opportunity Schools").

Aristotle wrote that we are most comfortable with those things about which we have intimate knowledge. One of Aristotle's essential principles states that the goal for men is most often agreed to be happiness (*Ethics*). Happiness is the opposite of fear. Plato, likewise, raised the same issue and asked, "Are we on the way to or from happiness?" Aristotle, elaborating on this point of view stated, "Presumably, then we must begin with things known to us" (p. 163). Thus, we begin to be happy only with things familiar. Expanding on this concept, it should be noted that happiness that envelopes all people will not be accorded to those with disabilities until those with handicaps are known to us for their positive, as well as negative, characteristics. Not only would the disabled have a better life, but the "normal" person also would exist more comfortably once stupid fears were taken away. Hesiod (Kaplan 1958) stated it well when he wrote in a fragment of one poem:

> Far best is he who knows all things himself;
> Good that he harkens when men counsel right;
> But he who neither knows, nor lays to heart
> Another's wisdom, is a useless wight. (P. 164)

This advice, ages old, was written while the Greeks were slaughtering handicapped individuals! Hardly did Hesiod or his countrymen take his advice seriously regarding those who deviated from the norms of human development. Education, the basis for human acceptance of mankind in all its racial and physical forms, is a slow, but nevertheless essential, process in the total evolution of a human or society. Until this process is consummated, the increasingly large population of handicapped individuals will continue as a misunderstood and often times rejected minority.

Guilt

Guilt and fear are closely interrelated, for the former is often the product of the latter. Fear of the unknown is based on ignorance and thus breeds feelings of guilt when social pressures are applied to the individual. Guilt is one of the most difficult emotions with which to deal. Guilt, like fear, often emerges from ignorance. Aristotle (*Ethics*) gives us a way out, however justified or not, when he says that "Everything that is done by reason of ignorance is not voluntary. . . . Acting by reason of ignorance seems also to be different than acting in ignorance" (p. 199). This has meaning for teacher education in the twentieth century.

Colleges and university schools of education graduate thousands of preservice teachers each year who have had no contact whatsoever with any type of exceptional child or youth during their period of training. In this circumstance, it is very possible that teachers extend to their children attitudes based on ignorance. One wonders where normal children learn positive attitudes about those who are handicapped in some manner—the mentally retarded child, those with physical or emotional handicaps. I recently visited a public school where all the pupils were attending an assembly. A film dealing with crippled children was shown as a basis for classroom discussions leading up to a mainstreaming program soon to be initiated throughout the school system. One teacher within my view sat with her hands over her eyes during the entire period of the film. One of her second grade pupils said to a friend within my hearing, "Who hurt Miss S? Why is she crying?" The teacher was not crying but was afraid to watch the film. This adult could not translate that film, excellent as it was, to a group of immature second grade pupils when her own life was so filled with fears, ignorance, and guilt regarding the very essence of the film that was presented. I firmly believe that guilt is the extreme opposite of reason. Fear and anger may be related to reason to some degree but not so with guilt, which is nonproductive and illustrates intellectual impotence.

Cicero (*On Moral Duties*), writing to his son Marcus many years after the death of Aristotle, emphasizes ". . . the conflict between the honorable and that which appears to be expedient. When interest drags us one way and honor calls us back, the mind is distracted with doubt" (Hadas 1951, 8). Further in his letter to Marcus he says, "The distinctive faculty of man is his eager desire to investigate the truth" (p. 9).

Too many people view handicapped people as objects upon which to bestow charity, to show compassion, to give gifts of money—to give but not to become involved in any direct and personal manner in order to erase guilt, to provide charity, but not "investigate the truth." Serving on a board of directors is not a true substitute for direct action. The former is the expedient of which Cicero writes his son (pp. 3–60). The honorable is the honest, direct involvement with someone who needs the personal support of a stronger, perhaps more affluent, human being.

Handicapped persons are neither "things" to be avoided nor to be relegated to the periphery of society. No man is perfect; each in the eyes of others has personal or physical characteristics that are sometimes far less than perfect.

Selfishness and selflessness are human traits related in the same manner as honor and expediency. I think of a Christmas a few years ago when my family spent the day with relatives. Our daughter asked her uncle for permission to invite some friends. They arrived—a man of forty-five years who was confined to a wheel chair and who could talk only as one who has quadriplegic athetotic cerebral palsy; a mature woman on a wheel stretcher who was in the advanced stages of multiple sclerosis; and Joey, a slight, petite, and cosmetically deformed man whose stutter was so severe that he could not communicate at all. These friends were driven to the Christmas celebration by a man with no arms, his wife with unusable legs, and their two physically normal sons of elementary school age who oversaw the entire operation.

The family that gave of themselves to transport severely handicapped persons to a holiday celebration is an example of honor. Expediency is the giver of fifty dollars to a Salvation Army collector, while others watched. This is the person who sits around a Christmas dinner table liking himself or herself for giving the gift; but also feeling safe because he or she never sees the recipient of the gift. The world has too few Tiny Tims with his renowned blessing, and certainly too few to receive it.

Cicero, it will be recalled, wrote to Marcus saying that it is "the distinctive faculty of man [eagerly to] desire to investigate the truth" (p. 9). Out of investigation there is a minimization of guilt. If I encounter something, the outcome of which is unknown to me or consists of something I cannot understand, I may react in a manner that elicits guilt. If, at a university swimming pool, I encounter a swimmer with upper extremity amputations, a dwarf struggling to keep her head above water at the shallow end of the pool, an obese individual who floats contentedly but makes little forward progress, I may tend to avoid each person as being unpleasant. Out of this personal reaction comes guilt, for subsequently I realize that a direct encounter might have produced a completely different reaction. I inquire. I find that the obese man has a remarkable sense of humor and is a delight to be with; the dwarf represents a degree of courage out of proportion to her size. The young man with no arms is studying electrical engineering at the university and is participating in a bioengineering research study as a subject, the goal of which is to develop prostheses that will operate on the basis of muscular-nerve stimulation. Each has something important to contribute to my life, directly or intellectually. None of their disabilities is contagious. Each person has enriched my life, and through Cicero's suggestion of a "desire to investigate" and to become acquainted with the individuals I have described, I find that it is not important that any of them is actually handicapped. Each survives in the swimming pool to his or her satisfaction, and each is making a satisfying life for himself in society generally. Guilt can be minimized by investigation, and investigation, with the quieting effect of knowledge rather than ineffective guilt, can lead to both friendship and mutual support. Reason supplants guilt.

What a valuable letter Cicero wrote to Marcus, his son!

How precious should we deem the gift of reason since man is the only being that has a sense of order, decorum and moderation in word and deed. No other creature is touched by the beauty, grace and symmetry of visible objects; and the human mind transferring these conceptions from the material to the moral recognizes that this beauty, harmony and order are still more to be maintained in the sphere of purpose and action; reason shuns all that is unbecoming or unmanly; all that is wanton in thought or deed. (P. 9)

One does not have to rationalize away the physical deformity of a handicapped individual in order to find a powerful violinist, a pianist (who happens to be blind), a poet (who happens to be deaf), a choreographer (who had a stroke), a surgeon (who happened to be cerebral-palsied), a dwarf (who is studying to become a journalist), an obese woman (who has five children who are loved and who in turn love their mother). False rationalization produces more guilt, but investigation as advocated by Cicero and direct encounters based on acceptance result in mutual trust and new horizons of experience for both the handicapped person and the so-called normal person.

We must teach children to investigate before opinions are formed, to seek out truths before fears and their consuming guilt become attached to an object or human being, and to honor all persons for what each can contribute. Society cannot afford self-defeating behavior that stems from guilt and fear. The handicapped population undoubtedly always will be with us and deserves something far more positive than being the object of fear, dislike, and avoidance. A lawyer representing the Office of the Attorney General of a large state is a member of that state's Planning Council for the Developmentally Disabled, established under U.S. federal law. He makes remarkable contributions to the deliberations of that council. The fact that he is confined to a wheelchair and is also a quadriplegic cerebral-palsied man makes his contributions no less valuable in the development of the state's program in the pursuit of legal solutions within the Attorney General's office.

We have always had handicapped people among us. It is argued that societies always have had to deal with this problem in one way or another, whether in a vicious or in a humanitarian manner. It should be pointed out, though, that no one would have to "deal" with the problem if it would not be considered as such. If a disabled person were accepted simply as a person who happened to have a disability and were accorded the full rights and privileges as a member of society, there would not be any problem. The United States abounds in service clubs with one or another motivation toward the handicapped. There is the Salvation Army and its annual Christmas-giving campaign. There are telethons, bikathons, walkathons, swimathons, etc., to raise money for cerebral palsy, mental retardation, and muscular dystrophy. Contests are developed in elementary schools that couple the number of books a child reads to the amount someone will give that child for some "cause." Students can "buy" an Asian orphan. One wonders how effective these short-term solutions are.

Mail rarely arrives but that there is another appeal for delinquent children; the blind, deaf, epileptic, emotionally disturbed, or other type of handicapped persons; for horrors of famine in Somalia, Cambodia, or elsewhere. These requests are not all bad, except for the awful administrative overhead that is never mentioned. But all would be unnecessary if education in the home and schools of this land made the acceptance of humans of whatever condition or ability a top priority in the development of children's minds, and if there were teachers and parents of these same children who without fear, guilt, or rejection could impart to young minds that men are created equal insofar as life is concerned.

A second lesson that applies to every citizen of a developed country is important to realize. It is not wrong to give to those who need, but giving does not free us from guilt. We must recognize that the actual cost of rearing a handicapped person within a family is too great for the family to assume. It must be shared by the total community. Further, it is too great a cost for the school system or any other agency in the community to assume, hence, the state must assist to the maximum. Finally, it is too great a burden for most states, and for that reason, the issue must become a federal policy. In the latter, we find the burden as it should be shared as equal as taxes are ever equal by every citizen of the country. But in the twentieth century we must go further. The concept of world federation is a necessity and must become a reality. If Somalia, India, and other countries face famine or lack the ability to provide within bounds of human dignity for those who are handicapped in some manner, then the world community must share and share equally. The unwieldly bureaucracy of the United Nations and its UNICEF is obviously not the answer as it currently functions. But humankind is brilliant enough to devise a method that can work if the members of the world community are committed. The UNICEF Year of the Disabled Person could be considered a fiasco in terms of both impact and results. By the middle of the "Year" no program existed, even on paper, and territoriality within the United Nations and certainly within and among the many national UNICEF committees was rife with tensions. The purchase of UNICEF stamps and Christmas cards, as a single example of many, lulls citizens into believing that all is well. If one can get beneath the surface veneer of the "good cause," one finds bureaucracy, mediocrity, and personalities that fight for their personal security to the point where international education cannot and will not ever become effective. Those for whom millions of dollars are raised still starve and lead inhuman lives. It is a situation that causes anger in the minds of those who know and discouragement in the minds of those who wonder why decades of international efforts have proven to be futile. Guilt cannot be reduced—national or personal—under circumstances such as exist in the national and international charitable agencies of the world. Handicapped persons continue to live; some exist in unknown numbers.

Fears and guilt can produce tensions that often may be reflected in personality characteristics, physical mannerisms, and, of course, in an individual's productions. Tensions can have positive attributes too. In visiting the Picasso *Museo* in Barcelona, Spain, our young German colleague who was accompanying us, stated that Picasso's paintings to him often reflected tension. In the Spanish culture this is often observed. The flamenco dances, full of beauty and excitement, are the essence of tension and rhythm. Even the bullfight possesses tension—tension of the ballet of the opening ceremony, the posturing of the matadores and toreadores. Tension, discipline, and precision. Tensions, uncontrolled, however, produce little of a positive nature as do fear and guilt. They are nonproductive for the most part.

Rejection

When fear and guilt exist, the sequel is rejection. We tend to ignore and reject those things we do not understand. Certainly this is true if fears predominate. In Christian folk history there is a parallel. The beautiful contralto recitative toward the middle of Handel's *Messiah* begins with the statement, plaintively sung: "He was despised and rejected of men, a man of sorrows and acquainted with grief." Whenever I hear this poignant sentence and its accompanying intense and tearing melody, I am startled into the comparative reality of the handicapped person and the situation that faces him. While death may not be imminent, as in the oratorio, the emotions surrounding handicapped persons are not greatly different.

It is not socially acceptable openly to despise someone, although the emotion is observed frequently even among friends. Generally speaking, however, it is an attitude foreign to well-adjusted human beings. We tend to cover it up with more socially acceptable characterizations if it exists at all. In the same manner, the hidden fear and guilt that many carry toward the handicapped person are not or cannot be exposed openly. Regardless of the social status of the individuals concerned—the handicapped person and the one who has unresolved feelings about him—it is socially unacceptable to expose raw emotions in a way that would allow society to make negative judgments about the person who holds them. This creates another cog in the vicious circle. Fear stimulates guilt, and guilt prompts rejection. Rejection fosters emotions that cannot be exposed without shame or damage to the holder of the emotion. This produces more guilt and animosity, more rejection, more guilt—a spiral that in effect is an offshoot of the original unresolved matters of fear and guilt. A good example is the controversy over whether to allow black people to buy homes in all-white neighborhoods. It is socially unacceptable for a knee-jerk liberal family to scream "We don't want 'niggers' living in our neighborhood." So they explain that they don't want their property value to go down: "It's not that we have anything against blacks, we're all equal after all, it's just that, well, uh. . . ." They cover up fear, feel guilty about, then reject. It is a mighty complicated, unresolvable emotional dilemma into which the rejecting individual has consciously or unconsciously floundered.

The problem contained within that individual is even more perplexing to the handicapped child, youth, or adult. While they view themselves as ones who often cannot compete, they do not see themselves as ones to be rejected totally by others. These handicapped individuals do not view themselves as so repelling that society does not wish to be seen as a part of their social life: a blind child whose teacher refuses to touch him or her, a child with seizures who cannot understand the fear provoked in others by his or her behavior, or the ataxic cerebral-palsied man who is avoided on the street on the assumption that his unsteady gait means that he is drunken. "Why do people avoid me?" he queries to a friend. "The other day, one of many, a mother drew her small child away from me to her when we passed on Main Street. Why does this happen to me? I intend no harm to anyone." It is not just the physically, mentally, or emotionally exceptional people who experience these socially negative emotions toward them, but frequently the gifted child or young person as well. These remarkable young people constitute another group of "different" people. It is those differences that prompt fear and rejection.

"Don't play with Billy; he's funny," says one playmate to another. "I can't stand brains," says an adolescent to her friend passing another in the school hallway. An adolescent boy to a friend said of a third who had just left them during a period between classes, "I'll bet he can't even kiss a girl without having to have three intellectual reasons for it!" Differences produce distances, which often result in rejection.

Individuals familiar with the Rorschach Test know that in responding to inkblots, individuals report those things that they see as reality or that often are motivated by unconscious perceptions. The intellectually normal, mentally healthy person gives responses that are typical of those generally seen by society, often reporting responses that are known clinically as "popular" (i.e., very frequently reported by otherwise normal and emotionally healthy individuals). It is a unique and exceedingly significant tool in the hands of a competent clinical psychologist or neuropsychologist.

The disturbed individual or the individual whose perceptions are motivated by the unconscious often gives poor form responses.

At the same time, the content of the response is also poor, indeed often pathological. A typical response on one of the inkblots by a normal, healthy individual is a "bat." This is such a typical response that it can be termed popular (i.e., it is expected to be reported by the viewer).

I use the Rorschach Test frequently as a clinical tool, recognizing its limitations as well as its virtues. In my files are dozens of Rorschach protocols of subjects who either live in the same house with a disabled person or who are closely related in some manner to a disabled person at work or in study. Consider the following response to the inkblot that normal people perceive as a bat. It is reported by a twenty-three-year-old man, a college student, who all his life shared his bedroom with a seriously physically handicapped, mentally retarded brother who is entirely dependent on other adults for all his needs. This young college student reported the typical bat, but one that was either trying to escape or was about to eat its prey:

> I see heavy wings about to fold around its enemy, an enemy who is not really an enemy, but is something the bat hates and which has ruined its life. The bat will be happy when it either kills the interference or is able to escape from the same cave.

It doesn't take too much imagination on the part of the clinician to know who the bat is and who is being rejected or against whom a killing or escape maneuver is attempted.

Among many other similar responses, I will report only one other. On one of the cards is an inkblot that is often referred to by clinicians as the phallic card, for there is a portion of the card that depicts, quite clearly, a phallic symbol. Normal individuals either ignore it or see it as it is, as do persons who are emotionally disturbed. However, it is merely the reporting of a reality for most.

A forty-five-year-old father of a twenty-one-year-old disabled son who is disabled to the extent of requiring complete care following a serious skiing accident when he was seventeen, went to a psychological clinic for assistance. In an attempt to get a relatively quick understanding of the man's problems over and above those that he was able to verbalize, the Rorschach Test was administered. On the above-mentioned card, he said he saw a phallus made of steel: "It's the kind I'd like to shove through my son; he's no longer a man. Maybe with the pain he'd receive he'd know the pain he dishes out to me every day." The hostility, rejection, and total denial of his son is fully depicted in the response of his father. These are not extreme cases in psychological experiences within a typical clinic or mental hospital. They are extreme insofar as "normal" society is concerned, but then one has to ask "What is normal society?" And how much of the so-called normal society harbors responses similar to these two examples in terms of partial or complete denial of the physically handicapped group of citizens, regardless of age?

A young father looks at his mildly deformed son when first visiting him in the hospital and says, "He'll never accomplish what I had hoped for," although the child really was only mildly handicapped. Hospitals often report attempts on the part of parents to place a handicapped infant up for immediate adoption. This is complete rejection. "Why did it happen to me," says a father of a newly delivered Down's syndrome infant. "I had such plans for him. No quarterback was to have been as good as he. Now what?"

Administrative and Agency Guilt and Rejection

The dollars collected and spent on handicapped children and adults total billions of dollars, and still are insufficient. At the same time, the federal cutbacks of fundamental services for the disabled, argued and effected by the Nixon and Reagan administrations, are little less than national tragedies and are certainly individual tragedies for many. They illustrate an insensitivity inappropriate to a nation's leader. Indeed, these actions can be interpreted as a punitive measure against a population that cannot effectively fight back. These measures represent a national political rejection. Our leaders fail to recognize the fiscal return to the nation through taxes that handicapped individuals can produce if they are appropriately treated and trained while young. These measures smack of the alleged characterizations of black children by Richard Nixon as being less intelligent than white children. Unfortunately, the domestic policies of the Nixon and Reagan administrations are not far different.

Private charities are to be lauded once certain guarantees are insisted upon by those who give. First, issues of territoriality must be completely negated. Consider the administrative duplication and costs of organizations that have worked separately on eyes, ears, spine, heart, and individual disease entities such as cancer, osteomyelitis, Reye's syndrome, autism, dyslexia, learning disabilities, sickle-cell anemia, cerebral palsy, mental retardation, prevention of blindness, and many others, each with its own territory to be protected and its own administrative costs. These issues rarely are mentioned and often never reported publically. Second, in a good charitable agency, overhead will be near zero levels. That goal cannot be acclaimed even by so-called community chest organizations where administrative overhead is more or less carefully monitored.

Third, somewhere in the charter of the agency, there must be a declaration that the agency and its "good works" are not covers for social guilt. Handicapping conditions are a fact of modern and ancient life. Individuals who smother handicapped children for public display and who use charities to salve their own guilt feelings, or who believe that in giving they have fully discharged a personal responsibility, are living falsehoods and are not facing the reality in any sense whatsoever.

Both private and public charity agencies often work to defeat programs for handicapped individuals. Hundreds of examples are available, but I shall select only two. Some years ago after much more effort than the result warranted, the Junior League of Syracuse, New York, gave Syracuse University approximately three thousand dollars to establish a nursery school program for blind children. The gift, following accounting procedures that almost demanded a separate bookkeeper, was renewed for two additional years; the university provided many times more than the league's gift from other sources in order to operate a good program. The league's gift was essential, however, and the organization took full public credit for the program. Then with little notice, the league officials announced to the university that they had a policy of not funding programs for more than three years in an effort to spread their funds to a broader base (and to take credit in the community for more than their just efforts).

Grants from the federal government for work with handicapped children and youth also rarely are made for periods exceeding three years. Three years may be too long for some inappropriately funded proposals, but for good programs that produce solid results it is far too short. The government reasons that its money should be replaced by local funds from the state or the university or the community when the three-year limit is exceeded. If local sources have been unable to finance worthwhile projects in the past, though, it is difficult to believe that they would do so after the federal government discontinued its funding. This is a fickle and erratic type of funding at best. Programs are aborted and money and time are wasted. Good research cannot be tied to a calendar. If a decision to fund is made, twenty-year life programs would be appropriate for some and indefinite funding as in the U.S. space program would be appropriate for others. Federal grants are too often programmed by the whims of individuals within the federal bureaucracy, and certainly national leadership in special education has never come from this group of civil servants. Congress is at fault here as well, for its mandated policies of short-term financing of basic service and research programs produce an easily obtained shield behind which insecure federal employees can hide or a platform from which they can dictate terms for the award of monies. These unfortunate barriers have caused more than one outstanding researcher in the area of disability studies to refrain from applying for or accepting federal funds. The five national research centers for learning disabilities had their funds terminated at the end of five years. Reapplication was required. Some good programs that have added to our knowledge were terminated, first, because of "Reaganomics" and, second, because bureaucratic representatives urged that available funds be used to stimulate "new" programs. Little is accomplished by this shortsightedness.

These issues are part of the concepts of fear, guilt, and rejection about which I have spoken in this chapter. They are complicated human characteristics. They can come from many sources, as I have noted. They may be personal and stem from early religious or home training. They may emanate from early role models in the form of parents, teachers, or relatives. On a more subtle level, they may originate in the actions of civil servants, those who superficially are "doing their duty" (i.e., rejecting research proposals of competent persons on the basis of bias, occasionally ignorance, or from recommendations of field readers who do not represent the best minds of the profession). I am not criticizing with malice, but I do mean to raise questions regarding the psychological motivation of decision makers and whether or not it is time to look carefully at all those who hold positions in federal, state, and local agencies involved with human services and funding. The question must be raised as to the focus of the most outstanding research completed in special education in the past three decades, and who funded it. Equally as important are the questions of what potentially outstanding research has not been funded, who made those decisions, and what forces motivated such decisions. What is the psychological base from which agency personnel operate and to what extent are their actions protective and consist of covers for basic and controlling emotions yet unresolved? These questions are each and all germane to the future of a national program of services to handicapped persons.

In his dedicatory address at the opening of the Syracuse University Special Education Building, the late John J. Lee, professor at Wayne State University, quoted a Chinese proverb to the effect that "all boats rise on the same tide." The "weakest link" concept is inherent in Lee's quotation. When total and uniform strength exists in all links, then "boats rise" equally with whatever type of tide, albeit political, social, psychological, or other.

Quality and allocentricism, when they exist, are based on good personal adjustment: intellectual and emotional acceptance of others rather than rejection; rational understanding of physical and intellectual differences in and among human beings rather than fear; and wholesome and aggressive actions against those things that connote unpleasantness to some rather than guilt. When these positive psychological and behavioral characteristics are incorporated into the lives of citizens, then equality of opportunity and life potentials for exceptional children, youth, and adults more nearly will become a reality.

References and Related Readings

Anastasiow, N. J., ed. *Social Emotional Development*. San Francisco: Jossey-Bass, 1981.

Ausabel, D. P., and Kirk, D. *Ego Development and Personality Disorders: A Developmental Approach to Psychopathology*. New York: Grune and Stratton, 1977.

Erickson, E. H. *Identity: Youth and Crisis*. New York: Norton, 1968.

Hadas, M., ed. *The Basic Works of Cicero*. New York: Random House, 1951.

Kaplan, J. D., ed. *The Pocket Aristotle*. New York: Pocket Books, 1958.

Loevinger, J. *Ego Development: Conceptions and Theories*. San Francisco: Jossey-Bass, 1976.

Chapter 4

Growth: A Developmental Process

The growth and development of a child should be like an inverse toboggan slide. The latter is long, smooth, and straight—downhill. The child's growth and development in contrast should be long, smooth, and straight, but *upward* from infancy to adulthood. The toboggan slide of my youth is remembered as being a quarter of a mile long, a straight track, ending in the expanse of Green Lake onto whose ice the toboggan would race and go into whatsoever direction we as children wished to direct it—or sometimes we let it direct itself into controlled but erratic or purposeless patterns. So with the growth of children, in the inverse, the graceful track of normal development is upward in a sloping curve, gradual yet steady, ever rising to a peak. It is directed to the peak after which it may plateau and thereafter in controlled, erratic, or purposeless patterns form the life arrangement for the mature adult.

The parallel I describe is highly oversimplified, yet it depicts for me the smooth progression of development I believe we seek for children and youth. The development of a child is far more complicated than the mechanical actions of a sled or a toboggan coasting down a man-made track. The growth climb of a human organism includes not only the physical and neurological growth that follows a genetically controlled track, but at the same time it must encompass emotional and intellectual growth, social adaptation, sexuality, and complicated educational achievement intimately intertwined with some of the other factors mentioned. Most of these latter factors are learned; all, the results of environmental conditioning. Danly speaks of this as the "precariousness involved in passing from one age into another" (Danly 1981, viii). Adult human beings have in their hands an immense power as they mold positively or negatively the development of their offspring.

The Well-Rounded Person

Popularly, people speak of some as "well-rounded." "He is a well-rounded young man," says a teacher of one of his pupils. What is meant by this characterization? The youth is emotionally well-adjusted. He is intelligent, and he uses his native abilities appropriately. He is thoughtful and analytical. This youth is physically mature and appealing to others in behavior, physical characteristics, demeanor, and speech. He is creative in some or many aspects of social activities. He is socially and politically conscious. He is multifaceted in his interests—art, music, contemporary values, sports, social and political concerns and obligations. He is some or all of these in dynamic combinations that fit the social milieu in which he finds himself. He can modify his behavior in keeping with the group with which he associates without appearing artificial. In all things he can be genuine and unaffected. This is the product that education seeks to produce. The goal is the same for the exceptional child and youth as it is for the young person who is physically and intellectually normal.

It appears to me that it is not necessarily absolute perfection we seek in the individual. That is an unlikely goal ever to be obtained, and the end result would probably be a boring race. What we seek is an individual who understands the dynamics of his life activities, and one who can predict or make judgments regarding the effects of his actions before they take place. The ideal youth is not one who is always happy, but one who can balance sadness with happiness and analyze the reasons for both emotional experiences. He is one who can risk and can assume responsibilities for those risks that fail. He is one who can observe and understand the behavior of others and can adapt his own behavior to draw the best from those with whom he is associated. He can be independent in his function, asking for advice as it is needed, ignoring the behavior in others that runs counter to his own standards of life and living. He is interested in others, can identify with those he selects as friends, is disappointed when others let him down, but joyful not only in his own successes, but in those of his friends. He is firm in his beliefs but listens to the opinions of others. Is this the essence of development and education? Can this be translated into a human being? I think so, although not frequently enough.

I think of Tony, exceptional only in that he is such a remarkable young man. He is six feet four inches, tall and straight with blond curly hair. He looks you in the eye when he talks, and conversation comes easily with this nineteen-year-old young man. He is a beginning junior in an eastern university, which gives one an understanding that he is probably advanced. He is, but not as much as he could have been. He is a gifted person with wide-ranging interests. It was his decision as an elementary school pupil not to "skip a grade," but to "explore more widely," he says, "those things that I especially liked." This he did, simultaneously taking piano lessons, becoming expert in most aspects of the percussion instruments, and studying the flute. He manages and plays in a band. His high school years were filled with baseball and golf, receiving varsity letters in both sports; he composed musicals that were broadcast locally on commercial television stations and were well received. He is vivacious, and his face is usually pleasantly animated. He is politically aware, pacifist in his point of view, socially conscious of those less fortunate than he, and concerned to help other students who have less resources than he. He is not wealthy, but he can stretch a dollar to see that a friend also eats. He has earned at least half of his university costs. Tony is an independent thinker, one who reads widely, and one who has sampled life as fully as possible without excesses. He has been sexually active since he was sixteen, and he assures me that this phase of his life can be well accommodated whenever he feels the need. He understands the physiology of sex as well as its emotional components and responsibilities. He also is fully aware that life in his time requires a delay in marriage and the acceptance of its responsibilities. He appropriately rationalizes his own needs and the necessity of delay in getting married.

He seeks advice when it is needed, for example, coming to me when his parents separated and asking if he could from time to time talk through his anger, disappointment, fears, and anxieties for both himself and for his father and mother. Living with divorce is not something he and his sisters were prepared to meet, yet he fully understands the need for both a separation and the impending divorce.

Tony enjoys music of all varieties. He is no sissy. He has some personal defects of which he is conscious. So long as these do not get in his way of personal success nor turn off his friends, he does not worry too much about them, and indeed they are insignificant habits and mannerisms. He does not smoke or drink, but he doesn't avoid either when the social situation requires them in others to make others feel comfortable. The personal disturbance that he deeply feels regarding his parents is complicated by the fact that he and his girlfriend have recently broken up ending a four-year romance that continued from high school into college. The fact that his best friend replaced him with his girl hasn't helped matters significantly. However, as he says, "So long as I can talk these matters through impassionately with someone; so long as I can hear myself saying things which reflect accurately my problems, then I'll be OK. I don't want someone solving my problems, but I do want someone to listen to me and check me out and my thinking." I have often heard others say to his father, "You are lucky; Tony is a wonderful boy." It is my opinion also that in Tony, through his parents, his schooling, and his friends, there has been achieved the "well-rounded" individual, and one who will carry into adult life values and habits that can be passed on appropriately to another generation. At the same time his well-balanced point of view will expand his horizons of experience and permit him to live the "Good Life" of which Professor Franklin Bobbitt of the University of Chicago used to speak and write.

Can American education guarantee to result in the well-rounded child? Education in the United States is in a seriously confused state. There are those on the one hand who espouse "education for life and living," yet are unable to define how one achieves these goals.The extreme of this point of view is to be found in the delightful novel of Patrick Dennis, *Auntie Mame,* but fortunately this extreme is rarely if ever observed in community education. On the other hand one finds the philosophy of "return to the basics," and here the emphasis on teaching and learning the fundamentals of reading, writing, and arithmetic is to be found. At more advanced levels Latin is regaining a foothold in the curriculum, and emphases on history, English and American literature, sciences, and mathematics are foremost. In between these extremes one finds all measures of variety, often with little consistency even between the schools of one community and those of its immediate neighbor. Standards and curriculum vary between states, and, within a given state, variation in educational programs is often at a level to be defined as confusion. In some communities children appear to grow, mature, and intellectually develop in spite of the schools. Parents often complain, pupils object, but little change is forthcoming. Occasionally there is a serious community explosion—school board members are recalled; school administrators released from their posts—but when one examines the effects of these actions two or three years later, one sees that changes in educational opportunities for the youths of the community have been minimal or none at all. In the United States we tolerate mediocrity in public education, and only when a situation becomes volatile is anything done about it, and then the effects are usually only temporary. The well-rounded youth appears forgotten.

In the early paragraphs of this chapter I spoke of the fact that the achievement of children in learning situations should be that of a smooth upward curve. General education, however, in the majority of communities is a graded experience. Children are expected to achieve one grade per year, or every 180 to 190 days of instruction. There is little wrong with this plan, except that educational growth and development should be a smooth and ever-increasing advancement. Too frequently grades in school are turned into watertight compartments, independent boxes that are seen to have little or no relationship one with the other. Classes in history are taught, for example, with no consideration of what was taking place simultaneously in the fields of art, music, literature, or science. What was going on in literature, art, and music during the Napoleonic Wars? Who was writing what during Cromwell's time, or who was fighting whom while the prolific Mozart was living? Politically, what was the stimulus for Handel's *Fireworks Music* and *Water Music?* What was the political milieu surrounding Michelangelo and his painting in the Sistine Chapel? Who was the Pope at that time, and what was his political influence throughout Europe? I recently talked with a social science teacher in a local high school. We somehow spoke of President Franklin Roosevelt. This relatively young man, a teacher of some ten years' experience, had to be reminded of the social and economic reasons for the development of the New Deal legislation! As an aside one might ask of high school students what the impact of the WPA under Roosevelt might have been on the development of the national interest in the United States in ballet. Who were the American composers and musicians who grew up during these depression years and later reflected this period of American history in their music? Education should stress interrelationships. In the United States education is segmented. Rarely does instruction move out of its single-minded track to encompass the intellectual universe. Rarely do pupils in elementary or high school programs have an opportunity to see, feel, or hear interrelations that have had a vital impact on their lives. A high school teacher of physics sees no reason for "taking time" to help his students understand the background and development of Alfred Einstein as a person. "All they need to know is the formula for the theory of relativity," he stated.

Often in teaching graduate students I am impressed with the fact that many appear to believe that events take place in a vacuum. In special education, for example, what did the impact of the growth of cities have on the development of special classes for children with retarded mental development? Was there an interrelation between the two world wars and the greater acceptance of physically handicapped persons in the community, and, if so, how did this come about? What were the spin-offs, if any, of the development of the transistor battery, the vacuum tube, the radio, the television, to the improvement and efficiency of hearing aids for use with those who have hearing impairments? I am reminded of students who fail to recognize or know of the relationship between World War II and the development of the field of neuropsychology; that Rorschach was a man, whose first name was Hermann; that he was a psychiatrist in Switzerland working essentially with schizophrenic patients. His test is not recognized to have any impact on an understanding of the complications of adolescents or adults with learning disabilities, for example. Significant events are seen in isolation from one another. A holistic point of view of human growth and development in a social, political, and scientific setting is not appreciated or valued.

The Exceptional Child

I have been writing in the preceding paragraphs of the development of normal children and youth. While exceptional children have all of the primary characteristics of normal children, the idiosyncratic elements inherent in their physical or mental disabilities have significant implications for their development. I have written on numerous occasions that there are more similarities than differences between exceptional children and their normal peers. The differences, however, often visually minimal to the observer, can be of a staggering magnitude insofar as learning and development are concerned.

I will later discuss the issues of intellectual differences, both the extremes of *mental retardation* and *giftedness*. Here it is only required to state that variance from the norm of intelligence has enormous implications for all aspects of development. While Kirk (1958) has pointed out that early education for the mentally handicapped child has significance for development and results in a smoother educational growth curve in subsequent years, the fact of retarded mental development nevertheless has a significant impact on almost every aspect of growth through adolescence and into the adult years. The growth curve may be smoother as the result of early education, but gross differences from the normal are maintained throughout the life span. Skeels and Skodak (1939) demonstrated this in their famous longitudinal study. This fact has meaning for the current educational fad called *mainstreaming,* normalization, or integration so woefully operated in many school systems of the world, following the unfortunate lead of the United States. In the retarded child population, the fact of restricted mental development has significance for the acquisition of readiness to learn, rate of learning, and level of ultimate achievement, among other things. There may be a smooth developmental curve with some of these children, but it cannot be compared favorably to normal children in rate or ultimate level even when optimal home and school educational opportunities have been available. When less than optimal circumstances prevail, growth plateaus occur, and with these less than satisfactory adjustment often results.

Mental retardation is not limited to the clinical classification of retardation. It cuts across all clinical categories of child deviance; hence the categories of *multihandicapping*. Mental retardation is a respector of no other clinical group. Cerebral palsy and retardation are closely related in some degree in about 75 percent of the former individuals. Learning disabilities and mental retardation, although a relationship denied by many parents of learning disabled children, is a fact and a very common one at that. There are mentally retarded blind youth, deaf youth, children with epilepsy, and with any or all other clinical problems. When the coupling occurs the possibility of smooth and progressive growth and development is almost never obtained, and when it is it varies with the degree of intellectual retardation and the severity of the physical problem. Mental retardation will have a detrimental effect on all aspects of growth: academic, physical, emotional, and social.

This latter statement is not equally true with intellectually *gifted* children. William James wrote "The greatest gap in nature is between two minds" (1890). If this be true, its paraphrase is almost equally as true, namely, the greatest gap in nature is between the two extremes of the intellectual spectrum. While James stressed individual differences between and among the minds of men, I stress here the developmental differences of groups when differences are so intimately related to intelligence.

Although studies indicate that there is a positive correlation between superior intelligence, health, and physique, between intelligence and other developmental factors, there is not in any degree the social or physical stigmata present in the gifted as when clinical problems are coupled with retardation. Even the stereotype of the gifted child always wearing horn-rimmed glasses is a fallacy! The development of the gifted child when carefully nurtured can be smooth and steady, ultimately reaching heights that can and often do change the direction of societies through music, art, literature, or the sciences. Unfortunately little research has been done related to the ways in which gifted and talented children learn. Since the famous Genetic Studies of Genius Series, authored by Lewis Terman and his associates and published between 1925 and 1959 in five volumes, few if any substantive studies of gifted children have been realized. There are exceptions to this statement, and some of these should be noted. Certain school systems, particularly at the secondary levels have made significant contributions to the growth of the gifted child. Notable is the Major Work Program of the Cleveland public schools, which operated for many years under the leadership of Dorothy Norris; Cass Technical High School, Detroit public schools; the Bronx High School of Science and the High School for the Performing Arts, both of the New York City public schools. There are other separate schools, for example in New Orleans, which serve the gifted children of that parish. However, the list is very small, and my statement that the schools of the United States essentially ignore this significant national resource stands as true. The result of this can be developmentally devastating.

Cerebral Palsy

Cerebral palsy, a long-term, nonfatal, noncurable disease involving the neurological system, is probably the best example we have of the unevenness of development in children. It is a disease in the accurate definition of the term meaning a *deviation,* and from almost any point of view the term is also synonymous with *complexity.* Cerebral palsy is made up of numerous subtypes (Winthrop Morgan Phelps identified twelve different types of athetosis alone). It is further complicated by the affected human geography from monoplegia to quadriplegia. There is a higher incidence of hearing impairment and visual impairment found among cerebral-palsied children than in the normal population of children of like ages, and the incidence of speech defects is extremely high in cerebral palsy. I have already commented on the very high incidence of intellectual retardation in this clinical population. There are, of course, some children with cerebral palsy who are intellectually gifted, but these comprise a very small minority. The heroic efforts of many clinicians often effect astounding levels of self-sufficiency, but a totally smooth developmental curve is difficult, if not impossible, to obtain. Consider the realities of a ten-year-old child with a quadriplegic type of athetosis, one whose measured IQ is about 105. He is simultaneously characterized by a moderate hearing loss, perceptual processing deficits, and is on a pharmacological regimen for the control of grand mal seizures. He has a severe speech disability usually associated with athetosis. A legitimate question may be asked. With the goal of a smooth developmental curve, how indeed can the best clinicians achieve this in the face of the complexity—not in any manner unusual—depicted in this child? Only the combination of disabilities may change in many others, if not most, cerebral-palsied children. However, it is not only the clinicians and parents who must be complimented in their efforts to achieve good developmental progress in these children and youth. The efforts of the child himself and his self-engendered ability to progress are often observed to be a little short of valiant.

However, I write here of the goal of even and gradual development. In contrast to normal children who are reared in a wholesome and secure environment and whose various aspects of growth are coordinated and related, the growth curves of those with cerebral palsy are uneven and disrelated. The concept of an integrated organismic age as conceptualized by Willard Olson and Byron Hughes (Olson 1949) is not reflected in cerebral palsy. Here physical growth may, for example, mirror normal trends, but simultaneously motor coordination and motor skills may be at a much lower level. Speech and communication skills may be three or four years retarded in children with cerebral palsy in comparison to their understanding of and ideational capacity for linguistic concepts. If all developmental skills are placed on a graph, they will represent a disorganized picture with high and low achievement levels being very obvious. It is a record full of "spikes." One of the things that is to me remarkable about young people with cerebral palsy is the fact that many develop into well-adjusted adults in spite of the frequent developmental plateaus they have experienced. Regardless, the neurological impairment this disease represents does not insure consistent growth and development of all the variables, and a smooth developmental curve is impossible.

Perceptual Processing Deficits

Almost all children with any form of neurological dysfunction also will be characterized by perceptual processing deficits that may take a variety of forms. Children with cerebral palsy, particularly those with athetosis and spasticity, are included in this group. In addition, children with epilepsy, autism, dyslexia, and aphasia will often be characterized by these added problems. Likewise, hyperactive emotionally disturbed children, blind children whose disability was caused by rubella, exogenous mentally retarded children, children who have survived Reye's syndrome, each and all among other clinical groups, may demonstrate the impact of perceptual processing deficits.

Perceptual processing deficits are of a neurological origin and are the result of various forms of neurophysiological dysfunction. In turn the resultant problems may affect any of the various aspects of learning and development—gross- and fine-motor development, learning dependent upon any or all of the sensory modalities, and the more complex learning related to intersensory and interhemispheric neurological activities.

Perceptual processing deficits take many forms. Erratic and shortened attention span may result. Figure-background pathology, dissociation, closure problems, and perseveration may be related to forced responsiveness to stimuli of an auditory, visual, or tactile nature. Both long- and short-memory functions may be impaired. This list is not inclusive, but serves to indicate the nature and causes of serious discrepancies in children's growth be it academic, social, physical, or emotional. Maturation may be on the side of many children, but equally as frequently and perhaps more so, children with perceptual processing deficits show terribly uneven development and often arrive at adulthood as confused and maladaptive individuals. Positive growth will not take place in the face of perceptual processing deficits without extraordinary educational measures being applied involving a total program of structure and motor training. Perceptual processing deficits are antithetical to the harmony required for the total integrity of development—for a developmental gestalt, not fragmentation.

Epilepsy

It is not necessary for us to trace this issue through all categories of physical or mental disability. The point we are intent to stress has been made. However, the issue of epilepsy contains some elements not common to other forms of disability, and thus it warrants some attention. As with children who have a perceptual processing deficit, those with epilepsy have a hidden disease until the seizure is experienced. Studies Earl X. Freed and I completed in the 1950s of a large number of adolescents who had disabilities, indicated that those with nonvisible physical disabilities were not considered different by their peers. This would include those with cardiac disease, a group of children sufficiently large in our research to ascertain that the issue of visibility versus nonvisibility of the physical condition was a significant factor in the evenness of the youth's development. So it is with epilepsy when, through medication, it is under control, except for those (such as parents) who know what the child's problem is. Clinically I have counseled many individuals with epilepsy. It is reported by these people that when their condition becomes known to others (socially visible), a distinct change in the attitude and the behavior of others toward the individual with epilepsy is noticeably different than formerly. "I am always on the defensive when that happens, and I look for the things in the way others treat me that indicate that they know about my problem," reported one high school student. Epilepsy constitutes a serious psychological as well as a physical problem for those who have it, and the reasons for this are many. Epilepsy is historically endowed with misconceptions, fears, unreasonable characteristics, and absolute untruths. From Biblical times until the present those with epilepsy have been isolated socially and certainly psychologically. Those with epilepsy have often been made to feel that they are different and unacceptable. Until very recently numerous states in the United States have had laws forbidding those with epilepsy to marry, and even more have refused them drivers' licenses. While such laws have fortunately changed almost everywhere, they nevertheless illustrate the degree of rejection society has imposed upon this group of people. Good human development cannot take place in this climate.

In public schools there are many examples of children with epilepsy who have not been permitted to take physical education, particularly swimming, when it is available to others, for fear that the child would have a seizure while in the pool or in other ways injure himself. Not true. Some teachers have requested that these children not be enrolled in their class but be assigned to another teacher's group.

Occasionally, but fortunately not often, a child may have the first seizure in a classroom. Such an example is known to me, for the family soon after engaged themselves in family counseling and became an administrative responsibility of mine. Except for some extremes in behavior, the child in question had not been considered different through his first nine years of life. One day in school a grand mal seizure was experienced with the accompanying loss of consciousness and bodily tremors. The teacher, unfamiliar with this problem, ran screaming out of the classroom leaving the rest of the children in the room alone with the child in question. They were generally stunned, not only because of the behavior of their friend, but because of "what he had done to their teacher." Even with careful explanation by the principal who soon came to the class and who also returned the next day to talk with the children, the impact on the teacher by the child in question could not be completely erased. For many months, this little boy was shunned by others in the class and was avoided because of what "he had done." The seizure per se can be a threatening thing, and to anticipate its reoccurrence sometimes places a severe strain on the relations between the individual and those around him or her who know. While control of the seizure is a possibility in the majority of instances, there is often the concern that "one may occur" at the wrong time, as one high school girl stated to me.

Children and youths with epilepsy often report an overconcern by parents. Elsewhere in this volume some of these examples have been reported, i.e., a mother informing other mothers of her son's epilepsy when the boy had attempted to date a girl; mothers preventing a son or daughter from riding a bicycle; mothers and fathers not permitting their son or daughter to go swimming with friends at a nearby lake. One set of parents even refused to allow their son to go to movies for fear he might have a seizure in a darkened movie house and "no one would know to help." In a sense, all of these restrictions seemingly may have some degree of logic, but for the most part they are as baseless as the laws regarding marriage and driving we noted earlier. However, such behavior on the part of adults, be they parents or school personnel, have detrimental effects on the way children grow and mature—the way the youth sees himself and the way the self-concept develops regardless of the age or the sex of the young person. "I look normal," says one, "but I know I'm not, even with the medication." Many young people do not know that if they are seizure free for a period of two or three years (variance with state law), they legally are not considered epileptic.

There are numerous types of epilepsy, and all of them do not have the same characteristics or behavioral manifestations. Since epilepsy is a neurological disease, some will be complicated by perceptual processing deficits but not with all such individuals. Differential diagnosis is important with all children, but with this group of young people, it is particularly important. Insufficient research has been done with children who have epilepsy to be able to make many clinically substantiated generalizations.

. Many children and young people experience an aura of a widely diversified nature a short time before the seizure actually takes place. Often this warning permits the child to remove himself from a classroom or social group before the seizure happens. The nature of the aura is interesting and significant in the life of the individual with epilepsy, and many of these young people feel that the fact of the aura has many advantages as a warning signal. They feel more comfortable about themselves because of this "safety valve." This facet of the problem has received little psychological research.

The relation between epilepsy and positive child growth and development is not so much a factor of the seizure per se as it is the emotional displacement surrounding the seizure. The fact of a seizure means many different things to friends, relatives, and to the community in general. Attitudes held by people toward the child or adolescent with epilepsy is interpreted or misinterpreted in many different ways and with a multiplicity of meanings. The psychological discharge on the part of the affected individual due to the knowledge that he or she "has" epilepsy may affect school achievement, choice of friends, withdrawal from peers, family relationships, jealousy among siblings, and indeed in some instances career choices.

I am aware that in at least one medical school, applicants who are honest enough to indicate they have had a history of epilepsy are not admitted to the school. I have sat on admission committees for graduate schools of education and have heard otherwise knowledgeable professors discourage the committee members from accepting an applicant because epilepsy appeared in the record. To change such a point of view is indeed a difficult job and usually is accomplished only with extreme reluctance on the part of the complaining professor. All of these environmental factors impinge on the good adjustment of the individual concerned, and if he or she is a young person, impinge on the developmental curve with which we here are concerned.

Summary

The point has been made, and it is not necessary to pursue it further. In concluding this brief discussion, it needs to be pointed out that not all exceptional children or youth are permanently derailed in their development because of their disability. The human organism, figuratively speaking, is extraordinarily resilient, indeed elastic. It can, and often does, take many blows, and survives. Well-adjusted handicapped adults are the result. I am reminded of Pepi, a fifty-year-old woman living in her own rented apartment. At the age of nineteen years she experienced multiple sclerosis. Now she is confined to a bed stretcher wheelchair, has limited vision, hardly understandable speech, and requires twenty-four-hour-a-day attendance by four paid persons. But Pepi is a well-adjusted person, more so as she consumes one scotch and soda one after another at parties! A good sense of humor, an active mind, an appreciation of the theater and opera help her, with assistance, to overcome man-made barriers (including the Metropolitan Opera House in New York City) to partially achieve the full life. Her condition has not changed in the ten years I have known her. Pepi—perhaps an extreme among those with physical disability—is not atypical of many handicapped persons who are "making it" from the point of view of personal adjustment. She is not making it economically and is being supported through Medicare and social services. Undoubtedly she would wish for a different life-style. But she is making it in terms of adjustment and against the extraordinarily negative odds of her physical disease. So it is with children. Many well-adjusted children with good school achievement survive the rigors of parental divorce, hunger, drunken parents, or poor teaching. Some do not. A majority of young adults were psychologically unaffected by the Vietnam war; many others were not. Although there is no census of those with physical and mental handicaps who are able to maintain a smooth growth curve in spite of disabilities, there are undoubtedly many others who are not. It is for these latter young people in particular that the total resources of the community must be appropriately organized and effectively utilized.

References and Related Readings

Brin, O. G., and Kagan, J. *Constancy and Change in Human Development.* Cambridge: Harvard University Press, 1980.

Crain, W. C. *Theories of Development: Concepts and Applications.* Englewood Cliffs, N.J.: Prentice-Hall, 1980.

Cratty, B. J. *Perceptual and Motor Development in Infants and Children.* Englewood Cliffs, N.J.: Prentice-Hall, 1979.

Cruickshank, W. M. *Selected Writings.* 2 vols. Syracuse: Syracuse University Press, 1981.

Cruickshank, W. M., Junkala, J. B., and Paul, J. L. *Misfits in the Public Schools.* Syracuse: Syracuse University Press, 1969.

Danly, R. L. *The Shade of Spring Leaves*. New Haven: Yale University Press, 1981.

Gabel, S., and Erickson, M. T., eds. *Child Development and Developmental Disabilities*. Boston: Little, Brown, 1980.

Illingsworth, R. S. *The Development of the Infant and Young Child: Normal and Abnormal*. 6th ed. London: Churchill Livingston, 1975.

James, William. *Principles of Psychology*. 2 vols. New York: Dover, 1890.

Kirk, S. A. *Early Education of the Mentally Retarded*. Urbana: University of Illinois Press, 1958.

Kretchmer, N., and Walcher, D. N. *Environmental Influences on Genetic Expression*. Washington, D.C.: U.S. Government Printing Office, 1969.

Maier, H. W. *Three Theories of Child Development: The Contributions of E. H. Erickson, Jean Piaget, and Robert R. Sears, and Their Applications*. New York: Harper and Row, 1969.

Olson, W. C. *Child Development*. Boston: D. C. Heath, 1949.

Paul, J. L., Turnbull, A., and Cruickshank, W. M. *A Practical Guide to Mainstreaming*. Syracuse: Syracuse University Press, 1979.

Skeels, H. M., and Skodak, M. "Adult Status of Individuals Who Experienced Early Stimulation." *Proceedings of the American Association on Mental Retardation* 44 (1939): 114–36.

Vander, Z., and Wilfrid, J. *Human Development*. New York: Alfred Knopf, 1981.

Chapter 5

The Psychology of Difference

The concept of individual differences is not in any way new to readers in the fields of psychology or special education. The powerful writings of Anne Anastasi (1958), albeit not contemporary, were significant in driving into the minds of many the uniqueness of the varying personal characteristics of individuals and the part these differences play in adjustment and growth. For many years, the concept of individual differences has been stressed in colleges and universities with preservice teachers, who were preparing to begin a career of teaching within the public or private schools of the nation, and with young psychologists who were beginning to move into the field of diagnosis and evaluation. As much as the concept of individualization has been stressed, we see very little evidence of its implementation in school programs. Basic tests and workbooks common to all pupils, or at best adjusted to "slow," "average," or "fast" subgroups within a given grade, characterize the instructional procedures utilized in the great majority of schoolrooms in the nation. As a matter of fact, a great number of teachers have never been taught how to individualize instruction and simply do not know how to approach a group of children from this point of view. We still receive reports that in certain school and agency situations, for example, the psychologists are expected to complete eight to ten psychological evaluations of children per day, although this is by no means universal. There are good programs of psychological evaluations in many communities. There are also too many poor ones remaining, and these can easily be documented. Children are seen as in a mass rather than as individuals. It is yet worth spending some time on the concept of individual differences, particularly as it relates to the exceptional child or youth.

Homogeneous Grouping

One of the persistent fallacies of psychological or educational research pertains to the oft-cited statements regarding homogeneous grouping, control groups, experimental groups, and related types of subject groupings. In one of two very recent reports of research that pertain to learning disabilities in children, the following statement appeared:

> The experimental group of learning disabled children between the ages of ten and fourteen years chronologically included thirty boys and girls. All significant variables were controlled for this group, and matched groups, i.e., homogeneous control and experimental groups reportedly were obtained. No significant differences between the groups were found insofar as the control variables were concerned.

The following statement appeared in the second report:

> Two homogeneous groups of subjects were obtained for this study, control and experimental. Both groups consisted of twenty carefully selected children characterized by similarities in chronological age, sex, and the essential characteristics of learning disabilities.

Before these two statements are examined, it is warranted that the concept of *homogeneity* and that of *homogeneous groups* of exceptional children are considered. Later, the characteristics of specific clinical clusters of exceptional children will also be considered. Too often, researchers in the fields of psychology and education, in particular, fail to recognize the limitations of the concept of homogeneity. The situation is different than when dealing with research problems in the chemistry or physics laboratories, or indeed in the field of genetics, in hematology, or with evoked responses related to electroencephalography. In these latter fields, all relatively exact sciences, it is much easier to consider the control of variables than in social sciences, which include psychology and education. Homogeneity can be defined. The word is of Greek derivation: *homos* means the same. If the word *same,* either in Greek or English, is examined, it will be learned that the definition and derivation permit no deviation from the concept of identical, exact, or alike in every detail. In psychology and education, we have permitted researchers, including me, to become careless in the use of terms, specifically in the use of the term *homogeneous.* It has become an accepted assumption in these professional disciplines that if one controls age, sex, and intelligence, one has a homogeneous group, or worse yet, two homogeneous groups if the concept of experimental and control is employed. The two disciplines that have been singled out for attention here are not the only culprits utilizing very loose definitions of grouping. Sociologists, economists, psychiatrists, and disciplines such as cardiology, pediatrics, and radiology frequently employ terms just as loosely as do the social sciences. The utilization of terms based on popular usage rather than exactitude has come to be an accepted degree of freedom permitted to authors and designers of research projects. In turn, this lack of exactness has led to hundreds of misleading conclusions regarding all kinds of problems related to human development and to the relationship of learning characteristics, for example, between exceptional children and youth and their so-called normal counterparts.

It is unlikely that a homogeneous group of humans ever exists. If *group* means cluster and if homogeneous group means an exact cluster with no deviation between or among members, then what is a homogeneous group of human beings? Assume that certain controls can be maintained among subjects—i.e., exact moments of birth, exact similarities in weight, height, color of eyes (much more difficult to control), color of hair, and race—what is this "group" of variables that remains uncontrolled yet significant in considering, for example, research with children with learning disabilities? Among others, they might consist of ages of mothers at times of delivery, chromosomal contributions of both fathers and mothers, similarities or differences in the size of the pelvic arch of the mother, and the similarities or differences in the degree of extension of the pelvic cartilages during the birth process (both possible factors in perinatal brain stem cranial damage), the duration of the perinatal activity, to say nothing of postnatal characteristics. Postnatal characteristics could include similarities in rearing procedures within the homes of the various children, teachers' personalities, emotional experiences surrounding first entering school, teaching methodologies employed with the children, interaction between subjects and school peers over the years, numbers and position of the subject among siblings, age of onset of puberty and child's attitude toward it, ad infinitum. Were the study being done in India and with children whose parents were believers in astrological phenomena, then a specific variable, rather difficult to control, would be the exact moment of ejaculation of sperm under conditions of a full moon, as I was reminded during a public meeting one day in New Delhi. I suspect that it would be possible to match two children on a majority of these variables, each of which is significant to the research task at hand, but I do not believe by the greatest stretch of the imagination, that it would be possible to match them on all human variables that might be germane to any psychological or educational research project. Ad infinitum is used here consciously, for the number of variables relevant to research with human beings is indeed practically unlimited. As a matter of fact, logically, no two people can be homogeneous: (1) they do not have the same parents, or (2) they were not born at the same time and/or did not have the same parents, or do not have the same mixture of genes. On a practical basis, we may have to sacrifice research exactness for clinical results, but in doing so, we should not mislead ourselves in that we are doing controlled research, and this caution should be a preface to every study purporting to utilize a controlled or homogeneous group.

With reference to the two statements noted at the beginning of this section, let us examine this situation still further. Both statements were made by authors reporting the results of studies that involved learning disabled children, one a group of such children between the chronological ages of ten and fourteen. In considering this "experimental group," one wonders if the author has considered the fact that his cluster of children vary on a myriad of elements, although he states that all "significant variables were controlled." What about the fact that within the group, there were ten-year-old children still in the later stages of childhood and at the same time there were others who were undoubtedly pubescent. Are girls and boys the same in terms of learning characteristics and particularly boys and girls with learning disabilities? We do not know this one way or another. But then, let us consider other uncontrolled variables within this experimental group of learning disabled children. The author implies similarities of subjects by giving them each the same clinical name, i.e., learning disabled. In my clinical experience, there is not a greater example of individual differences and deviations than in the field of learning disabilities. Merely to classify a number of children or youth into the same category does not result in homogeneity.

Learning disabilities are characterized by a variety of perceptual processing deficits related to any one or all of the sensory modalities. Here are gross differences that must be controlled if homogeneous groups are sought. However, within a given sensory system, there may easily be as many as twenty quite different processing deficits that alone or together in varying constellations go to make up the concept of a learning disability, i.e., memory deficit, sequencing problem, attention disturbances, intersensory dysfunctions, perseveration, dissociation, closure problems, and many others. Likewise, the impact of neurophysiological dysfunctions, their localization and extent, undoubtedly is a significant factor that is absolutely impossible to control. Age of the child and the physical condition at the time of the neurological shock are significant variables, and although we know too little about the process as yet, the issue of variability of nerve regeneration in human beings and subsequent possible reestablishment of certain degrees of function is a factor that cannot be discounted. Just how does one go about obtaining homogeneity in a cluster of learning disabled children in the face of these and a myriad of other variables that have not been mentioned? I often read research studies wherein children are lumped together on the basis of mental age and wherein the psychologists have employed accepted standardized instrumentation. Matching on the basis of mental age or performance or verbal intelligence quotients is possible, but what about the dissimilarity of the elements that contribute to the weighted scores (the qualitative diagnostic profile) culminating in a performance or verbal IQ score? Have the subjects performed equally as well, one with the other, including all the intrasubtest elements, on such categories as Coding, Similarities, Object Assembly, Block Design, and other items of the Wechsler Intelligence Scale for Children (WISC), for example? Matching or grouping is rarely, if ever, carried to this extreme. It must be if homogeneity is to be obtained, and even when this is done, the many other variables I have previously mentioned must somehow be considered. Matching, on the basis of a matrix of variables is essential, but it is unlikely to be obtained. Statistical manipulations may be employed to minimize the matching impossibilities, but this produces contrivances that must of necessity cast suspicion over the whole effort. Psychology may not yet have sufficient maturity or possess sufficient skills to be able to create a homogeneous group. Until it does, research based on purported homogeneous groups must be considered in a guarded manner and its results open to serious question. I am undoubtedly not saying anything new here, but I am reinforcing a long held concern that most research based on group comparisons that has been published in the fields of education and psychology, particularly with exceptional children of whatsoever clinical type, is essentially worthless because of the fallacy and myth of the homogeneous group. (For further information see Keogh et al. 1982.)

Let us examine two simple profiles (table 1). Although incomplete, they may shed some light on the grouping problem with

TABLE 1. Sample Profiles of Variables

Characteristic	Profile 1	Profile 2
Sex	Male	Male
Age	9-5-23	9-5-23
Height	4'9.5"	4'9.5"
Weight	85 lbs.	85 lbs.
Race	white	white
IQ (WISC)	100	100
Performance IQ	95	95
Verbal IQ	103	103
Weighted scores		
Coding	5	10
Block Design	9	12
Picture Completion	11	11
Picture Arrangement	11	5
Processing characteristics		
Dissociation	yes	no
Perseveration	yes	no
Memory problems	no	yes
Sequencing	no	yes
Attention span limitations	no	yes
Closure problems	yes	no
Visual figure-ground reversals	yes	no
Auditory memory problems	no	yes
Auditory figure-ground reversals	yes	no
Intersensory disorganization	yes	yes
Gross motor dysfunction	yes	no
Neurological dysfunction		
Frontal lobe dysfunction	yes	yes
Anterior parietal lobe dysfunction	no	yes
Temporal lobe dysfunction	no	yes
Occipital lobe dysfunction	yes	no
Birth history	negative	prolonged and "difficult"
Position among siblings	3 of 5	1 of 0
Age of mother at subject's birth	28	19
Age of father at subject's birth	30	22
Positive familial characteristics	father: nonreader	none

which I am here concerned. Two boys are involved, and both are diagnosed as learning disabled.

Depicted here are two learning disabled boys, similar in basic characteristics of sex, age, height, race, and intelligence (insofar as IQ is concerned). The two are extremely different, however, insofar as the characteristics of learning disabilities are considered, neurological dysfunction, and certain familial characteristics. If these two youths are included in the same group of subjects is the group homogeneous? Can they be considered "the same" insofar as grouping is concerned? I believe not. Here there are twenty-two variables among others that could be listed wherein the differences exist between the two subjects. The list of variables in this comparison is in no way exhausted.

An Alternative to Groups

If group studies with human beings have all the limitations that I have suggested in terms of noncontrolled variables, then either research does not get accomplished or an alternative must be found. The alternative in the form of single-subject research is a significant opportunity and should be widely employed. One of my former students has prepared a fine summary of the issue of single-subject research, Dr. Steven Russell of Bowling Green State University. With acknowledgments to Dr. Russell and with his permission, I am including his statement here as an excellent, brief outline of a very positive alternative to the issue of grouping and all of its pitfalls that I have already mentioned.

A significant approach to this problem, albeit rather apolitical, but one which has received a great amount of attention recently, is that of single-subject research. As advocated by Kratochwill et al., single-subject research should be an integral part of the research endeavor [and other areas of childhood exceptionality]. They continue by stating the apparent benefit of such a research design—individual case studies which can be compiled, leading to the formulation of hypotheses and future research.

Johnson suggests that although $n = 1$ as a research design is currently unusual in educational research, it can yield data that do not oversimplify the situation. Through this method and design, the analysis of results, and the comparison of different cases, can be facilitated by the profiles of each case available from such designs. Johnson suggests, for instance, that it might be found that a disability can be corrected in one case, and that this method of correction found to be useful in this single case might well be applied to another case with little, or no change. However, Johnson cautions the researcher, and practitioner alike, by stating that although the disabilities in both cases may be the same (e.g., both being learning disabled), due to the individual differences between the profiles of each (e.g., one individual having significant auditory processing deficits while the other has significant visual processing deficits; one individual exhibiting significant reading disorders while the other demonstrates little or no reading disorder), the method found to be effective in the first case may have to be adjusted for the second case, in order to be effective.

Various designs for conducting single-subject research have been suggested by Hersen and Barlow, Kratochwill, and Guralnick. Among the designs suggested have been the case study, $n = 1$, intensive, operant, time-series, and multiple-baseline. These methods suggest the same type of research; however, certain procedures in the design or method of analysis change from one type to another. Moreover, with all of these methods it is necessary to specify the subject's (or subjects') characteristics, to specify the treatment variables if a treatment is employed, and to specify the relationship of the relevant subject's characteristics to the observations or treatment variables. In addition, replicability becomes key to establishing generality with the above designs.

As Chassan has stated in support of single-subject research, each case serves as its own control. Statistically significant results cannot be an artifact of a lack of homogeneity between cases. The common fallacy is to assume a significant effect demonstrated in an extensive (group) design exists for every, or for most, or even an appreciable proportion of the members of the population—as is often the case with much of the learning disability research. This assumption is false. The extensive (group) model does not permit identification of the subject's (or subjects') characteristics that accompany the tested effect. Therefore, with special populations, in particular the learning disabled, the need for single-subject research, and recognition of the heterogeneous nature of this population, must be supported. Researchers in this field need to feel the importance of this issue.

Nowhere has this concept been more evident, nor more strongly advocated, than in the research conducted by Keogh and her colleagues. Keogh and her associates designed a three-phase, three-year project to "identify, define operationally, test, and evaluate a set of 'marker variables' which can be used to guide empirical research and program evaluation." Marker variables were defined as generally referring to a common core of characteristics and information regarding samples on which research is being conducted within the confines of a particular field, in this case learning disabilities. More specifically, "Marker variables reflect the constructs which characterize a particular field and may tap cognitive, psychological, social, motoric, or demographic dimensions." The inherent value of marker variables for the learning disability field is nearly implicit in their description. Marker variables "will facilitate the development of a reference base for researchers and program administrators in order that they may compare research findings, generalize results, develop theories, and reach policy decisions.

Though the method chosen by Keogh and her associates for the identification of marker variables was through the use of an extensive review of previous research studies in the field of learning disabilities, followed by refinement of the marker variables, and concluded with a field test of the usefulness of these variables, additional variables of this sort, particularly those not yet identified within the existing body of research, can be discovered and identified through the use of single-subject research. Additionally, both extensive (group) research and single-subject research will profit through the employment of marker variables in that the applicability of the results will be more clearly delineated.

Finally, though it is recognized that the results of such investigations as those that employ a single-subject research design will not be generalizable to the entire population of learning disabled learners, nor to a significant proportion of this population, the results will provide the bases of future research through the generation of hypotheses that will subsequently be testable in experimental designs. Through the generation of these hypotheses, and the subsequent testing on a larger population of like learning disabled learners, it will be possible to define new variables that will assist in the definition, identification, intervention and remediation, and program evaluation of the learning disabled population and education.

Clinical Variables

It is undoubtedly trite to remind a reader that individual differences exist in practically all things. Steel molded to an exact specification may be an exception, but even here, minute differences in components do exist. Bach (Mass in B Minor), Beethoven (*Missa Solemnis*), Verdi (*Requiem*), Bach (*St. Matthew Passion*), and Brahms (*Ein deutsches Requiem*) have each written magnificent orchestral and choral works. Some contain, in part, the same words: "Kyrie eleison," "Christe eleison," the "Sanctus," the "Agnus Dei," and others. Yet each is unique and, within the first few bars, it is possible to tell one from the other, as well as who composed each. The individual differences of the composers each using essentially the same text has resulted in something so personalized that no other composer can come near the resounding magnificence of the first.

On the other hand, each of four conductors—the late Eugene Ormandy, Leonard Bernstein, Seiji Ozawa, and Georg Solti—conducts the Verdi *Requiem*. None is like the other. Each man lends his differences to the work in a manner that imprints it with his mark. The strings of the Philadelphia Orchestra, under the baton of Ormandy, glistened like those of no other orchestra; they were his trademark. The emotion that Bernstein transmits to his orchestra produces a fire unlike that of any other conductor, and so with Ozawa, Solti, and before them, a long list of conductors each of whom has added his expression to a composer's work. The notes and markings the conductors read do not vary from the initial composer's writing. The interpretations do.

Muralists abound, but what differences exist between those of Hockney, Rivera, or indeed of Michelangelo. In the arts we speak of character. The work of Picasso or Dali can be identified at a distance and from a brief glance. The sound of Rampal can be recognized after a few phrases are heard by those who know flute. The poetry of Milton is easily distinguished from that of Ibsen even though identical verse forms are utilized by the poets.

The early scholars of Greece and Rome were more interested in the characteristics of man than they were in the differences between men. The philosophical constructs of the good life were their forte. Cicero, however, in the last years of his life writes *On Moral Duties,* and in so doing emphasizes the issues of individual differences to which this chapter is addressed. While not emphasizing physical differences between men, Cicero stresses character differences on a higher plane. Writing to his "dear son," he states,

In the next place observe that Nature has invested us with two characters. The one is universal, inasmuch as all men participate in reason and in that excellence which lifts humanity above the brute creation. This is the one source of honor and decorum and of the very idea of right and wrong. The other character is individual. Great as are the diversities in the constitution of the body—one man is a swift runner, another a strong wrestler; one has a stately, another graceful figure—the diversities of character are greater still. L. Crassus and L. Philippus possessed great wit, Caesar, the son of Lucius, even greater, but his was more labored; on the other hand, their contemporaries, young M. Drusus and M. Scaurus, were remarkable for their gravity, and C. Laelius for his vivacity, while his friend Scipio united a loftier ambition with a more solemn demeanor. Among the Greeks, we are told, Socrates had a winning, playful, sprightly manner, and his discourse was full of that roguish humor which the Greeks call irony; Pythagoras and Pericles on the other hand had not a spark of gaiety and yet attained commanding influence. Among the Punic leaders Hannibal was as shrewd as Q. Maximum among our own; both had the gift of silence and the art of hiding their own stratagems and stealing a march on the enemy. For such qualities the Greeks assign the palm to Themistocles and Jason of Pherae, and we have a remarkable instance of astuteness in the artifice of Solon, who feigned madness in order to save his life and benefit his country. In contrast with these there are men of frank and open character, who love the truth, hate deceit, and set their face against craft and treachery; others again like Sulla and M. Crassus, would stoop to anything and cringe to any man, if only they could gain their object. . . . Besides these there are countless varieties of character, none of which is to be condemned, though they all differ from one another. (Pp. 41–42)

One cannot help but wonder about the impact of such a letter from a father to son, this section only a small part of the much longer discourse on moral duties that Cicero imparted to his son who was about to depart on a long journey to England. The father's astute perception of the significant characteristics of the national leaders of his time, in combination formed for young Cicero a behavioral model, but as well illustrates a unique set of observations regarding the differences among men.

Books have been written that stress the clinical differences between and among human beings, exceptional children as individuals and as groups in particular. Here only the most significant differences will be emphasized.

The impact of a physical, emotional, or an intellectual difference in an individual immediately sets him apart insofar as group similarities are concerned compared to nonexceptional children. There are tremendous differences among so-called normal children, differences of height, weight, sex, religion, ethnic background, genetic history, birth history, postnatal illness history, and many many more significant variables. The fact of a disability, whether physical, intellectual, or psychological, provides a variable that may in one degree or another impact on each or all of the "normal" differences in human beings.

Vision. There are the usual intragroup differences in any category of exceptional children or youth. On the basis of visual acuity alone, one must consider differences of unique proportions among, for example, three children, one of whom has 20/20 vision (normal) in both eyes corrected, one of whom has 20/90 vision in both eyes corrected, and one of whom has a 20/200 vision record in both eyes corrected. The first has normal vision for all intents and purposes, the third is legally blind. The second individual would fall into the category of the "partially sighted." These three examples are just that, merely examples of extremes in visual acuity. Within these arbitrary degrees, there are dozens of other degrees of visual acuity, each of which would have to be considered if a homogeneous group of visually handicapped subjects were to be organized as a research group. An individual with 20/200 acuity is legally blind with sight, but are two individuals, both legally blind, comparable for careful research if one has 20/200 vision and the other 20/400? If psychological research of an exactness comparable to space orbiting research is the end goal, then the example we have used here provides too much of an uncontrolled variable to rest assured that controls are indeed in place.

One can progress further than mere acuity. In a study in which I was once engaged, I thought we had at least controlled for visual acuity. Careful measurements had been made, and we were ready to proceed. One child in a group called my attention to the fact that he thought he had an eye that resembled my own. When I pursued this, I discovered that somehow his 20/20 vision had only been measured in his right eye. His left eye—like mine—was a prosthesis. What impact does monocular vision have on studies involving binocular activity? Depth perception will be affected, the visual field will be reduced, and fine visual-motor activities may be impaired. If the study involves driving an automobile or piloting an airplane, then it is likely that little effect of the monocular issue will be important.

Tunnel vision, glaucoma, muscle imbalances, and a myriad of other clinical problems involving vision may serve as significant variables that must be considered in good research plans. These variables are important in considering the psychology of difference, and they cannot be ignored in developing homogeneous groups of visually impaired persons for inclusion in studies.

Hearing. If vision has its multiplicity of variables, hearing has more. Not only are the matters of frequency and decibel loss significant variables to be considered, but outer ear, middle ear, and inner ear localization must be considered. Within the inner ear and within millimeters of space, defects of such significant structures as the organ of Corti, the aqueous and vitreous humors, the ciliary hairs on the tectorial membrane, may individually or as a whole produce variance that would be virtually impossible to match accurately with another subject. While the age of onset of hearing loss forms a significant variable, the ability of researchers to match on this variable with other than very rough measures is well nigh impossible. For example, two children may have exact hearing losses as measured on good audiometers. One experienced his loss apparently prior to birth (a congenital loss); the other, following measles at the age of three years (an adventitious loss). The former has had no association with sound or its meanings; the latter, some experience with sound but not enough to support him in the development of adequate speech as he reaches the fifth or sixth year chronologically. We have matched here only on the basis of auditory acuity. Consider the complexity of the matter if type of loss is controlled: important is the IQ if it could be accurately measured; parental attitude toward hearing losses; acceptance-rejection ratio of both children by peers, by grandparents within the family, friends and other adults; and on through a long list of significant research variables. The issue of self-concept of these two children and its impact on the capacity of the two to be similar for purposes of research is a variable that is almost never considered by persons planning research.

Cerebral Palsy. I do not intend to point out what is becoming the obvious for each clinical category of children and young people found in special educational programs throughout the school systems. However, with cerebral palsy the issues of complexity and difference become extreme. Cerebral palsy is not just cerebral palsy:

a. Cerebral palsy is a variety of subtypes, clinically, i.e., spastic, athetoid, ataxia, rigidity, mixed, rare, among others. Winthrop Morgan Phelps identified as many as twelve subtypes of athetosis alone.
b. Cerebral palsy consists of differences in human "geography," i.e., quadriplegia, right and left hemiplegia, paraplegia, and, although some dispute their neurological existence, monoplegia and triplegia. Athetosis is characterized by a preponderance of quadriplegias; spasticity, by the hemiplegias.
c. The etiology of cerebral palsy varies widely and may be further related to prenatal, perinatal, or postnatal factors, one complicating the other.
d. Cerebral palsy is associated with a higher degree of seizure states than found in the general population.
e. Cerebral palsy is associated with a higher degree of visual impairments than found in the general population.
f. Cerebral palsy is associated with a higher degree of auditory impairments than found in the general population.
g. Cerebral palsy is associated with a much higher degree of speech impairments than found in the general population.
h. Cerebral palsy is associated with an extremely higher degree of retarded mental development than found in the general population.
i. Cerebral palsy in one major study was found to be associated with perceptual processing deficits of multiple dimensions in nearly 90 percent of the subjects studied.

What is the possibility in the face of these nine facts of obtaining homogeneity in groups? One child with cerebral palsy is a male, eight years of age. He had a measured IQ of 119, a mental age of nine to eleven years. He is emotionally well adjusted. His cerebral palsy was apparently of prenatal origin. His mother died in childbirth; the father remarried and cares for the child. This subject's cerebral palsy is associated with a hearing loss. He is athetoid and quadriplegic, and speech is severely impaired. He has a visual impairment and grand mal seizures at the rate of five to seven per day. His psychological assessment, insofar as it can be completed satisfactorily, shows numerous processing deficits and a short attention span, among which are dissociation, closure, figure-ground reversals, sequencing and memory problems, and both visual- and auditory-motor coordination problems. Here is one subject. Try to match him controlling just the variables mentioned here so that a homogeneous duet would be obtained. How about a homogeneous group of thirty boys? Keep in mind the degrees of difference in the example we have employed here are not fully inclusive, i.e., no mention of emotional overlay has been included, the attitude of the parental stepmother is not assessed, the roles of siblings are unknown, school placement is not accounted for. There are other important uncontrolled variables if matching is to be accurately accomplished. The single-subject research designs may be the solution to many of the perplexities of studying exceptional children.

Other Variations. The matching of groups of *multiply handicapped* children or youth undoubtedly provides the most challenging issue in the total field of exceptionality. Here the psychology of difference reaches its zenith. This problem has been described earlier, but probably needs to be identified as a separate matter in this discussion. I do not wish to grind the issue of matching variables to the ultimate, for the point of difficulty has probably already been made sufficiently. One of the most interesting of all of the "groups" of exceptional children is that of the multiply handicapped, however, and this one needs some attention. Recently a journal article was devoted to two "matched" groups of multiply handicapped children. Both groups were considered to be homogeneous; the variable in this study is that of two different teaching methods. "The groups were homogeneous in that controls were established for sex, age, race, intelligence (estimated), and length of time in the facilities where the training program was to be undertaken." If these limitations comprise homogeneity, a new definition of the term is required. We will have no argument with race, and probably none with sex. Age, however, was only to the rounded-out year. Is a child of nine to ten years the same as one nine to eleven years? What is "estimated" intelligence in the group whose members were ultimately described as "having a variety of physical and mental handicaps?" One was characterized as having quadriplegic athetoid cerebral palsy with petit mal seizures of frequent occurrence, a mild cardiac problem, and estimated intelligence quotient on the Columbia Mental Maturity Test of about 110. I wonder if the author recognized the fact that the CMMT tests about 15 points higher than some other intelligence scales? In addition to using an estimated test score, what is the effect of such a score from a test that itself produced results that are at variance with those of other standardized instruments? A second child included in this report was "a blind boy with left spastic hemiplegia, had grand mal seizures of frequent occurrence, a hearing and language problem, and a measured IQ of 89" (no test indicated). Regardless of the fact that these two subjects were members of larger groups and that the purpose of the project was to test the effectiveness of training techniques, what is the value of the so-called homogeneous groups in the first place? I see none. This naive "researcher," knowing little about grouping, and seemingly less about statistical procedures, has contributed nothing to the literature. Where are the reviewers who permitted such conceptual and methodological inadequacies to pass them and to allow such an article to get into print in the first place?

The Challenge of Individual Differences

A few years ago there appeared on the bookstands a document that is almost impossible to understand in the light of what is known about learning in children and youth, namely, a volume authored by a "panel of prominent educators," ostensibly headed by Mortimer J. Adler. The thesis of this publication, *The Paideia Proposal: An Educational Manifesto* (Adler 1982), is that there shall be a "one-track system" of schooling for all children. It advocates the "same objectives for all without exception." This is ludicrous, if not idiotic, and one wonders about the intelligence of those who comprise the so-called panel. *Paideia,* a Greek word, roughly can be translated as the upbringing of children and is barely germane to the book's contents. If the volume had remained concerned with the upbringing of children in the broadest sense and in the light of what is known about individual differences, little criticism could be brought against it. But the authors do not do this.

In spite of what is known about different rates of learning among children—the retarded at one extreme, the gifted at another, and those of normal or average intelligence at still another level—this panel of educators recommends an essentially uniform curriculum for all children. It carries education back into the nineteenth century and is a reflection of the worst in conservative thinking among educators. The Paideian goals of education are to prepare children "for the continuation of learning in adult life, during their working years and beyond." No one can dispute this as a desired goal, but the means to the end as advocated by this "panel" defy logic. How in the name of conscience can a single approach to education in a democracy effectively encompass the needs of a child with an accurately measured intelligence quotient of 75 on the one hand and those of a child with an accurately measured quotient of 140 on the other hand? Adler has long been an advocate of an educational program incorporating the Great Books—a program of which he was one of the conceptualizers. He has had so little contact with children who deviate from his perspective that all children are possessed of superior intelligence that his current advocacy of the "Paideian" point of view is little short of foolish. It violates all that is known regarding the individualization of instruction, different growth rates of children of the same chronological age, and different levels of optimal attainment in the acquisition of skills. It would be interesting indeed for Professor Adler and his panel of associates each to be assigned as the teacher of a school class of children under the philosophy of mainstreaming and to face on a daily basis thirty or more children, heterogeneous as to race, with variation in intelligence levels between 70 and 135, including two hyperactive emotionally disturbed children, three children with perceptual processing deficits resulting in learning disabilities, and two Hispanic children who do not speak English. This is not an extreme situation in most large school systems of this nation. Just how his "educational manifesto" calling for a single-track system of education for all children would work under this situation and hundreds of other classroom situations in the United States like the one described is impossible to conceptualize. Adler, the director of the Institute for Philosophic Research, has stepped so far out of logic and a rational approach to education as to make thoughtful persons lose any confidence in the institute, if indeed they ever had any. If what has been written were not so absurd and dangerous, it would be humorous. There is indeed no humor here, however, when those reputed to be leading thinkers on matters as important as education, recommend an attack on a national problem that ignores psychoeducational facts and research and is as unrealistic as the Paideia proposal.

I began this chapter with the statement that while the concept of individual differences was in no way new, its implementation in the schools of this nation either with normal children or exceptional children is rarely seen. We diverted to a consideration of the inherent individual characteristics of children and youth and the impossible situation that these create when researchers, thinking that they can achieve homogeneity, seek to secure and to study homogeneous control and experimental groups. If this is impossible, the alternative of studying individuals is not.

In a research sense I have already emphasized the importance of considering the single-subject research concept as a significant attack on research with exceptional children. But of equal importance is the clinical and educational implication of the psychology of difference.

The uniqueness of children is undoubtedly the single most important factor that has kept me working in the field of the exceptional child for as long as I have. What intrigues people about people and about children and young people in particular? Is it their differences?

With all of the emphases that have been made on individual differences over the last many years, it is almost absurd to remind ourselves that no two individuals are the same, that any two children are remarkably different one from the other, even though they may be of the same sex, parentage, and possess all of the common traits usually associated with siblings. Nevertheless any parent who attempts to approach his children with the same tone of voice, the same disciplinary methods, the same motivational techniques, the same suggestions regarding clothing, toys, or recreational activities, is daily reminded that extreme differences often exist. A teacher who attempts to deal with her class group as a single entity rather than as a collection of thirty unique personalities is bound to a life of frustration and continuous challenge from her pupils.

The extreme in the concept of individual differences became obvious in the 1960s and early 1970s among young people who, becoming disenchanted with the hypocrisy of adult society, often stressed their individuality to the point of running away from home, separating themselves from their families, and establishing themselves in a society essentially of their own making and illustrative of their own beliefs, personality characteristics, and modes of behavior. These young people were not in any sense the dregs of society as some conservative adults would have characterized them, and did. These were often charming, socially concerned, and politically conscious individuals many of whom had a common goal, namely, to make the world a better place in which to live. That they accomplished their goals in large measure is a fact of history. Had it not been for the discouragement of the Vietnam war, the oppressiveness of the Nixon administration, and the creeping bigotry of conservative religious groups, these brave young people with all of their unique individual differences could have turned the nation around, almost a full 360 degrees. They nearly did so in many universities and colleges, and to the better. It was the extreme in individual differences that made these tens of thousands of adolescents so interesting and to many so challenging. There was a common thread among them—a drive to make the world a freer and better place to live. Their methods of attaining their goal differed, and it was this that made them so attractive. One did not necessarily have to agree with them; in a democracy differences of opinion make the nation strong. However, for one interested in differences among human beings, this generation afforded a laboratory the nature of which has rarely been seen before.

I began these last paragraphs by stating that it is the uniqueness of exceptional children that makes them attractive and has motivated professional people. This is true also of the generation of young people about whom I have just written. Let me examine three youths to further elaborate the point of individual differences. Two are seventeen years of age, one is nine.

The two seventeen-year-old boys are members of a class of boys and girls in a rural high school. There are sixteen young people in this group, each carrying the label of learning disability, although the basis for this diagnosis is vague and incomplete in numerous instances. Two of the youths stood out from the rest as having very severe learning problems, and these two were selected for intense clinical study: Dave and Scott.

Both boys were brought to a university clinic where a wide variety of clinical skills was available. Dave was six feet four inches tall, thin and handsome. He was a farm boy, mature beyond his years, and had a community reputation as a woman's man. He was literally on call from many farm women to engage in sexual relations in the absence of husbands, and while this reputation was ego building among his immediate coterie of friends, he basically was a worried young man because of it. "Why me," he often asked the clinicians. More important was the constant fear that his parents would find out about his peccadillos, for he came from an extraordinarily conservative religious family. While sexual activities are common among seventeen-year-old youths, the nature of this boy's behavior, its frequency, and its involvement with women who considered themselves friends of his mother and father, constituted an individual difference that set Dave apart from his friends and that constituted a fear-ladened emotional overlay to his learning problems. All else had to be interpreted with this behavior factor in mind.

On a clinical basis Dave was a nonreader. At seventeen years he functioned on a Grade I or low Grade II reading level. Academic skills were not valued highly within his family unless it be to be able to read the Bible, and his mother said that Dave's wife would someday do that for him. Little did the mother realize that Dave and some of his immediate friends were frequent purchasers of pornographic materials, and these were read to him by his friends during what they assumed to be clandestine sessions.

Visual motor problems were predominant in Dave's clinical records. He was as nearly a classical dyslexic student as could be imagined. In spite of his adolescent development and sexual activities, Dave was a well-adjusted person insofar as friends and teachers could ascertain. He was liked probably in large measure because of the aura of mystery that his behavior held for his peer friends. He was hyperactive and had not yet been able to master driving an automobile. This came two years later. Eye-hand coordination was poor; as a matter of record almost everything that required visual input was poorly developed. He did not swim. Riding a bicycle was difficult, although he operated a motorcycle by dint of extreme effort. Auditory perception was good, and most of his school achievement was obtained by careful listening. Visually, the attention span was useless; aurally he could listen to pop records or to a story being read to him for long periods of time. Most important of all he was likable. He was pleasant to be with. He minimized his disabilities, but he begged the clinicians to help him "be a better person." By "better person" he meant two things: first to overcome some of his learning problems in order that he could acquire a driver's license, and, second, to assist him to get over his fear that his father would find out about his community sexual affairs. "He'd kill me if he knew."

Scott is Dave's closest friend, a member of his learning disabilities class, and a constant companion out of school. Scott is the one person to whom Dave has confided all of his after school and nocturnal escapades in the farm community and all of his fears, and Scott is sworn to secrecy. Scott violated this one day when he told me that his friend had an "awful problem." My response was noncommittal, but I did tell Scott that if it were a secret, then he had better treat it as a secret. However, if he wanted Dave to know that I knew there was a secret, but not its contents, and that Scott too was worried about it, Dave, not Scott, might want to seek me out and we could talk about it. Little did I know the magnitude of the problem being carried between the two boys. On one of my visits to the high school, Dave sought me out and asked if we could walk outdoors alone. I agreed and moments later with the help of many four-letter words Dave's problem came tumbling out. He was a scared boy who wanted a way out of his dilemma. We talked about two things, first, what would be his father's real attitude if he knew, or more realistically if it were brought to his attention in the company of a third person? Second, which woman had started this, and which had obviously spread the rumor among friends that a willing adolescent was at hand? The father issue was slow in coming; the woman identification was easy to bring to the surface. Calling her, insisting that she come to the school principal's office, Dave and I easily confronted her. There was no way she could deny the situation, although she threatened to tell Dave's father. Contributing to the delinquency of a minor, however, is a relatively easy way to silence that type of threat, although it made Dave realize that his father needed to be brought into the picture quickly. The woman was required to promise that she would speak to every person she knew with whom Dave had been involved, and Dave had a complete list. Demands on Dave stopped; the telephone no longer rang for "after school work, if Dave were free."

We turned to Dave's father, and I took the lead only bringing Dave into the conversation after the problem was fully presented. Dave's father was outraged, not so much at his son, as at wives of his friends in the community. He talked to Dave "like a man," leaving all religious issues aside, sharing some of his own boyhood experiences, and accepting his son as a friend who had made some tragic mistakes. The presence of a third person during the conversation was important. Finally the father asked Dave how I had found out, and what Scott's role was in telling me that a secret existed. The father stepped to the telephone and asked Scott to come to the farm immediately. When Scott arrived, the father congratulated him on keeping a secret, taking the right step in letting me know that something was troubling his friend, and insisted that the secret be continued so that no one in the community would further be hurt. Although there were other matters to consider, the issue essentially was closed at this point. Two boys became even closer friends and more dependent on one another. More important both boys had an adult in Dave's father with whom they could and did communicate in the future. But what of Scott and his personal differences? He was also labeled as learning disabled.

His birth history was positive; it had been long and difficult. Injury had obviously taken place, although the medical records in the small rural hospital were less than complete. As a sixteen-year-old youth he had learned to utilize a number of "crutches." His parents had secured a Talking Book, and many records were constantly on order and used. He was a seriously dyslexic youth. His memory was short, and sequencing was a real problem. His mathematical skills were better than those connected with language in any form. He was personable and polite and had many friends. He was not a sissy, although he was reticent and a follower, particularly a follower of Dave. He was too scared to enter into any of the sexual activities in which Dave participated, although Scott had been invited to do so several times. Scott had honor and class, and high respect for his parents, and a great admiration for four older brothers and a small sister. His parents were open and very supportive. He had never experimented sexually; protested that he had never masturbated; and claimed that he would never have relations with a girl until after he was married. Four years later he is living with a young lady, a college classmate.

Both youths were popular; both were unique in physical build and personal characteristics, ethics, responsibility, and leadership. Both had significant, and somewhat similar, perceptual processing problems. Both were seen as school failures. Dave continues on his father's farm, unmarried but now an adult to pursue his own ways. Scott who remains a friend, struggles through the third year of a state university, secure that he will "make it," and happy that he has found a girl he thinks he loves and about whom he has shared the fact of his living arrangements with his parents. Two youths, similar learning problems, individual ways of coping with them, and significantly different ways of grappling with adolescent social adjustment: one essentially a willing pawn; the other, a loyal and insightful follower.

Tommy, the nine-year-old boy, was a human battering ram. A learning disabled boy with somewhat limited mental ability, Tommy has discovered that he could control his world by using his head literally as a battering ram. Tommy was an adopted child, reported by school personnel as having an intelligence quotient in the trainable range. Actually, it was much higher than this, although below normal. Tommy too, when his attention could be controlled sufficiently to gain cooperation and make measurements, was visually, aurally, and tactually disabled insofar as perceptual-motor abilities were concerned. He did not read. He was not psychotic. He was scared—scared of himself, scared of his adoptive parents, and scared of all people. His attention span was limited to a few seconds; his teacher had a twenty-five minute reading session daily. Tommy was just about completely uncontrollable.

On one occasion I was preparing to work with this youngster in attempting to ascertain what skills were intact insofar as visual-motor perception was concerned. As I was leaning over to arrange some materials on a low table before me, Tommy got up, moved quickly away a few feet, lowered his head and with a force not expected from a child of nine, threw himself at me first hitting me on the side of my head, and rendering me unconscious for a few seconds. This was his method of control—and it succeeded in most cases. His foes—human beings—were afraid of him. Although intensely disliked, he was in control and was the boss. His unique controlling behavior was also dangerous. He had knocked many children and fewer adults unconscious on the playground of the school and elsewhere. Right or wrong, I decided that behavior in kind had to be utilized to illustrate to this child the insult he was causing others. Quickly and when the field was clear I lowered my head and as he had done, rammed him sufficiently hard to throw him across the room, and stunned him. He was not hurt fortunately; he was shocked and very surprised. With me, at least, this behavior never occurred again, and it reduced as he began to realize with others that his behavior was essentially unproductive. Whether I used approved psychological behavior in the treatment of this child is a bit more than questionable. It is not my usual approach to children. It was premeditated, however; I knew what I was going to do if confronted.

The primary point being made here is the set of unique differences that existed between David, Scott, and Tommy—all children and youth with a common diagnosis. These differences are the clinically fascinating elements in children that attract professional people, that constitute challenges, and that make teaching and psychotherapy worthwhile when problems can be rectified and solutions found. In most cases wrongs can be righted, and adjusted youths can take their places with some degree of positive security as adults.

References and Related Readings

Adler, Mortimer J. *The Paideia Proposal: An Educational Manifesto.* New York: Macmillan, 1982.

Anastasi, A. *Differential Psychology: Individual and Group Difference in Behavior.* New York: Macmillan, 1958.

_____. *Fields of Applied Psychology.* 2d ed. New York: McGraw-Hill, 1979.

Cruickshank, W. M., ed. *Psychology of Exceptional Children and Youth.* 4th ed. Englewood Cliffs, N.J.: Prentice-Hall, 1980.

Keogh, B. K., Major-Kingsley, S., Omori-Gordon, H., and Reid, H. P. *A System of Marker Variables for the Field of Learning Disabilities.* Syracuse: Syracuse University Press, 1982.

Stubbins, J., ed. *Social and Psychological Aspects of Disability: A Handbook for Practitioners.* Baltimore: University Park Press, 1977.

Telford, C. W., and Sawrey, J. M. *The Exceptional Individual.* Englewood Cliffs, N.J.: Prentice-Hall, 1977.

Thomas, D. J. *The Social Psychology of Childhood Disability.* New York: Schocken, 1980.

Willerman, L. *The Psychology of Individual and Group Differences.* San Francisco: W. H. Freeman, 1979.

Chapter 6

Quantitative or Qualitative Assessment and Testing

When the administrators of the public schools in Paris, France, asked Alfred Binet to devise a method to screen mentally retarded children from the Parisian school system, they really started something. The most famous of the early intelligence tests were the revisions of the Binet-Simon test. With these 1916, 1921, and 1937 revisions, intelligence testing in the United States became the vogue, and few children escaped. The 1960 revision ensured still more.

With the publication of the first Wechsler Intelligence Scale for Adults, nearly as many adults as children faced testing. When the concept of the Wechsler test was taken over by the United States Army during World War II for use in induction centers and elsewhere in psychological work, untold thousands more young men experienced "testing." The Army General Classification Test, the "Wechsler" itself, and other forms of so-called standardized intelligence tests at that time were utilized widely with adults. If one extends the concept of testing to include group tests, such as the Stanford Achievement Test, the California Test of Mental Maturity, the Detroit Learning Aptitude Test, the Progressive Achievement Tests, and dozens more that have appeared to harass children who were already in trouble, one wonders when teaching per se actually took place. Oftentimes, it did not and still does not!

There were many other tests that appeared during this period than those already mentioned: the Healy Picture Completion Test, the Kohs blocks, the Porteus Mazes, the Grace Arthur Performance Test and its later revision, and still later, the Leiter International Performance Scale. This list is not complete, but it illustrates the armamentaria that psychologists soon had at their disposal. The most recent to appear in the psychological marketplace is the Woodcock-Johnson (Developmental Learning Materials/Teaching Resources, Allen, Texas). It has been well received by professionals and is becoming widely utilized. While conceptualized for children and youth with learning disabilities, it is often used with intellectually normal children who have other forms of disabilities. The Columbia Test of Mental Maturity (CTMM), initially devised for use with physically handicapped children, especially those with cerebral palsy, has many positive characteristics, but has not received the wide use that others have. Its standardization is relatively weak, and its comparability to other intelligence tests for the same age group is not good. However, the concept of the CTMM is excellent.

The Leiter, while somewhat popular, has so many built-in defects that it could not be recommended for use with physically handicapped children. It is composed of dozens of wooden pieces of approximately one-half-inch width that must be fitted together to form concepts. I would have much less objection to it if the pieces were twice the size. As they are not, they are almost impossible to pick up by a physically handicapped cerebral palsied child. The test certainly has proven a detriment to learning disabled children with almost any degree of dissociation (including those learning disabled with multiple problems of cerebral palsy, dyslexia, aphasia, and some hyperactive emotionally disturbed children) who are characterized by visual perceptual processing deficits, a problem the author of the test had not considered at all.

One cannot fail to recognize the long-standing New York State Regents Examinations, which have haunted students in New York State high schools for generations. When one thinks that every child in the state in certain grades takes the same examination at the same moment under conditions that often are far from ideal and under the watchful eye of teacher-monitors, one realizes that education in the United States has not progressed very far in some localities. Citizens in the United States bow to testing, and the futures of young people hinge on limited performance opportunities of a short duration, usually carried out under less than decent conditions of mental health.

The alliance that exists between the Educational Testing Service of Princeton, New Jersey, and admissions offices of colleges and universities, schools of medicine, schools of law, and practically all other professional schools illustrates a reliance on impersonal appraisals of young people that is hardly warranted. When one experiences the inadequate personal adjustment of many graduate students in professional schools and the preservice students in medical schools and schools of law, one quickly loses faith in testing as a method of screening into schools those students with desired skills (especially now that affluent students can spend approximately one thousand dollars to take a course in how to take these kinds of tests). For example, most students who strive to get into a good law school nowadays take one of these classes and treat it as more important than their coursework. They do well on the Law School Admissions Test because they have learned how to take the test. It is not a matter of ingenuity, either, but only a matter of having enough money to afford the course. This is relevant only in that it bothers me when I talk to one of these students, who brags to me about his or her high test scores—and I don't consider that person particularly bright. I recognize that the tests of the Educational Testing Service are not personality tests; I use this service as an example of the testing contagion that has swept the United States and for which no immunization has yet been found. America has sold its soul to testing, but look at Europe, the Soviet Union, and Japan, especially the latter. If a four year old does not test well there, the child will not get into the "good" kindergarten, therefore will not get into the "good" grade school, high school, and could never hope to enter Tokyo University. Their lives are shattered before they're old enough to tie their shoes. America is not that bad yet. Fortunes have been made for authors and corporations who market these tests. No one knows how many children and youths have had their careers blunted or have been diverted to second-choice careers because of a test itself, because of the testing situation, or because of the emotional tension created in the pupil who knows that his or her future depends, in a significant measure, on the results of the test. The unfortunate situation is that the students or the parents have little recourse when some or all of these negative elements exist.

While some may disagree with these statements because of their apparent heresy, I have taught graduate psychology courses in testing for many years and am well acquainted with the strengths and the weaknesses of all quantitative tests on the market today. Some of the tests are good, if appropriately handled. Unfortunately, too few school psychologists are able to disregard test instructions and rely on unimaginative, practical applications, or disregard a test when the results are inconsistent with the rest of the information gathered about the person tested. Some graduate schools place a heavy emphasis on the Miller Analogies Test as an element in their admissions policies. A one-hour test of one hundred analogies seals the fate of many potential graduate students in many colleges and universities. Usually a cutoff score of 70 is required for admission to a doctoral program, and it is rigidly enforced. This brings to mind a nurse, long in practice, who at the age of forty-six years entered a university program and completed her undergraduate degree. This was followed by the completion of a master's degree with universal faculty congratulations. She desired to go on to a doctoral program but was not admitted because of a Miller Analogies Test score of 17. Through some connivance, however, this score was easily changed to a 77, and she was admitted! She completed her degree; the dissertation was considered outstanding; her committee members gave her a standing ovation at the end of her oral defense of the dissertation. For twenty years, thereafter, she held a leadership position of major responsibility in a western state.

I am reminded, also, of a young man whose Miller score was 34. He was denied admission to a graduate school. Mysteriously, the 34 was discovered to be actually an 84 by a knowing secretary in the graduate school admissions office. This young man, whose work in human sexuality has received national attention, completed his doctoral program with the enthusiastic support and applause of a large faculty group. His career is assured, not by tests, but by his intelligence and skills that were not reflected in this single test administered by a graduate school admissions office. These two examples, I suspect, could be replicated a hundred times over. The tragedy is the hundreds of young people who, for various reasons, are unable to meet minimum requirements established arbitrarily by admissions offices, and who, therefore, are unable to pursue careers that are satisfying and are needed. There must be a better way to recruit students, to prepare them for careers, and to provide an ever-increasing supply of competent professionals.

Although at first glance, changing test scores, or being a passive observer, could be considered unethical, there is a more significant moral question involved. The arbitrary quantitative cutoff point established by a faculty committee is not the important element in permitting, or not permitting, a student to pursue his or her life goals. The important issue is not the test itself, with all its defects of standardization, administration, tension production, or other negative factors. The significant issue is the qualitative evaluation of a student by competent faculty members, who judge a student to be competent by considering more than the raw scores of standardized tests. Thus, changing a test score is justified from many points of view. Objective tests undoubtedly have some advantages if they are properly utilized, but when a young person's life hangs on the threads of a man-made instrument, whose reliability is subject to question, and when tests are too often unreliable statistically, then it appears to me to be less than professional to perpetuate the use of inadequate instrumentation.

The way psychological tests and psychologists are utilized in some settings leaves much to be desired and is the basis for the endless flow of criticism that is leveled against psychologists. I am familiar with a school system, for example, that employs approximately thirty master's degree level psychologists. Each of these people is expected to examine a minimum of ten children per day with the Wechsler test. I am also well acquainted with the psychological department of the largest prison in the United States. Approximately twenty psychologists are employed in only one of the divisions. Clerks, of all things, administer the Minnesota Multiphasic Test to prisoners, some with extraordinarily complicated personality problems. These same clerks also administer the Bender-Gestalt in large groups, utilizing huge cards that are shown to the group by the examiner. The Rotter Sentence Completion Test and certain achievement tests, likewise, are administered by untrained personnel to persons with complicated problems. The clerk-administrators also are expected to obtain a manual dexterity test score on the subjects tested. The psychologists are expected to take these test results and review them, formulating six reports per day on men whom they have never seen. In addition, the psychologist is expected to review the prisoner's records, some of which involve one-to-six-inch thick volumes. A good treatment program cannot develop from this inadequate program, particularly when one considers that the quarters that house some or all of the psychologists, in the prison mentioned, are unheated and winter clothing is required throughout the day. Further, many of the offices are aviaries for sparrows, whose presence is evident everywhere. In case the reader is not familiar with psychology clinics, this is an example of the worst type of setting. The psychologists serve, in reality, as a rubber stamp to incompetence.

Use of Tests in Special Education

Quite often I serve as a consultant to public school systems. The purpose of the consultation is almost always related to the adaptation of instructional programs to children with various intelligence or achievement levels. With equal frequency, some form of the Wechsler intelligence scales is used as a method to ascertain abilities in a given child. Often, multiple intelligence tests are utilized. The most extreme situation I have ever encountered was a psychologist's report on a single child that exceeded two hundred pages of typewritten manuscript. It must have taken hours to prepare. Regardless of this professional misjudgment, more appropriate reports in terms of length still include much unusable data from the educator's point of view. I am impressed that the often tedious work of psychologists results in negligible changes in the instructional program for a child. One often wonders what happens to results of tests administered, as far as improved teaching methods are concerned.

Children may be classified as mentally retarded or normal as far as intelligence is concerned, which has impact on fiscal reimbursement for the school system from state departments of education. This accounts for the IQ test. In some school systems, children are still placed in self-contained classrooms on the basis of intelligence quotients, although this does not happen with a great deal of frequency. The IQ test, therefore, may have value as far as finance and some placement decisions are concerned. The test contains much more than this, though, but is not very often fully utilized. Tests still are utilized primarily for classification; rarely are they utilized for instructional modifications or to better meet the individual differences of the children in need.

The Wechsler test contains qualitative data that would be significant to teachers if they would use, or knew how to use, the information. For example, a tremendous amount of language information is contained in the verbal portions of the test, which should give the teacher a series of leads related to the level of instruction required for a child. Information regarding memory function also can be found in the test. The relation between this information, level of instruction, and such specifics as memory for spelling or for multiplication tables then becomes obvious. In the performance aspect of the test, dissociation is apparent in the Object Assembly test and in the Block Design test (as in the Grace Arthur Revised Form II and other tests). Once a dissociation problem becomes apparent, a teacher should recognize that the child has problems in letter or number formation. The test picks up perseveration as well. Sequencing is tested in the performance part of the Wechsler. This is related to operations in long and short division, in multiplication, and to relationships among words and letters in spelling and reading. But the raw or weighted scores are not often interpreted in this manner for the educators, who might utilize the information. The Coding subtest provides important clues for teachers, as far as the child and "new learning" situations are concerned. These issues are seldom discussed. The average intelligence test contains much information regarding curriculum readjustment, but few psychologists or teachers have ever had testing courses approached from this orientation. The value of the tests for instruction purposes is essentially nil, and much time is wasted both for the child and for the professional personnel involved. During IEPC meetings, I often ask the attending psychologist the meaning of his or her findings for either placement or instruction. The responses too often are a wistful facial expression or an honest, "I really don't know."

To make matters worse, recently I have become aware that some states mandate specific tests to be used. Two states at least require the Wechsler Intelligence Scale to be used by the state department of education. Some officials learn a little about one test and consider themselves to be knowledgeable about testing in its entirety. Unfortunately, this ignorance is disastrous as far as accurate testing is concerned. The state of California has declared such actions to be illegal. One wonders how long it will take the other forty-nine states to reach the same conclusion. The Wechsler test, prepared in English, is inappropriate for black children and for Hispanic children. (This writer is aware that the test is translated into Spanish, but to what degree satisfactorily?) The test would also have to be translated into Japanese, Chinese, into Vietnamese, French, or into the languages of nearly forty minority groups of children who live in Detroit, Michigan, alone. I am told that the languages of one hundred and forty-one minority groups are used in the homes of children in Los Angeles County, California. Culture-free testing has been a subject of much controversy over the years. As such, one wonders how appropriate it is to use a test that cannot be guaranteed accurate to everyone's satisfaction.

This situation is almost as serious as a recent experience that I had when visiting an elementary school in a midwestern state. There, the principal said to me on arrival, "Oh, I wish you had been here last week. We just finished 'Frostiging' the entire school." No wonder some leaders in psychology and education age more rapidly than they ought. If this situation were not so sad it would be funny. Sadder yet, neither the principal nor most of his teachers knew what to do with the volumes of "Frostiged" materials that were produced. It can only be hoped that pupils, parents, and the community, in general, will not tolerate such incompetence and will not submit to wasted dollars for very much longer. Dr. Marianne Frostig produced excellent, highly individualized diagnostic materials. To apply them wholesale to every child in an elementary school, though, is the height of administrative incompetence and absurdity.

Should Binet, Simon, Arthur, and their successors be thanked for the never-ending stream of tests that have been developed and applied to children? Is testing a hallmark in the progress of educational or psychological growth? Consider the generation of men and women who were completing college—if they went to college—in about 1930. Prior to that time, there were few tests available and certainly fewer school psychologists to administer the tests to unsuspecting pupils. While the present generation has produced at least three depressions and four wars in which men and women from the United States have participated, it can be said safely that these economic and social disasters would have occurred regardless of whether its members were tested with the Wechsler Intelligence Scale. The future "tested" generation, in all likelihood, will have an equally poor performance. Of course, there are alternatives to the slap-dash testing methods that occur today. If tests are fully and imaginatively utilized and the results analyzed individually rather than en mass, intelligent decisions can be reached that will help rather than hinder those tested.

Qualitative Analysis of Children and Youth

One of my greatest complaints, as the reader will have noted by this time, is when an educational program is derived only from quantitative scores, often based on doubtful statistical data. With the exception of grouping children into self-contained classrooms, IQ test results have never told teachers how to teach. There is nothing in the IQ that dictates the curriculum unless it is the general knowledge to lower or raise the difficulty levels that are given the children "to learn." The same point could be made with lesser emphasis regarding the mental age, a figure obtained from some intelligence tests, which relates the intelligence quotient and the chronological age. Often, however, this information is not given to teachers; they receive only the IQ. At other times, tests such as the Wechsler are used, which do not produce mental ages. Most of the issues, however, revolve around the point that in certain tests, a series of mental ages may be developed (or in the case of the Binet, only one), but teachers do not know how to relate mental age to achievement levels, which are not necessarily synonymous. A teacher reported to me, "I have the mental age, but I don't know what to do with it. How do I relate it to what he can actually do in reading and arithmetic. The mental age is 10 years and 10 months but he is working at a second grade reading level. What do I do?" One cannot help but wonder how much insight this teacher has into the problems of the learning disability group of children she teaches. It also reflects on the type of teacher education young people are provided in colleges and universities. Reliance on quantitative information from psychological tests leaves much to be desired, to say the least, and misleads well-intentioned teachers on too many occasions to the disadvantage of the pupil.

In contrast, I place my faith on the judgment of skilled professionals who have learned how to understand and assess children and their deviations. I do believe that testing can be helpful if psychologists are prepared to be something more than IQ mechanics; if they can match quantitative results with qualitative characteristics, and in turn translate the data to teachers in a vocabulary that makes educational modifications possible; and if psychologists can learn to match psychopathology with educational methodology. For example, *perseveration*—the prolonged aftereffect of a stimulus—is common to many clinical problems in children and youth. But the effect of perseveration has to be looked at from a variety of angles. (I.e., What is the meaning of perseveration in mental retardation and what is its impact on learning? What is the meaning of perseveration in learning disabilities, and how does this factor interfere with learning? What is the meaning of perseveration in the life of an emotionally disturbed child and his or her learning? What is the meaning of perseveration in the life of a childhood psychotic?) There are modest differences in each of the clinical groups I mentioned, but they are differences that must be considered in order to treat the child or youth properly.

We turn, again, to an alternative—the qualitative assessment—and in a brief discussion will attempt to make a point. The late Newell Kephart, although writing of children with learning disabilities, speaks of the "perceptual-motor match" (Kephart 1970). I spoke of the same concept, the "psycho-educational match," in a later book (Cruickshank and Hallahan 1975, vol. 1). Kephart and I, among others, are essentially concerned with qualitative evaluation of children. This means that the psychologists or other diagnosticians must know children and their normal and psychopathological traits and characteristics so well that they can match these with the child's test performance on whatever activity the psychologist places before them. A few examples will illustrate this point.

The Group Interview

A technique of assessment exists that is midway between quantitative and qualitative assessment, and in a sense, is like neither of the two, namely, the group interview. It is often utilized in industry. The group interview is a technique that divorces itself from quantitative data and relies on the qualitative evaluation of individuals by a group of individuals. It was used effectively for several years at Syracuse University, for example, with students who were applying for admission into the School of Education and for many years by the Board of Examiners of the New York City Public Schools.

The group interview involves six to eight students meeting together at a single time with a committee of five or six faculty members. The students know the reason for their presence. The group of students is given an oral question or a described situation. Usually the latter is controversial; sometimes no answer or solution is possible. The students are asked to discuss it.

Examiners are thoroughly briefed prior to the group's arrival. Examiners are asked to assess not only information possessed by a given student, but personality characteristics that might or might not be appropriate to a teacher. Aggressiveness, intolerance, shyness, dominance, submissiveness, and other similar traits are to be noted. Is a given student unwilling to listen to others or to accept a valid point of view on a given question? Does a student force his or her point of view on another? Was the question twisted so that it could be dealt with, or did the student(s) ultimately come to the conclusion that they were presented with an impossible situation? Are the students dressed appropriately for the situation? What is their general use of oral English? Do they interrupt, or are they courteous of the time? The list of observable characteristics is almost endless. Together, they serve experienced faculty members with a remarkable opportunity for evaluating both general knowledge and personalities of those applying for admission to a professional school. Admittedly, this is not an appropriate tool for elementary school children. It is for high school youth. Experience and living are required. I have used it rather effectively with high school pupils, particularly in orientation sessions around the topics of human sexuality. It is, however, most appropriate for use as a diagnostic tool with college-aged young people. It contains more of the advantages of the nondirective, qualitative assessment technique than that of the quantitative tests.

The Psycho-educational Match

Although I shall be writing about children with learning disabilities in this section, the technique described here is appropriate for any child. IQs and mental ages are unnecessary insofar as classroom instructional programs are concerned. For research, however, another issue may be germane.

If one were to examine the known and obvious characteristics of children with learning disabilities, and I have already mentioned the characteristics of perseveration, other problems would be seen readily. These children have their progress impaired by the presence of dissociation, figure-background pathology, perceptual-motor dysfunctions, closure problems, malperception of the human form, directionality problems, time and space disorientation, sequencing problems, reduced attention span, and a variety of other issues (Cruickshank 1981).

I usually use one or two cards from the Rorschach Test when I begin to work with a child, not as a personality test, but as a technique to give me clues as to the approach a child takes to a new situation and as an indication of the length of his or her attention span. Often a single card, Card I, is sufficient. On this card, a response from an intellectually normal, mentally healthy individual is often a "bat." I know there is something wrong when a ten-year-old boy immediately points out a small white dot that is followed by a "bump here," a "black line here," a "dot there that isn't on the other side," a "white line here," and four or five minutes of similar responses describing and criticizing the blot. Never is an accurate percept reported. The child jumps from one portion of the inkblot to another, never relating elements. This is an excellent example of a response to rare details and a short attention span. The teacher of this boy tells me that he always is glancing around the classroom, is very distractible, and that he has practically no usable attention span. Both the teacher and the clinician have reached the same conclusions. It is now possible to match these independent observations with modifications in the educational setting that will minimize the child's dependence on external stimuli and make it possible for him to attend more satisfactorily to that which the teacher has placed on his desk before him. We now have one piece of the education puzzle in hand—a piece that would hardly come from the routine administration of an intelligence test.

Turn now to the Bender-Gestalt Test, or more satisfactory if the subject is a child, to the Benton Visual Retention Test. One of the Bender-Gestalt cards, which involves the intersection of two curved lines, is most helpful. If instead of crossing the lines, the child puts them in some sort of parallel fashion and on the previous Rorschach card has been unable to put parts together into a meaningful whole, there is considerable evidence of *dissociation*. Dissociation is the inability to put parts together into meaningful wholes. This, for example, affects handwriting. It affects forming a letter *t*, an *H*, the *x*, *F*, or almost any other letter that puts parts together into a "new" whole. Unless the teacher understands the psychopathology of dissociation in a child and can match or minimize this with a teaching method that reduces the disability, the child is going to have serious learning problems in writing, reading, and number concepts regardless of his or her intelligence or clinical diagnosis. Children with cerebral palsy, exogenous types of mental retardation, dyslexia, aphasia, and other forms of central nervous system involvement have the same characteristics of psychopathology as do those children called learning disabled.

In terms of more functional aspects of learning, children with problems of dissociation may have difficulties in learning how to tie shoes, how to lace shoes (relating the lace with eyelet of the shoe, and the operation of crossing the laces), buttoning clothes, putting a belt into the pant loop, ad infinitum. These characteristics of learning disabilities do have a functional implication and relationship (Cruickshank 1981).

Closure is closely related to dissociation and can easily be picked up by the discerning teacher or psychologist. The numeral *6* or *9* appears as an almost straight line in children with closure problems, as do the lowercase letters *c* or *a* or sometimes *d*. This issue along with dissociation occurs regardless of intelligence level or mental age.

The *distractibility* observed in the first example is closely related to both short- and long-term memory. Memory dysfunction is closely related to failure of the child in many aspects of his daily life—memory for multiplication tables, in extreme cases, memory for dressing functions, memory in carrying out instructions given by teachers or parents, memory for grocery lists, memory for dates and activities related to certain days. Digit memory subtests from various intelligence tests may provide the same information.

Memory deficit leads to still another processing dysfunction related to learning, that of *sequencing,* which is involved in all arithmetic operations—addition and borrowing, subtraction and borrowing, in multiplication, and in the steps involved in long division. Sequencing is involved in dressing oneself, in setting the table for dinner, in going to and from school and home, in starting an automobile in drivers' training classes, in social dancing, and in a multiplicity of other significant home, school, and community activities of children and youth. Simple sequential-type activities not related to intelligence tests can be devised by the psychologists to measure these skills and whenever deficits are observed in order to provide teachers with insight into the behavior of the child in question. They are not related to IQ and mental age.

The capacity to *differentiate figure from background* is somewhat more difficult to assess than some of the other characteristics mentioned here. It is an issue that certainly can be picked up by the Rorschach Test, and it is easy to infer from the Marble Board Test (Cruickshank et al. 1965). Both of these are qualitative tests with observation by the examiner the crucial element. The Marble Board Test is also very helpful in determining distractibility, issues regarding concept formation to a certain extent, and attention span limitations, each a fundamental factor in classroom or home teaching situations. Figure-ground problems and distractibility to extraneous stimuli are significant issues in learning to read and must always be accounted for in assessing the reasons for reading failure. These issues simply do not come to light sufficiently through the use of standard intelligence tests or commonly used achievement tests. As a matter of fact, most psychologists never receive training in these issues when they take graduate courses in "testing." Kephart's concept of "perceptual-motor match" or the "psychoeducational match," which I espouse, are essential elements in the attempts of educators and psychologists to relate teaching method and materials to processing deficits, and in this case, to figure-ground pathology.

Some quantitative tests do give information regarding *directionality* (i.e., the Porteus Mazes), although these are not used very often anymore. Directionality is, however, an aspect of social behavior that must be evaluated and understood. I have often demonstrated to teachers simple techniques of directionality problems so that they get some understanding of the difficulties that both children and youth could have with respect to left-right, above-below, up-down, front-back. When one considers how often in the course of a single day directions form the basis of a child's behavior, it quickly becomes obvious that this aspect of processing needs much attention by a diagnostician. "Write your name on the line in the upper, right-hand corner of the paper." This request could leave a learning disabled child in a bad predicament.

Concept formation is a significant element that must be assessed by a psychologist who is intent upon providing teachers with information that is significant to the child's development. A variety of qualitative instruments are available. Goldstein and Scheerer have developed well-known tests for this problem, and not one of them should be omitted from the instrumentation used by psychologists: the Color-Form Sorting Test, the Weigl-Goldstein-Scheerer Color-Form Blocks, the Goldstein-Scheerer Stick Test, and their adaption of the Kohs block design materials (Goldstein and Scheerer 1941, 1–151). All are excellent. I find that the Color-Form Sorting Test is better for young children, while the Vigotsky (or the Hanfmann-Kasanin Test in the United States) is much more satisfactory for adolescents or adults. The latter tests not only get at problems of concept formation but are excellent in picking up issues such as perseveration, as are the Kohs blocks. However, qualitative observation by skilled examiners is the clue to their successful usage.

Strauss and Werner (1942), and a replication by Dolphin and me (Dolphin and Cruickshank 1958) provide both an interesting and stimulating way to obtain information regarding concept formation in children with both perceptual processing and emotional problems. These tests involve the grouping of familiar objects together and in the grouping of objects in front of pictures. In all cases, the child must indicate the reason for the grouping or placement of an object. In addition to conceptualization, such characteristics as dynamic-concrete formalism, distractibility, utilizing secondary characteristics of objects as the basis of grouping, use of uncommon objects and reasons for grouping, and a variety of other cognitive principles become apparent in ways that are not negatively challenging to the child.

There are many other characteristics of children that affect learning and performance and that do not become apparent easily through quantitative tests. I shall treat only a few of these. Directionality has been mentioned. Similarly, many children with central nervous system dysfunctions present both *time and space disorientation*. These children constantly ask about the time; they constantly need to be reminded as to where they are, where they have been, or where they are going. These issues can be determined by the psychologist or by the astute teacher, and can be incorporated into the educational regimen of the child. Once again, a match is made between a deficit and the educational program to the advantage of the child.

Ayres, as well as others, has stressed the significance of sensorimotor foundations to academic abilities. The characteristics that we have thus far mentioned are significant parts of this issue, but the problem must be dealt with carefully by those who are knowledgeable. Occupational therapists can be of much assistance in this field of evaluation, A single, concise statement of this issue can be found in A. Jean Ayres "Sensorimotor Foundations of Academic Ability" (Cruickshank and Hallahan 1975, vol. 2).

Intersensory organization or disorganization is related to this issue. It has to do with an appraisal of the child's behavior when two or more sensory systems are put into operation at a single time. How many times in the course of a day does the teacher say: "*Listen*, boys and girls. Listen to me. *Look* at the blackboard. See what I have written there. *Copy* what you see onto your paper." Visual-motor, audio-motor, and motor skills per se are involved insofar as the successful performance by the child is concerned. Many children with central nervous system dysfunction are unable to function properly when they are confronted with tasks that involve the integration of two or more sensory systems into a single act such as described here.

Children with various types of handicaps, particularly those with central nervous system dysfunction, have had developmental histories that are characterized by failure experiences. As a result, the capacity of the child to perceive his own body as well coordinated is uncommon. Failure is interpreted as a lack of control of the body and its parts. His body, upon command, will not write his name, cut his food at the dinner table, help him dress, bat a ball, run properly, or do the same other things that the child sees others around him doing. The Draw-a-Person Test, as described by Karen Machover and others, can be helpful, although I do not use the test as a personality test. At frequent intervals, I simply ask the child to draw a picture of himself. I am interested at this time only in the degree to which he is able to draw himself as a coordinated entity. Are fingers on hands, hands on arms, arms on body? Are feet separated from legs? Are there facial characteristics and other elements to his drawing that lead one to believe that he sees himself as a coordinated being? Most learning disabled children show many errors in the conceptualization of the human form. Until they conceptualize their own bodies as coordinated, totally functioning organs, many if not all, will have difficulties with academic learning. The latter requires the simultaneous total operation of the body—eyes, ears, bodily stance and position—as well as an orientation to body functions and directionality. Reading, writing, and number concepts involve the body as a totality, and until the child realizes this and achieves these coordinated skills, difficulties will lie ahead. The concept of a well-coordinated body image is one of the last developmental functions to be achieved by the learning disabled child, and sometimes it is never achieved. This evaluation is the responsibility of the psychologist. However, when the child is unoccupied, the teacher can be helpful by asking the student to draw a self-portrait. Thus, a record is available of the developing self-concept and body image that may be of significance in assessing the development of the child. We could carry this discussion further, but I think the point has been made.

From observations of child performance on things that produce information regarding the characteristics briefly discussed here, competent psychologists, teachers, and other professionals are in a position to develop an educational program of instruction that matches the disability with a teaching technique or method. The psycho-educational match then is complete to the advantage of the child. Placement of the child does not depend upon IQ cutoff points. It depends solely on the perceptual processing deficits and characteristics that the child demonstrates.

One further point needs to be made. The discussion contained in this chapter has centered almost solely on *visual perceptual processing deficits*. All of the sensory modalities may be involved, but the second most significant sensory system to have an impact on learning is the *auditory system*. Unfortunately, still too few audiologists are prepared to examine children for auditory perceptual processing deficits. Audiologists understand how to measure hearing losses, and they accomplish this with skill. But when it comes to examining a child for auditory figure-ground pathology, for auditory dissociation, or for other auditory perceptual processing deficits, skills are too often lacking. The same may be said for tactuo-motor perception and, undoubtedly, for the other sensory modalities as well. All of this is part of the qualitative evaluation of children. Out of this approach comes an understanding of what the child needs insofar as an educational regimen is concerned. Dynamic and effective educational programming becomes a possibility when this approach is utilized.

Katórthoma is a Greek word derived from the translation of the twelve labors of Hercules, and it means a challenge, with a successful completion of the task. In assessing handicapped children, any professional is confronted with a Herculean task that involves at least twelve parts, undoubtedly twice that many. Diagnosticians are confronted with a katorthómian task in meeting the challenge of the complexities of the nervous and psychological systems and of successfully completing any understanding of the deficits that these systems portend to the end that a smooth and progressively even development is achieved by the child. This is not easy to accomplish; it can be accomplished.

References and Related Readings

Cruickshank, W. M. *Selected Writings.* Vol. 2. Syracuse: Syracuse University Press, 1981.

Cruickshank, W. M., Bice, H., Wallen, N., and Lynch, K. *Perception and Cerebral Palsy.* 2d ed. Syracuse: Syracuse University Press, 1965.

Cruickshank, W. M., and Hallahan, D. P., eds. *Perceptual and Learning Disabilities in Children.* Vols. 1 and 2. Syracuse: Syracuse University Press, 1975.

Dolphin, J. E., and Cruickshank, W. M. "Pathology of Concept Formation in Children with Cerebral Palsy." *American Journal of Mental Deficiency* 56 (1951): 386.

Goldstein, K., and Scheerer, M. "Abstract and Concrete Behavior." *Psychological Monographs* 53 (1941): 1–151.

Hunt, M. L. *The Hunt Adaptation of the Bender-Gestalt Test.* New York: Grune and Stratton, 1977.

Johnson, O. G. *Tests and Measurements in Child Development: Handbook 2.* San Francisco: Jossey-Bass, 1976.

Kephart, N. *The Slow Learning Child in the Classroom.* 2d ed. Columbus: Charles E. Merrill, 1970.

Knobloch, H., and Passnanich, B., eds. *Gesell and Amatruda's Developmental Diagnosis: The Evaluation and Measurement of Normal and Abnormal Development in Infancy and Early Childhood.* 3d ed. New York: Harper and Row, 1974.

Knobloch, H., Stevens, F., and Malone, A. F. *Manual of Developmental Diagnoses: The Administration and Interpretation of the Revised Gesell and Amatruda Developmental and Neurologic Examination.* New York: Harper and Row, 1980.

Krajicek, M. J., and Tearney, A. I. *Detection of Developmental Problems in Children: A Reference Guide for Community Nurses and Other Health Professionals.* Baltimore: University Park Press, 1977.

Lidz, C. S. *Improving Assessment of School Children.* San Francisco: Jossey-Bass, 1981.

Mauser, A. J. *Assessing the Learning Disabled: Selected Instruments.* San Rafael, Calif.: Academic Therapy Publications, 1973.

McLoughlin, J. A., and Lewis, R. B. *Assessing Special Students.* Columbus: Charles E. Merrill, 1981.

Miller, P. J., ed. *The Psychological Assessment of Mental and Physical Handicaps.* New York: Harper and Row, 1973.

Sanders, M. *Clinical Assessment of Learning Problems: Model Process, and Remedial Planning.* Boston: Allyn and Bacon, 1979.

Strauss, A. A., and Werner, H. "Disorders of Conceptual Thinking in the Brain-Injured Child." *Journal of Nervous and Mental Diseases* 96 (1942): 153.

Wallace, G., and Larson, C. *Educational Assessment of Learning Problems: Testing for Teaching.* Boston: Allyn and Bacon, 1978.

Chapter 7

Categorical versus Noncategorical Education

During the decade of the 1970s and perhaps a little earlier, parents and general educators became disenchanted with special education, with self-contained classes, and the latter in large measure, with all of the financial and political support that special education was receiving from the federal government. These attitudes spawned two nationwide movements: mainstreaming and noncategorical education of the handicapped child. A nationally recognized special education leader stated, "Everything which we believe is good for handicapped children has been swept into a dustbin." His comment expresses my concern, and my concerns will come out in this chapter, I am sure.

I can well remember the first time I heard the term *noncategorical*. I was sitting in the audience at a national education conference. A speaker was reading a paper that dealt with "pressing issues" in special education. I was startled into more attentive listening when the speaker stated, "Of course, we are all acquainted with the concept of noncategorical teacher education. This is undoubtedly the single most significant development in all of higher education, .certainly during this past decade and probably for several more decades into the future." The date of this conference was the spring of 1975. "What is noncategorical education?" I whispered to a colleague sitting next to me. "Beats me," was the reply. "Sounds like mixing peanut butter and catsup in a sandwich!" he continued. During a question-and-answer period, the speaker was confronted with this question by another member of the audience. In a sarcastic manner, as if the questioner were simply not up-to-date educationally, the speaker stated that anyone "who has been around special education for very long certainly knows about this concept, knows its value, and is aware of the immense changes it will effect in special education." At that, several others were on their feet asking for a definition of a concept with which we were all supposed to be familiar. None was forthcoming, and the speaker finally stated that he had to leave for another meeting. He could not define the term himself.

Today as I write, I still am not really certain what noncategorical education is. It is startling to me that the term can be accepted and used functionally when there is no research to support it and when the concept negates the uniqueness of the different types of handicaps, as well as the educational needs of each. It is a term that easily can be misconstrued by novices in any form of education. It is a misleading term. Noncategorical education, as it is generally understood, contradicts the best concepts in special education.

I have many times stated that there is something special about special education. I think noncategorical is more a reflection of special education and society's fear of incorrect classification, with its hesitancies in saying words such as black person, Negro, Hispanic, Puerto Rican. People fear being caught unenlightened and "unhip." People do not know the terminology for handicaps, so do not want to get caught being incorrect. Who knows what upsets minority groups anymore, except the experts? Who knows if calling a person cerebral-palsied is the same as calling a Hispanic a PR, or a black person a nigger? Not many people want to be called an Archie Bunker. One needs only to look at a group of handicapped children to be impressed with their often peculiar and special needs in order to accomplish even the most simple physical or intellectual activity. This becomes evident, for example, when comparing "mild cerebral-palsied children" with physically normal children. The differences are not all physical. They involve both fine- and gross-motor functions, and may characterize one or all four of the extremities. A range of speech, vision, and hearing problems may be present in the children. Although not generally recognized, a major percentage of children with cerebral palsy will have perceptual processing deficits, a large number will have emotional overlays; and about three quarters of the total group in some degree will demonstrate retarded mental development. This is only the "mild" classification of these children.

A cerebral-palsied child usually can be called a multihandicapped child. As one moves up the imaginary scale from mild to "moderate" to "severe" degrees of disability, the physical and psychological aspects of cerebral palsy become more and more pronounced. Also as the physical and psychological manifestations become more severe, academic achievement appears to become more retarded. The discrepancy between the cerebral-palsied individual and his normal peers, insofar as reading and other cognitive areas are concerned, is illustrated by differences rather than similarities. The issue here is not mainstreaming; the issue is noncategorical educational placement. The two terms have overlapping meanings, but they are used quite separately by many educators. In my understanding of the terms, noncategorical implies the inclusion of a variety of children with different clinical problems in the same classroom, self-contained or a regular classroom. In teacher education there are broader implications.

When cerebral-palsied children are put into a noncategorical framework, their disability is minimized in the minds of many, including their parents. Further, the training that is so necessary for successful adult living also is minimized. The fact is that cerebral palsy is a bona fide medical category characterized by factors that preclude easy integration with others. Perceptual processing deficits, for example, whether with cerebral palsy or in learning disabled children, are powerful determinants to learning and preclude almost any sort of noncategorical stance. They are eccentricities that must be overcome by highly specialized teaching procedures before any thought of integration with other children can be considered.

When I speak to my medical colleagues in the university and consciously use the term *noncategorical,* I invariably receive a response of "what do you mean?" The orthopedic surgeon and the pediatric neurologist are as interested in moving their young patients into the stream of normal community living as anyone concerned with handicapped persons. Yet, those in the medical professions related to special education rarely, if ever, use the term *noncategorical.* They realize that the differences that are so obvious in the physical and psychological arenas are those things that must be put into appropriate working order before a child can be considered "normal" or permitted to function in a noncategorical sense. We speak here not of *severe,* but of *mild* or, at most, *moderate* problems in handicapped children and youth. For years, teachers were told to "teach to the disability." Only when the disability is minimized through education can the child or youth be considered to exemplify the noncategorical.

The blind child is perhaps the easiest exceptional child to integrate into a regular grade in the public schools, and this has been done for many years. Experience has demonstrated that with appropriate assistance, the child can function quite fully in an otherwise ordinary class. However, even with this group, the noncategorical classification negates the concept of appropriate assistance. Blindness is a category within the broad spectrum of exceptionality. It is a disability, and no one can deny this fact. Blind children need braille materials, including books, dictionaries, reference books, and daily assignments, because of this disability. They need braille typewriters and Talking Books. Furthermore, both the children and their regular classroom teachers require itinerant specialists, who can come into the regular classroom, ascertain that the children have what they need to succeed, teach them braille and its progressive variations, and determine that the teachers have the items necessary to teach these young people. The noncategorical advocates are unable to respond to this dilemma with lucidity or logic. They say that these children are too severely handicapped to remain in regular education. For example, it no longer matters that a blind boy has been able to function quite well in regular education for the past three years with the help of some special services. That child suddenly becomes too seriously handicapped to function in regular education, despite evidence to the contrary. He is blond, smiles, and jokingly kicks his neighbor. He acts in many ways as a normal child acts. But he is blind; he belongs to a category of clinical problems called blindness. This cannot be denied. Now, he is referred to as a child with a noncategorical disability and is placed in a noncategorical class with a miscellaneous group of other disabled children. Unfortunately, this term is confusing to general educators, who have done a superb job with this child. Before, these educators could work from the standpoint that the child in front of them was blind, he then becomes noncategorical, next, without doubt, an even vaguer and more confusing term will appear to the detriment of both the child and his teachers. It never becomes clear just whom the term noncategorical benefits. Why is the term under any consideration?

There is nothing noncategorical about a dozen blind children I see every week who live, breathe, play tricks, laugh, cry, swim, and are proud of their accomplishments. The same holds true for children who wear hearing aids. Although the term "hard of hearing" is not very good, it is ignoring their problem to call them noncategorical. Realistically, children with handicaps are only being moved from one category—blind, deaf, cerebral-palsied, etc.—to another—noncategorical. The problem of how best to help them still remains. But just as the author of this book is bald, so these children are blind. Both can and historically have been categorized appropriately. If a program is an honest program, from the point of view of curriculum and teacher effectiveness, it matters little what it is called. It must, however, be called by a realistic and honest term; noncategorical is not that term.

In other chapters of this book, I mention children with retarded mental development and still others with intellectual superiority. The noncategorical classification cannot possibly be beneficial to them. We have been struggling with the special needs of the disabled since the seventeenth century and perhaps before. Look at the impetus for private schools for gifted youth because parents feel that public educators are not meeting their children's needs. Look at an emotionally disturbed child. Look at the multitude of disabilities, whether physical or emotional. They all have problems different from one another and cannot be lumped together under the noncategorical label. I once worked in a state institution with five hundred adjudged delinquent boys, each of whom presented serious personal problems and needed help in order to live in so-called normal society. They were certainly a category of disturbed young men, many of whom seriously were seeking special help with the goal, as one fourteen-year-old youth said to me, "to be able to go home soon." One wonders what noncategorical means in the provision of services to these youth.

Within this framework, I would like someone to define educationally the child with epilepsy, with orthopedic disabilities, with quadriplegic congenital amputations, with diabetes, asthma, autism, dyslexia, learning disabilities. There are many more, and additional categories continue to develop. Look at Reye's syndrome.

Category means class, group, classification. The argument for noncategorical becomes ludicrous rather quickly in terms of semantics. How can exceptional children (a category) be nonclassed, nongrouped, or nonclassified? The problem would be inconsequential, except for the fact that both children and teachers of these children may be hurt educationally and psychologically in the use of the concept of noncategorical.

I often wonder from what source the term came, who created it, and how it became fastened to the field of special education. We have redheaded boys and girls, a category. We have obese men and women, a category. We have tall basketball players, a category. We have alcoholics, a category. I discovered that I am a statistic and became part of a medical category a few moments after having a heart attack. I am even a statistic in a subcategory of those with a particular type of heart attack and am treated and conceptualized as such. I conceptualize myself in this way also. If I and my doctors did not, then every time I had a heart attack, we would have to start from scratch to determine what my heart was doing when it went wrong. Categories are a part of any social order.

Today, our society is euphemism oriented. Mothers are no longer called "housewives." They are now called "domestic engineers," whether they consider themselves as such or not. People who used to be called janitors are now "custodians" or maintenance engineers. Ditch diggers are now called "construction workers;" garbage collectors, "sanitation workers." Secretaries are now called "administrative assistants" or "clerical workers." Computer programmers are now called "programmer analysts." No longer does a title mean anything. One has to look up the job description. Perhaps that is what is happening with noncategorical. People are afraid to commit themselves to a label, however helpful it is to have that label. Society is a vast social worker, with jargon that tries frantically to avoid being offensive. What happens is that it becomes meaninglessly generic.

Religion is full of categories and subcategories. It is nearing the absurd to conceptualize a noncategorical religious world made up of Christians, Jews, Catholics, Black Muslims, Islamis, Zen Buddhists, and all of the subgroups of protestants—high and low church Episcopalians, Hassidic Jews, and born-again fundamentalists. Comparatively, the same issue obtains when one group, for whatever purposes is given an honest label, youths with epilepsy, blindness, emotional disturbances, autism, mental retardation, etc.

It would be wonderful if physical disabilities did not exist or if all those with physical disabilities were of the same category. Of course, that is what the term *noncategorical* does. It becomes meaningless because it lumps different kinds of people into one category, regardless of facts. Just as one does not do home canning by placing in a single bottle one strawberry, a cherry, a radish, a pickle, and one each of pears, peaches, grapes, and onions, so one does not group children with a variety of different and distinct problems into one classroom. Just as with the example of canning fruits and vegetables, each of which involves different cooking times, seasoning, and preparation—not to mention taste continuity—so disabled children of different categories need and require different approaches, equipment, teaching methods, and are characterized by a variety of different personalities that makes grouping for teaching both difficult and often impossible.

The concept of noncategorical special education is indeed an absurdity. As a matter of fact, special education per se and general education itself constitute two historical categories. Except with the artifact of mainstreaming, those who advocate noncategorical education are careful to retain the concept of special versus general education. One wonders when there will be a national council for noncategorical education that will do away with the American Foundation for the Blind, the Easter Seal Society, the United Cerebral Palsy Association, the Association for Children and Adults with Learning Disabilities, and others. To keep the latter and simultaneously advocate noncategorical education is both illogical and indicative of the fact that those who advocate noncategorical education have not thought the matter through fully. Fortunately, these organizations thus far have no intentions for abrogating their important categorical roles. The instances of these established organizations and the simultaneous advocacy of noncategorical special education represents one of the too many inconsistencies that exist in this thinking and of the fallacious conclusions too quickly drawn. One of the things that surprises me not a little is that the national organizations I have mentioned in this paragraph have not taken a stand against noncategorical education in special education; the purpose of such a trend would be to protect the very children that, over the years, these organizations have purported to serve and represent.

Noncategorical education is a meaningless philosophy and certainly does not represent the best in those who advocate it. The concept of individual differences originated from special education as educators learned that there were children within their grade groups who did not fit the mold filled by most of the others. As in the 1930s and the late 1920s, public community education began to extend itself to the service of handicapped children and differences between and among children became more and more obvious. It was soon recognized that there were children of school age who did not meet the criteria for inclusion in the regular grade groups of the schools. Special classes, poor as some of them were, became viable efforts on the parts of school administrators to meet the needs of children with differences. Categories of children in the best sense of the term became the customary approach. First, there were special schools, then special classes—each for a different category of children, each with a cadre of specially prepared teachers and representatives of other professions to meet the growing needs of these children and their unusual challenges. Noncategorical education has no rightful place among thoughtful educators and administrators. It is an attempt to be compensatory to the criticisms that have been leveled against special education during the last few years. Rather than to improve special education and make it as great as it should be, unresearched and thoughtless movements of noncategorical education have been launched that will never provide equal educational opportunities for the children involved. In the years ahead if not already, noncategorical education will be a laughingstock. Lawsuits will be the next obvious step on the part of both parents and noncategorized children.

Noncategorical Teacher Education

I visit numerous colleges and universities during the course of a given academic year. I frequently am informed that "we are following the noncategorical plan of teacher preparation at this university." What that plan is, I shall discuss momentarily. Meanwhile, it appears to me essential that we examine what it is that special educators have been seeking vigorously in teacher education for the past several decades.

In the early 1930s, teacher education for exceptional children was nothing of which to be proud. Teacher selection was poor and certification—built upon elementary certification—consisted, for example, essentially of instruction in handicrafts and some supervised practice teaching for teachers of mentally retarded children. There was an occasional methods course included, but this was not universal. No state had anything like an optimal program, although a more sophisticated program was in place in Michigan, where special education really began. Separate certification existed (and still does in some states) for each clinical area of special education. These teachers were prepared to be specialists in their subject matter field on the premise that unique characteristics did exist in the children who would be taught and educated by them. Each of these programs was based upon the completion of a certification program in either elementary or secondary education.

Mental Retardation. Any program of teacher education in special education is premised on the fact that differences unique to the group of children being considered do exist and that these differences dictate differences in the teacher education program being offered. To believe that all exceptional children can be grouped into a single category is the height of absurdity and is contrary to what research and practice has demonstrated. Mentally retarded children and youth are different from other types of handicapped individuals and more so when mental retardation is combined with other disabilities. Even then, the interplay between the second disability and mental retardation results in a different dimension as far as the retardation is concerned.

Educators of mentally retarded children need a different type of education from those who teach intellectually normal children. These future teachers require a fundamental course in biological (à la Halstead) intelligence, including a thorough understanding of the degrees of intelligence within the range of retardation. In keeping with this, they need to understand the major classifications of mental retardation (i.e., endogenous, exogenous, mixed, organic, neglected, and psychopathic) and the research and theoretical writing that is germane to each. Some of these classifications are related to intelligence levels and, as such, will be handled differently either within the public schools or within special day-care centers or sheltered workshops. Specific methodology is required for endogenous versus exogenous children, and this information must be known to the future teachers. In other words, a year-long methods course must be provided that is specific to the classification of children under consideration.

Preservice teachers of the mentally retarded also must know about issues of measurement as far as intelligence, achievement, perceptual-motor abilities, and social development are concerned. They must understand how to adapt teaching materials to the appropriate mental level. They must understand a philosophy of education appropriate to retarded children, hopefully a program similar to the concept of Occupational Education discussed elsewhere in this volume. The educational program cannot be a watered down academic program better geared to the intellectually normal child.

The concept of abstract and concrete learning with the retarded child must be understood, and the future teacher must know how to adapt abstract learning to concrete situations in order to begin to meet the needs of the retarded learner. The issue is not to make something easier or more infantile, but to adjust all learning to a vocabulary level commensurate to the chronological age and, simultaneously, written at a vocabulary level comparable to the child's mental age. This may mean that the same story or arithmetic lesson may have to be written at several different levels of difficulty in order for all children to be able to learn the same subject matter simultaneously at appropriate functional levels.

These teachers, like all teachers—special and general—also require a complete course in the psychoeducational characteristics of exceptional children. They need to know not only the problems of learning experienced by children with other types of disabilities, but something of the background of such pupils in terms of the issues of multihandicapping conditions. The history of special education is another fact of preservice education that these, and all other educators of exceptional children, should experience. Special educators need to know where their professional field fits into the historical development of all people and what its contribution has been to society and what its contemporary values are.

With respect to the mentally retarded, preservice teachers must be knowledgeable regarding the current issues pertaining to the field itself (i.e., issues of normalization within the public schools, community problems regarding deinstitutionalization, programs of sheltered workshops, the role of the institutions and residential facilities for those unable to cope with society in a communal living center, and state and national legislation in behalf of the retarded individual). The rights of the retarded adult, insofar as vocational rehabilitation, prevocational training, marriage, voting, property ownership, and related issues are each and all germane to the preservice preparation of these teachers. These issues represent vital elements of a categorical nature that must be assimilated by young students, and these hardly can be adequately conceptualized in a noncategorical setting.

Blind Children and Youth. While I will not discuss the total spectrum of teacher preparation and exceptionality, blind children and youth and one or two other examples will illustrate sufficiently the point that I wish to make. Hereafter, I will not repeat the need for all students of special education to understand the history of their professional field, nor will I mention the universal need to know of the psychoeducational development of children and youth. Suffice it to point out that these emphases are needed, indeed required, for all teachers and are as important for the other categories of physical and intellectual disability as they are for the seriously visually impaired.

Teachers of these children need to understand the mechanism with which they are working (i.e., the eye). Hence, a course in the neuroanatomy of the eye is essential to their preparation. They need to understand the physiology of the eye, the physics of seeing, and the diseases of the eye that impair vision. These areas of information are essential, not only as a general background for the teacher, but also so that the teacher can communicate intelligently with ophthalmology and other disciplines involving vision specialists.

These teachers must have courses in the learning and utilization of braille and its several grades. This implies knowledge of the use of the braille typewriter in order to be able to teach blind children these skills. Teachers of blind children need to know the use of Talking Books, sources of discs for them, the techniques of ordering materials for the machines, the use of experimental sensing devices, the availability of embossed maps, globes, and other supplies such as braille paper. These teachers need to understand how to utilize volunteers in the preparation of braille teaching materials so that all children have the necessary learning materials on the day and time when they are needed. Mobility training is an essential skill to be learned by teachers of the blind; this is not something left to the physical education teacher as one general educator once told me. Teachers of the blind must also act as resources to parents of these children and must be able to talk authoritatively regarding the use of guide dogs, canes, vocations, and a variety of other life-support functions. Piano tuning and caning chairs have long since given way to much more realistic and varied adult occupations, including teaching, research, journalism, and law. Recently, I was exploring some of the upper floors of one of the buildings while assessing a school for the blind. There, I was astounded to find thirty-four upright and grand pianos, an unlimited supply of piano frames on which pupils used to practice tuning. It was obvious at a glance what an essential element of the curriculum of that school used to be and probably not so long ago. Fortunately times have changed, and opportunities for blind youth and adults have expanded markedly. Teachers now need to understand these changes and be able to function in the positions of advisor and counselor.

As with the blind children and youth, readiness to teach or to work clinically with the deaf, the partially sighted, the hard of hearing, those with a variety of speech problems, aphasia, dyslexia, cerebral palsy, and other neurological diseases, orthopedic problems, epilepsy, autism, organic problems of speech such as cleft palate, and the talented and gifted are each highly technical fields that require extensive specialized preparation.

Socially and Emotionally Maladjusted. The final category that I wish to mention in this section consists of those children and youth with social and emotional maladjustments sufficient to bring them to the attention of school and community authorities. This is a unique category of young people whose personal problems are the results of environmental deprivation, broken homes, abuse, community disorganization, drugs, racial conflicts, and an almost endless variety of other problems, the impact of which is to disorganize learning. Social and emotional growth, to say nothing of academic learning, takes place but is of a type and nature that is contrary to the standards and customs of the surrounding society. As a result, in terms of the social milieu, child maladjustment and often family maladjustment exists, and the community reacts in strength.

With respect to teacher preparation, preservice students need a number of specialized elements in their programs. In addition to normative growth and development, the whole field of child psychopathology and abnormal psychology needs to be presented and understood. Teachers of these children need to dip into the offerings of the medical school and to become acquainted with issues of mental disease and psychiatric treatment forms. In the face of current social behavior, teachers of these children need to know much regarding drugs and substance abuse. Teachers of emotionally disturbed children will find themselves in frequent disciplinary activities, hence they need to have firsthand experience through a variety of practice with medical personnel, social workers, psychologists, and other professional groups each of which has a significant part to play in the education and treatment of these children. An acquaintance with psychological tests, their uses, and their interpretations is an essential element in the preparation of this group of teachers. None of the elements in a total training program can be assimilated in a short period of time. In-depth training and experience is a requirement.

In some larger communities—Los Angeles, for example—police departments are maintaining staffs of officers who are specially trained in the field of learning disabilities. The fact that the most learning disabled children also are represented by significant emotional overlays makes it important that teachers become acquainted with law enforcement programs that relate to these problems. In so stating, it is not implied that a direct link between learning disabilities and delinquency exists; this is a fallacy that has received too much attention in the past few years. What is being stated is that, with socially and emotionally maladjusted children, teachers need to be acquainted with all available social agencies that can be of assistance.

It quickly becomes obvious that teachers do not meet the needs of exceptional children through a superficial education. Each of the types of children and programs briefly described here involves an investment of time, energy, and thought on the part of the students and by the faculty of a university. Mediocrity can no longer be tolerated in special education and superficiality has no place in the education and treatment of children who represent the third or fourth standard deviation from the normal. Each of the categories of exceptional children that I have mentioned requires intensive study, as do those that have not been singled out for more elaborate description.

I have been in universities where a noncategorical teacher education plan was being followed. In some of these circumstances, preservice teachers were receiving only the most superficial type of university experiences. In one university, students "majoring" in special education had only a two-year symposium on exceptional children. In this experience, involving some sixty, two-hour lectures, professors representing different fields of special education each presented their information during four or five sessions. The field of the deaf, a complicated and technical aspect of special education was covered only in six lectures, never to be presented again in a more expanded manner. This is not only an impossible manner in which to prepare teachers to work with these children, but it is dishonest and unethical. School superintendents in the vicinity of this university told me that they were no longer employing teachers from this program because the teachers did not know anything. At this university practice teaching—never sufficient under any plan—was arranged in two-month blocks of time with exposure to as many different types of exceptional children as time permitted.

In a second university, the noncategorical approach consisted of a series of lectures that was comparable to the above example except that it lasted only one year, with the addition of a "methods sequence," which provided a year-long course on "Methods of Teaching Exceptional Children." How anyone can believe that methods of teaching the deaf, the cerebral-palsied, the mentally retarded, or any other clinical types of exceptional children can be considered sufficiently similar to be able to be approached by a single professor in a single class is beyond belief. To consider this foolhardy is to say the least.

The noncategorical teacher education program is carried to an extreme in one university, and this action follows the certification requirements established by the state in which the university is situated. A set of core courses, not particularly related to special education, is required of all future teachers of exceptional children. In addition, *one course*, for example in learning disabilities, is required and upon successful completion of that course, the individual is certified to teach learning disabled children. The same teacher may then successfully complete another single course, for example in the field of the emotionally disturbed, and with that is certified to teach emotionally disturbed children, also. The teacher is perhaps motivated to continue and complete still another course in the field of mental retardation. The state now has another teacher certified to teach mentally retarded children. This teacher is in fact certified to teach three different types of handicapped children on the basis of three, three-credit-hour courses. The teachers in that state speak of themselves as noncategorical and sometimes, "transcategorical" personnel. This is educational insanity and not teacher education. This type of program makes a segment of professional education the laughingstock of the field. One teacher reported to me that she was certified under this arrangement to teach emotionally disturbed children. An insufficient number of such children were available in the community to permit a class to be organized. At the request of the superintendent of schools, this person attended a three-week summer course in the field of learning disabilities, which provided three hours of graduate credit. On the successful completion of this course, that teacher was certified to teach learning disabilities. A sufficient number of these children was added to the group of emotionally disturbed children to make possible the organization of a class. This was seen as a noncategorical class under the direction of a dually certified teacher! I have to ask myself what it is that we have been fighting for during the past forty years in an effort to upgrade special education and special education teacher education? These examples push special education teacher education back to a point prior to the early years of this century. Parents are not going to tolerate this kind of mediocrity in the preparation of teachers to whom the most difficult children in the community are assigned for their special growth and development.

Exposing young preservice students to a little information about a number of complicated clinical problems is not teacher education at its best. Fortunately, the American Speech and Hearing Association, the Division of School Psychology of the American Psychological Association, and some other professional organizations have not succumbed to the noncategorical concept. High standards of professional preparation continue to be maintained by them. School psychologists have recently had to meet an increased number of clinical internship hours before certification could be achieved. In contrast, special education as a field has retreated to a noncategorical emphasis that is ill-defined and that graduates teachers with only a thin veneer of knowledge regarding a complicated aspect or series of aspects of child deviance. One cannot help but to wonder where the leadership of the Council for Exceptional Children, the National Association for Retarded Citizens, the United Cerebral Palsy Associations, and a dozen other professional and lay organizations rests while this retreat from quality teacher education is taking place. Where is special education leadership, and why does it sit quietly while ineffective inroads are being made into a field that deserves much more, not less? As in the musical, *Damn Yankees,* to whom have special educators sold their souls?

The education of exceptional children whether they be retarded or gifted, blind or hearing impaired, neurologically handicapped, learning disabled, or emotionally disturbed, represents the most complex educational challenge in all of elementary or secondary education. Research, some of it poor and leaving much to be desired, nevertheless is accumulating to provide educators, psychologists, and neurologists, along with other professional specialists, with a reservoir of technical information that, in combination, bodes well for exceptional children. There is no research, however, that indicates that educational standards should be lowered. There is no research to support the concept of noncategorical education or teacher preparation. There is a growing understanding of what the child with disabilities needs, but there is no research to indicate that it is better for these children to be placed in regular classes, assigned for short intervals each day to a so-called resource room, or to be provided for through other arrangements under the guise of noncategoricalization. These terms and arrangements are educational fads that have sprung up overnight like mushrooms and that will wither and evaporate soon, it is hoped. Meanwhile, children will be hurt, and the individual progress of those who cannot defend themselves will be stunted. Crimes against children are being committed by educators who have thoughtlessly given voice to untried administrative arrangements. Blatant unprofessionalism is observed in these thoughtless and ill-conceived arrangements that in large measure violate the best of what competent educators have attempted to accomplish over the years. The entire special education establishment—state department and federal agency personnel, college and university personnel, and school administrators alike—who espouse these procedures that violate what is known about exceptional children should be subject to the strongest criticism. What is viewed as the so-called noncategorical approach to special education is inexcusable and professionally unacceptable.

Mainstreaming

My point of view regarding mainstreaming has been explained in print sufficiently so that it would be redundant to discuss it fully again here. I shall include comments only to the extent that there be no misunderstanding as to where I stand on this debatable concept. As I have stated elsewhere, beginning in 1939 I have argued for the concept of selective placement of handicapped children in regular grades of the public schools (Cruickshank, Morse, and Grant, ms.). During every decade since that time I have written several articles in support of this point of view. Typical of the statements that appear in nearly a dozen papers is the following:

> Selective placement (of the child in schools) involves the careful and complete assessment of the abilities and limitations of the child, his home, and community by professionally qualified persons representing numerous disciplines and the ultimate joint recommendation of an evaluation team regarding the optimum educational placement in terms of the realistic opportunities which present themselves. (1967)

This sounds a great deal like the concept of Public Law 94-142 and the basis for the Individual Educational Plan nearly ten years before the idea in the law was advanced. Somewhere along the line there has developed an opinion by many that I am against the concept of mainstreaming. That is not true. I am a strong advocate of *selective placement.* I am positively opposed to the wholesale administrative actions that have taken place in too many school systems under the influence of administrators who are poorly oriented to the nature and needs of exceptional children and their decisions backed up by members of boards of education who have no background whatsoever in this phase of education. I have said earlier that exceptional children do have unique learning characteristics, and these must be met by well-prepared teachers who have been provided both academic preparation and supervised practicum experience so as to be able to meet these unique needs. This phrase will be repeated again in this book. These children, except in gross characteristics, are unlike normal children in terms of their learning needs.

Both special educators and general educators have adopted the concept of mainstreaming with little thought as to the implications of this approach to education. The former U.S. Office of Education some years ago sponsored and funded a large number of so-called

118 / Disputable Decisions in Special Education

Deans' Projects. These projects were intended to study various aspects of the mainstreaming approach. Individual projects have had specified responsibilities and were headed by both general and special educators. Very few were directed by leadership persons from either field, and the results to date have been practically worthless. Little of value that could not have been anticipated or has already been anticipated and said about this approach has developed from the Deans' Projects. The title comes from the fact that the project was supposedly placed under the general supervision of the dean of a school of education. In fact few deans are prepared to undertake such research, and many had only a dollar interest in the project in the first place. This aspect of "research" in higher education has not been complimentary to professional education. However, the projects continue, and mainstreaming with little or no research or philosophic orientation has also continued. In the aforementioned reference I have written a detailed position paper stating my position regarding mainstreaming. It would be inappropriate here to repeat the statement in its entirety, but I will abstract major points from it in order that my position be understood and cautions be in the records.

1. It must be recognized that a program of normalization cannot take place over night. It is more than an administrative decision. . . .
2. We must recognize that the concept of normalization leading to an appropriate understanding of least restrictive placement is a total community decision and as such requires total community orientation. . . .
   a. There must be a total understanding and a positive decision regarding normalization . . . by every member of a School Board. . . .
   b. All administrators and supervisors of the school system must have a complete understanding of the program. . . .
   c. All teachers, school nurses, social workers, psychologists, and whatever other professional staff is utilized within the school(s) must have a thorough understanding both to the psychoeducational characteristics of all types of exceptional children, and also to the concept of normalization and integration of various exceptional children within the ordinary classroom. . . .
   d. All support personnel in the school system, i.e., secretaries, bus drivers, custodians, and clerks, also need a good orienta-

tion to what may be a different type of pupil to appear in the school and on school buses. . . .

e. All of the so-called normal pupils in the elementary and secondary schools must have a full orientation to the exceptional child who may be joining their classrooms or their school. . . .

These issues, among others, are absolutely essential to complete before the first child is integrated. There may already be in the school classes some very mildly handicapped children or youth. These may be the core around which a broader program of normalization is developed. It must be remembered, however, that the program is not one of wholesale integration of handicapped children into schools and classes, but *selective integration.* Parents and community leaders should be made a part of the orientation program in order that total community support is given to the decision reached by the board of education members.

When this type of careful preplanning is undertaken, the concept of integration has a chance to work. Experience has demonstrated that it takes about eighteen months of preplanning and orientation before a school system is ready for this redirection of its programs, and even then all will not go smoothly. There is in the United States at the present time, a serious and appropriate backlash toward the concept of mainstreaming. It is being brought about by parents and teachers who realize that their children are not obtaining what it will take to make them as independent in adult life as it is possible to achieve. In large measure this is due to two things: first, general educators are in no way sufficiently prepared by attitude or technical professional orientation to serve the exceptional children in ordinary classrooms, and, second, when decisions have been made, they have been wholesale in nature and total populations of exceptional children have been integrated on a given date rather than selectively over a period of time.

I believe that every exceptional child should be educated in as nearly normal circumstances as it is possible to achieve. The disability per se will obviate against this, and human beings being what they are will find many general classroom teachers unable to accept exceptional children socially or emotionally. Under the latter circumstances it is almost criminal to place such children in such a psychologically hostile environment.

I take no credit for the development of the concept of mainstreaming, and as a matter of fact in view of its dismal record, I don't want credit. However, in *1957,* through funds received from *the* Ford Foundation, we did undertake a two-pronged program of inquiry regarding normalization. One was a program making possible the expansion of services by special educators to all children through the use of teacher assistants for exceptional children (Cruickshank and Haring 1957). Again this was long before Public Law 92-142. The second aspect of the program involved what eventuated in successful attempts to change teachers' attitudes toward exceptional children (Haring, Stern, and Cruickshank 1958). Both of these programs were effective, but their effectiveness was the result of careful preplanning and detailed supervision of the program as it was put into effect. No element was ignored, and all of this pertained to preintegration stages. Actual integration of the children was to come later. We were now dealing only with attitudinal change of general educators. It can be accomplished, but it is not an overnight matter.

Summary

Mainstreaming and the noncategorical classroom and teacher education are intertwined concepts. Neither is anywhere near the perfect solution to the education of exceptional children and youth. Both are faddist concepts developed out of frustration on the part of special educators, general educators, and parents of handicapped children. In the belief that special education was poor and could not be improved, these two methods of solving the problem developed rapidly and without complete thought. Special education as a discipline in professional education can be inspiringly good, but to achieve this high level of professional effectiveness, much effort and thought must be given to it. The educators of the deaf and those of the blind have come nearer than others in developing sound social and educational techniques effective in bringing these children to the maximum of their abilities. Even these fields, however, need improvement and attention. Educators of the mentally retarded have been content to follow a watered-down academic program. Even with all of the funding available from the former U.S. Office of Education, no one ever tried to determine the validity of Richard Hungerford's concept of Occupational Education, probably the best concept of education and training of these children that has ever been conceived. The education of gifted children is left purely to chance except in a few communities in the nation. Programs for neurologically handicapped children including accurately defined children with learning disabilities is so fouled in irrational personalities and antagonisms that what is known clinically has never had a chance to demonstrate its worth over time. Special educators have it within their abilities to provide a stellar program of educational services for all clinical types of exceptional children. It will take effort and concentration. Furthermore, it will take the support and encouragement of general educators who themselves understand the goals of special education. It will take insightful administrators who have an understanding of the total educational process going on within their schools. Special education cannot be a mere afterthought to general education. Some mainstreaming will be possible, and as much normalization as is possible should be undertaken within appropriate restraints. Both special education and general education are needed in order to serve the needs of all children in a community.

References and Related Readings

Cruickshank, W. M. "Self-contained Classes and Mainstreaming." In "The IPEC: A Step in the History of Special Education," W. M. Cruickshank, W. C. Morse, and J. D. Grant, chap. 5. Ms.

Cruickshank, W. M., and Haring, N. G. *Assistants for Teachers of Exceptional Children.* Syracuse: Syracuse University Press, 1957.

Dunn, L. M. "Special Education for the Mildly Retarded: Is Much of It Justifiable?" *Exceptional Children* 35 (1968): 5–22.

Hallahan, D., and Cruickshank, W. M. *Psychoeducational Foundations of Learning Disabilities.* Englewood Cliffs, N.J.: Prentice-Hall, 1973.

Haring, N. G., Stern, G. G., and Cruickshank, W. M. *Attitudes of Educators Toward Exceptional Children.* Syracuse: Syracuse University Press, 1958.

Hobbs, N., ed. *Issues in the Classification of Children.* Vols. 1 and 2, San Francisco: Jossey-Bass, 1975.

Lerner, J., and James, K. "Systems and Systems Applications in Special Education." In *The Second Review of Special Education,* ed. L. Mann and D. Sabatino, 273–307. New York: Grune and Stratton, 1974.

MacMillan, D. L. "Issues and Trends in Special Education." *Mental Retardation* 11, no. 2 (1973): 3–8.

Meyen, E., ed. *Proceedings: The Missouri Conference on the Categorical/Non-categorical Issue in Special Education.* Columbia: University of Missouri Press, 1971.

Warnock, H. M. *Special Educational Needs: Report of the Committee of Enquiry into the Education of Handicapped Children and Young People.* London: Her Majesty's Stationery Office, 1968.

Chapter 8

The Role of Disciplines

This chapter addresses the various types of functions of professional disciplines that influence programs for handicapped children and youth. This chapter has broader application than to this single group of individuals. My comments may apply to almost any program regarding disciplinary interventions. Although generalizations can be made regarding all interdisciplinary functions, several distinct types are addressed here; single discipline function, multidisciplinary programming, interdisciplinary programming, and transdisciplinary arrangements for the delivery of services. I also wish to discuss a number of observations I have made during my years of work in program administration for the handicapped. While these experiences have taken place within a university setting, my conclusions are not restricted to higher education. My concerns are relatively universal and may apply to agencies, public schools, and treatment clinics. In years past the disciplines worked independently of one another or were almost completely subservient to another, i.e., nursing to medicine, and as well as other disciplines to medicine. A single discipline was essentially seen as being omnipotent and controlled. The control often extended beyond the hospital or physician's office to other areas of social function.

Discipline in the Professional Setting

I have often wondered whether or not there would be a problem in effective multidisciplinary, or in any other types of interdisciplinary relationships, if there were not the discipline of medicine. Sometimes I think that if the medical profession were no longer necessary in an interdisciplinary program, then the program would work beautifully. I single out the medical profession because with excellent knowledge of their own field they extend this attitude and assumption to other fields where they have little knowledge, and thus they throw wrenches into the smooth systems of teamwork. Too many medical persons have not learned to work with people, only to lead them. Furthermore, as the result of their preservice training, this professional group has isolated itself from genuine cooperative programming for so long that there is an expectancy of difficulty by others when disciplinary interrelationships are attemped.

Part of this problem may come, as I have suggested, by the admission of less-than-well-adjusted, but dominant, students to professional schools. Part of it may come from the mystique that medical personnel always have assumed omnipotence in their understanding of all things. This attitude may have come also from the awareness of medical students that responsibility for life and death is enormous. Additional emphasis may have come from the historical position either self-assigned or assigned by the community to medical personnel. In raising this question, I may be labeled antimedical. However, I have worked closely and successfully with leading medical personnel for most of my professional life, and continue to do so. I have also attempted to integrate medical personnel into a variety of service and training programs. Some of these attempts have been successful; others, near or full failures.

Why is this effort so difficult and so risky? I have come to two conclusions. First, is the matter of individual personalities, and, second, is the issue of the historical position of the disciplines in a presumed professional hierarchy.

To paraphrase an old truism: no professional function will be stronger than its most insecure and maladjusted members. It is my considered opinion that medical school admissions committees put too little emphasis on the personality characteristics of candidates for the profession. During my directorship of a large interdisciplinary training program, we had a number of preservice students from medical schools come to us for experience and for rotations. In general, these young people had already adopted unfortunate superior attitudes that almost precluded their easy participation in an interdisciplinary program and often resulted in hostilities between them and students or faculty members from other disciplines. To get them to leave their white coats at home was a near impossibility.

In lecturing to the entering class of a university medical school on one occasion, I reminded the students that in the hospital my profession was and should be considered ancillary to medicine. However, in the school situation or in the psychological clinic medicine was considered ancillary to the educator or to other disciplines with a primary responsibility. Even at this early stage in their preparation, this concept did not rest well with the audience. Is ancillary a one-way concept? I do not think so.

There is a vocal and growing concern among many persons regarding the self-assumed and omnipotent role of the medical profession's tendency to remove itself from any realistic effort at interdisciplinary action or, for that matter, to participate in any but solo action. A recent publication of Brackbill and her associates contains an excellent statement and speaks of "medical power" as a historical reality, but also as a medical fantasy physicians attempt to implement (Brackbill, McManus, and Woodward 1985).

The Federal Food and Drug Administration abets and enhances this medical power play. For example, its officials reversed without approval the June, 1938, congressional legislation creating the FDA. The FDA, six months later, promulgated a regulation that all prescriptions will "appear only in such medical terms as are not likely to be understood by the ordinary individual" (U.S. FDA, 1938). *Ordinary* and *physician* appear as a class structure.

Pharmacists likewise support the medical fantasy of supreme locus of power. Unable to translate the pharmacist's label on a prescribed medicine bottle, I asked to know what the purpose of the medication was. "Ask your physician," was the reply. With that I asked for the return of the prescription form, went to another pharmacist who was a friend, and received the information I sought. This is unnecessary behavior on the part of the first pharmacist as well as protectionism in a bad form.

There is positively no legal or moral rationale for medical omnipotence—an issue that already in numerous quarters is beginning to bring the house down. The right to know all is inherent in American people; not the right to "know only what I tell you," as more than one physician has stated. Brackbill's excellent monograph underscores this issue in a remarkable manner. By secrecy, control is maintained. The medical profession has been granted control by its taking an unwarranted status. How society would scream if automobile mechanics adopted the same self-serving attitudes—lawyers, teachers, electricians, plumbers, or farmers, ad infinitum. Each is capable of doing so, but only one profession is continuing to attempt it along with other means via the vehicle of its national trade union, the American Medical Association, an effort supplemented by organizational sycophants such as medical societies, art museums, social groups, etc. There can be no such thing as a professional hierarchy.

A profession, each in its own way, is equal to all others, and no one of them can either function without the others or be considered more authoritative than its peers except in its own professional territory. How many times have interdisciplinary efforts failed or floundered because the physician was or could not be the captain of the team. At the University of Michigan institute I formerly administered, the coordinator of a client-patient team rotated alphabetically among the two dozen disciplines represented on the staff. It worked.

Having said all this, let me assure the reader that my own relationships with physicians who over the years have treated me has been excellent. They have been selected, not only in terms of their professional competence, but for their personalities. Often operating on a first-name basis, equality is quickly established, and these persons became good family friends. There are thousands of remarkable physicians who represent all that society expects in terms of honesty, competence, willingness to share their knowledge, and patience. Unfortunately, however, there are many, if not more, who represent the situation as it has been described here.

I have found it interesting that the same professional characteristics do not apply to the dental profession. Dentists wear uniforms, whether necessary or not. They prescribe drugs. They perform surgery on certain occasions. I wonder why they do not exploit their medical mystique. However, a feeling of equality exists between dentists and other professional personnel. The need for status is not obvious, and dental students and faculty members in university settings are social beings who fraternize with colleagues from other disciplines. The spirit of cooperation is obvious. The willingness to lead is manifest only when their discipline is needed for leadership.

The Institute for the Study of Mental Retardation and Related Disabilities at the University of Michigan was intended to be an interdisciplinary training center, serving students from seven of the university's colleges and schools and from fourteen departments. At its peak, its staff numbered more than one hundred persons, who represented between fifteen and twenty professional disciplines. It was a remarkable faculty and staff, and it had an accomplished record. This was achieved, however, not without pains and pangs. Several examples will suffice to illustrate my meaning.

On one occasion in the institute's early years, the program director for pediatrics came into my office to inform me that, because I was not a medical doctor and because mental retardation was a medical problem, all records for clients seen in the institute should be signed by him. Mental retardation is hardly a medical problem but I did not argue that point. I refuted his claim that he should sign the records and told him the diagnostic team leaders would rotate alphabetically among the disciplines represented as had been agreed upon, beginning with *Administration* and *Audiology*. When the letter *P* was reached, personnel from *Pediatrics, Psychiatry,* and *Psychology* would in turn become the team leaders. He disputed this decision, which had been reached by the staff, on the basis that he was a physician and had the sole responsibility for "patients." Suffice it to say that his decision did not hold, and he finally resigned because he could not rationalize his role with the other disciplines unless he were in total charge. This was true to lesser extent with his successor, although she learned to respect her role and those of other disciplines in the diagnostic and training process.

Another time, the program director for social work came to me not understanding why we needed a program director for nutrition in the institute. The program director for psychology was at one time irate because the program director for occupational therapy was doing "testing," and he believed all such testing should be done by a psychologist. Although at that time not certified as a psychologist in the state of Michigan, he presumed that no other discipline could function in a field related to his own. Ultimately, time erased these views, but much time also was wasted by the shortsightedness of professional territoriality. We had a rule that there could be no private practice conducted within the institute. A program director for child psychiatry once told me that because he was a physician, the rule did not apply to him. That was dispelled and quickly. The issues of disciplinary dominance and autonomy are not solely a criticism of the medical discipline. The latter is just more blatant, perhaps because the community also feeds this attitude.

The University Musical Society publishes an annual list of all donors. All physicians are listed as Dr., all other patrons as Mr. and Mrs. This public stroking is carried on in the face of the fact that probably one-third of the remaining contributors to the society are doctors of philosophy, education, microbiology, law, engineering, biochemistry, and a myriad of other doctoral degrees. If this sounds like sour grapes, it is not. It is a complaint against a public manifestation that one profession is better than another. It is a complaint against an institution that places one discipline on a pedestal to the detriment of true interdisciplinary functions.

As I stated earlier, under my direction the institute served seven schools and colleges in the university: the schools of Education, Nursing, Dentistry, Social Work, Public Health, the Medical

School, and the College of Literature, Science, and the Arts. With the exception of the Medical School, each of the university divisions gave the institute complete cooperation. The only form of cooperation received from the medical personnel were verbal promises. The dean, associate deans, members of the executive committee of the school, the chairman of pediatrics, and other departmental chairmen, all said they would cooperate, but they never did. Extreme efforts were made to solicit their support, e.g., transfer of salary funds to the Medical School, joint appointments, conferences with faculty members and departmental chairmen by the score, but all to no avail. A few persons came through, but the number was so insignificant that efforts to seek cooperative programming were stopped on my part. The chairman of the Department of Pediatrics thought he was working with me by asking me to take a member of his faculty full time because he viewed the faculty member at the Medical School as ineffective. Cooperation on the basis of equality, however, never was forthcoming from that source during my entire tenure. Cooperation can never be a one-way street.

In these examples, there may be a reason other than historical aloofness to explain why the medical profession cannot function in a cooperative manner. The medical faculty initially wanted the institute to be an integral part of the Medical School, and this was denied by the university administration. This type of program could not have been an interdisciplinary program developed within that kind of blatant disciplinarianism. No one would have been able to speak for the educator, the dentist, the occupational therapist, or other disciplines on matters of promotion, tenure, rank, and salary. The medical profession has not proven itself sufficiently mature in such matters to allow it to be responsible for a total interdisciplinary model. The medical model, as good as it is in the operating room, cannot prevail in a true interdisciplinary concept, and the university administrators understood this. That understanding, however, did not make administration of the institute any easier.

The field of learning disabilities is one with which I have been associated for many years. The first evidence of any state pediatric academy interest in this problem took place in Florida in the late 1950s. In a department of pediatrics with which I have had an association for some time, a faculty member announced during a staff meeting in 1977 that he was the responsible person for children with a "new behavioral syndrome," that of learning disabilities. When he was asked when this problem was first recognized nationally (1963), he responded, "recently." There is a role for the physician with learning disabled children. If medication is required, then a physician has that responsibility. However, the learning disabilities field is essentially a psychoeducational responsibility, as it has been in the United States as far back as 1936. Unless the professions can work together, learning disabled children and their families are going to be shortchanged. Pediatricians, as well as all professionals involved, must recognize this and must also recognize their appropriate supporting role. If each profession operates within its disciplinary limits and in recognition of its own skills, there is no need to overlap or to be threatened by other disciplines, and the medical profession too can relax.

As part of the national policy under the Kennedy legislation in mental retardation (P.L. 84-926) interdisciplinary training, research, and service centers were established in many universities nationwide (see chap. 9). They were erroneously called "university affiliated facilities," but in reality were not affiliated with anything. They were integral parts of the various university administrations. The University of Michigan had one of these, as did the universities of Wisconsin, Alabama, Miami, North Carolina, Washington, Oregon, California, and others. I was the first nonmedical director to be appointed to head one of these programs. Later, Harvey Stevens headed the Waisman Center at Wisconsin, and the Kennedy Center for Child Development at the University of Colorado Medical Center also was later headed by a psychologist. All others were administered by physicians. I was not well received when the administrators first organized themselves into a professional lobby. Further, there was also great concern in the federal funding agency about awarding money to a program with a nonmedical administrator. As other nonmedical administrators gradually found their way into these facilities, attitudes relaxed. The federal funding agency found it difficult to criticize quality programs only because they were not headed by physicians.

The controls the medical profession has attempted to maintain over programs for handicapped persons has been evidenced in other ways. Until the early 1950s, programs of education for handicapped children within public school systems often were located within the department headed by the school physician or the director of pupil personnel.

Institutions for physically and mentally handicapped residents have been under the directorships of medical personnel historically, both in Europe and the United States. While this is still the mode in many countries, the trend has been broken in the United States. There is absolutely no rationale for the chief administrator of an institution for mentally retarded residents, for example, to be a physician. There is nothing related to budget development, personnel policies, supply ordering, building maintenance, and related administrative matters that is medical in nature. Obviously, the chief of clinical services in a residential facility may well need to be a physician, but even that is subject to reasonable question. Physicians are needed somewhere along the line in the delivery of services, just as are members of other professions. They are not needed at the command post in every building of the institution.

One wonders why physicians must be the directors of state departments of mental health, a tradition that has been upon us for almost the entire history of such state programs. In one state there have been six directors of the department of mental health, five psychiatrists and one pediatrician (whose appointment was aggressively opposed by the members of the state legislature because he was not a psychiatrist) within the past fifteen years. The fact that these men were all physicians did not make them good administrators, nor did their medical preservice preparation provide them with administrative skills. In fact, only two of the six could have been given a high rating as administrators, and these were individuals who would have succeeded irrespective of their professional discipline. Their success could have been replicated by anyone from any of a dozen other disciplines, and basically their day-to-day decisions or year-to-year planning did not require medical backgrounds.

There was much interest in the state when the departmental program for mental retardation was placed under the direction of a psychologist and even more when a nurse succeeded him. From what source does the medical mystique persist that such administrative positions need be filled by physicians? Is it from the community? the administrative system? precedent? status quo? or from the medical profession itself? Undoubtedly each force, and perhaps others, plays an important role, but it is obvious that the American Medical Association and the medical profession as a whole perform the leads in the play.

These additional examples illustrate the disciplinary hold one discipline has on service delivery in areas wherein its skills are not needed and are self-serving in a primary manner. There are examples of persons from other disciplines who have successfully held these administrative positions: Richard Hungerford, mentioned elsewhere in this volume, was at one time the superintendent of the Franconia State School for retarded persons in New Hampshire. Mr. Hungerford was an educational administrator. Mr. Harvey Stevens, one of the most respected persons in the field of mental retardation, was an educator chosen for the superintendent of the Central Colony for the Mentally Retarded in Wisconsin. Since 1966 most Michigan institutions for the mentally retarded have been administered by persons from disciplines other than medicine. This action has been taken often in spite of the strong lobbying efforts of medicine. Decisions of others prevailed, however. The drive for medical control has prevailed for more than a hundred years in the United States. Returning this discipline to its proper role in American society has been an effort of the past four decades. This is not to deny that there have been some outstanding medical administrators. Dr. Robert Haskell, a pediatric psychiatrist who headed the world-famous Wayne County Training School near Detroit, was one of these. Others could be named. However, the administration of residential facilities and state departments has not always attracted the best of the medical profession, either administratively or professionally, and services to the citizens of the states often have suffered proportionally. Professional administrators, a discipline in and of itself, should replace other disciplines in these roles as a matter of national policy.

In concluding this section of the chapter, I need to reinforce a point. I speak here of the historical attitude that prevails today and is detrimental to service performance. Obviously society owes much to medical practitioners. Advances in medical practice have most often come, however, from other disciplines. Medical researchers have performed remarkable feats and subsequently have eradicated many handicapping conditions, vis-à-vis, poliomyelitis, osteomyelitis, some clinical types of mental retardation, disabling conditions as a result of rubella, the control of seizures. It may be that because of these remarkable successes the profession has been allowed to place itself upon a pedestal. Engineering, physics, chemistry, and mathematics have contributed equally as significant developments on society's behalf, but have retained a more humble professional position. It is important that perspective be maintained regarding the disciplinary contributions that have been made to human life, and not all of these in any manner have come from medicine. These points will be elaborated in the paragraphs that follow.

Controlling Personality Characteristics

It is important to establish certain essentials regarding disciplinary function in the delivery of human services of whatsoever nature. Most of my remarks here pertain to personality characteristics of individuals working within disciplines that affect multidisciplinary involvements.

Irrespective of whether there is a unilateral or multidisciplinary relationship being established between a professional person and a client, interpersonal relationships must be considered, i.e., teacher-child, physician-patient, psychologist-client, social worker-client, or any of these in an interrelationship between and among professional colleagues. It would be hard to conceive of a society that contained no personal problems within given professional persons. There is nothing about professional people that precludes personality problems, sometimes of great magnitude. Personal problems of individuals can get in the way of good professional relationships, either in client-patient or professional colleagues of the same or other disciplines.

An audiologist, or more accurately an educator of the deaf in this instance, whose aggressive personality traits were nationally recognized, caused me no end of administrative difficulties. Exactly nine faculty members over a decade's time resigned from the hearing and speech faculty because of this individual. He always had to have a scapegoat, a whipping boy, someone to put down and to criticize. Several times he was offered positions elsewhere, and I made successful attempts to retain the services of this person; his clinical skills with speech and hearing problems were so splendid. I now criticize myself for having made these efforts. I was crucified constantly by this individual, and many others were hurt in his flailing attempts to control. Better had I let him go, recognizing the fallibility of the faculty member and my inability to change deep-seated personality characteristics within the setting of a university academic program.

Over the four decades of my professional-administrative life, I have been in the position of employing many, many faculty members—perhaps as many as three hundred, although I have never kept a record of this. I have kept a record of another fact; eight times I have employed individuals whom I later wished had never come to my attention. All of these persons later left our employment. In not one of these instances did the new employer call me personally or in any fashion try to obtain a recommendation from me regarding the individual on whom he had set his sights. It is interesting that, except for two of these individuals, six moved again from the new place of employment after a short period of time. In two instances, when I later looked into the preemployment information of the persons, I observed that I had been given dishonest recommendations from current employers, who wanted to be rid of an employee so much that they falsified both letters of recommendation and telephone conversations. Obviously, one would never go back to those sources for additional faculty employees. These eight individuals—eight professional errors on my part—had personality traits that made it nearly impossible for others to work with them as colleagues. On a postemployment basis these people were characterized by others as lazy, "flaky," aggressive, unwilling to carry out responsibilities, both sadistic to and manipulative of students, hesitant to the point of withdrawal, noncommunicative, harsh to secretaries, and so on through a long list of traits that individually or together made cooperative efforts difficult if not impossible.

Given tenure and a university bureaucracy full of faculty committees, rules, regulations, and grievance procedures, the only opportunity administrators have to truly effect change in an academic program is when they are able to employ new people. This may undoubtedly be true of any large organization, but I only know of universities that, in spite of all their glory and remarkable social contributions, are often controlled by internal politics and individual attempts to maintain the status quo in order to cloud mediocrity.

There are certain personality traits that these professional people should have, regardless of the discipline. First, they must enjoy people of all ages. It is not necessary that the enjoyment be overwhelming; professional people basically must be satisfied with being in the presence of colleagues, students, and clients. I recognize that individuals are motivated by many things in their selection of a profession, i.e., the social status of the profession, their need to provide services to others to enhance their own status, and other dynamic motivating forces. The "call" to the clergy may be another reason for entering a profession; here, destiny is completely out of the hands of the individual. What a relief! Another desirable trait is an honest interest in the profession. For example, to be interested in the problems of children and youth, to thoroughly enjoy working with the disabled person, with adults, or aging individuals, is not only a compliment to the professional, but also a genuine source of satisfaction to the receiver.

Allocentricism rather than egotism is a desirable personality characteristic. Professionals need to reach out and be concerned with the problems of others in a sincere and healthy manner. Allocentric persons are open-minded and open in their relationships with others. Just as closed professional systems inhibit good professional programming, closed minds and closed personalities make professionally interpersonal relationships difficult to achieve. Allocentricism can also be carried too far, unfortunately. The visionary who can never deal with reality is not a helpful person in a staff meeting. I have been associated with such persons over the years, and they rarely are able to contribute anything to the decision-making process of the group. I knew a young prelaw student who was so allocentristic that he often overwhelmed those with whom he came in contact. Finally, he matured enough to see himself more realistically in relationship to others and modified his personality characteristics to the point where an even balance is his current behavior mode. He is a delight to be with, whereas earlier he monopolized any social situation in which he found himself. An appropriate outreaching to and encompassing of others is the desired balance to pursue.

Somewhere, there is probably a dominance-humbleness scale from one to ten. A disciplinary representative should likely fall somewhere in the middle of such a scale. Those who overpower others tend to be avoided whenever possible. Hostility often develops and renders group decisions nearly impossible to obtain when an individual attempts to dominate a situation or force his or her opinion on others.

At the other extreme, a team member who is so humble as to be seen as self-effacing is also inappropriate as a disciplinary representative. A withdrawing person may be unable to participate fully in group discussions, and accept the decisions of others, when in fact the opinions run counter to his or her own judgments or disciplinary positions.

Balance in personality characteristics, making possible full participation in group discussions, a defender of client needs, a good representative of the discipline involved, and a respecter of the points of view and comments of other team members are each and all characteristics needed and sought after in team members and in any type of group endeavor. Utopia is something for which to strive although unobtainable because it makes each person strive for more than mediocrity. Individual personality problems can get in the way of effective group action to the point of destroying excellent professional programs. Once, for a short time in an emergency, I was the chairman of an academic program in a major university. I inherited a total faculty group, and indeed, by action of the university administrators replaced an acting chairman who continued on the faculty. Within this faculty group of approximately ten individuals was a collection of personalities the likes of which I had not previously encountered. They varied from politically driven individuals who worked against others behind the scenes, to aggressive and dominant individuals who sought to manipulate others by sheer dint of psychological controls. Manipulation by rumor characterized another. Control by silence and silent participation in any group discussion characterized a senior member of the group. Still another, through aggressive behavior, ultimately was able to thrust aside my successor as chairman and put himself in that position. This is in spite of the fact that he had demonstrated in other ways behavior inappropriate to any administrator.

Academic brilliance does not ensure good personal adjustment. During an employment interview individuals are on their best behavior. It is only later that the true characteristics of the individual emerge and must subsequently be confronted. In the example I have cited, each faculty member had apparently been employed because of his academic strengths; no one had ever made penetrating inquiries regarding the nature of the mental adjustment of the individuals. Professional honors, publications, organizational memberships, or other similar items in a personnel resumé do not insure appropriate leadership in most university activities.

Omnipotence is another characteristic in professionals that can defeat team action. The individual who has all the answers to any situation cannot only be a bore, but often will mislead the remainder of the team members in decisions and actions that later prove to have been erroneous.

Throughout this discussion I have been very negative. Is it ever possible to find professional persons who meet the criteria I have implied or who are not characterized by the traits I have specifically mentioned? I fully believe it is possible. If not, I doubt I would have remained in academic life for so long. In university teaching, administration, and research, I have met some of the finest people anywhere, and have come to admire students, faculty members, and administrative colleagues fully, some as personal friends and others as professional colleagues. I repeat that the key to assembling a faculty group capable of great things individually and collectively is the care taken by the employer at the preemployment period. Written recommendations are hardly sufficient. Too much can be clouded by a present employer wishing to divest himself of a faculty member.

Visits by the employing university representatives to the candidate and to his or her university are important. There one can observe how the candidate relates to other colleagues, his or her behavior while teaching, and one can visit with colleagues to assess the individual directly. These are ethical and important procedures. When they are not welcomed, I would look for other candidates. It is too easy to make a mistake, which later will prove financially costly and academically or personally embarrassing, not to utilize all techniques possible to assure oneself that the best possible person is being employed. No employer is always right in his or her personnel decisions. Major effort to evaluate the future faculty member is nevertheless a primary responsibility of administrators in any college or university. To exert less than a complete effort is to render a disservice to the academic community. A university faculty must be characterized by allocentric behavior, cooperative attitudes, and the capacity for joint endeavor. Without these traits in individuals, academic competence will not be demonstrated.

Types of Disciplinary Cooperation

There are three distinct types of disciplinary cooperation, one of which is rarely utilized. Each of these requires that the disciplinary representatives possess in good quantity the personal characteristics and qualifications that I have stressed in the preceding paragraph.

Multidisciplinary Action. While no type of disciplinary cooperation is easy to implement, multidisciplinary programming is undoubtedly the easiest and perhaps the most likely to succeed. Under this approach, a group of disciplinary representatives simply agree to work together independently, and there is a high degree of independence for each discipline involved. Obviously such a consortium can become an administrative inconvenience if too many disciplines are involved. However, each discipline does its own work, regardless of who else may be providing services to the client. The disciplinary representative writes and files reports that are drawn together into a meaningful statement by an administrator or another person designated to do this work. The essential issue in this type of professional activity is that all personnel know what they are doing individually, i.e., multidisciplinary function means parallel responsibilities, not intrusions into the work arena of another discipline. Lines of responsibility are carefully drawn. The failure of multidisciplinary action is due to disciplinary representatives who have an erroneous notion of their relationship to other personnel within the hospital, school, or clinic. There is a high degree of independence of the single discipline in a multidisciplinary team. The chairperson of the team, or someone designated by that person, puts together individual disciplinary reports into a final statement. The disciplines remain relatively inviolate. If there are serious discrepancies, the chairperson may meet the individuals who have the difference of opinion and try to work things out.

Under the multidisciplinary approach, personality variance among team members can be tolerated to a larger degree than under other administrative arrangements because the disciplines essentially are independent of one another. During my experience as an administrator, I sometimes have had to use this approach where there were irreconcilable differences between two or more professional persons. Unfortunately, multidisciplinary teamwork places greater responsibility and work load on a chief of clinical services or on another administrator, but the clinical program survives until personnel changes can be effected. The reasons behind such a decision must be understood by all staff members, for it essentially means disciplinary independence rather then cooperative professional activity. Within a clinical service, hospital, or school setting, the multidisciplinary approach is characterized by a relatively watertight system of clinical units with a "head" or "chief" or "chairperson" of each discipline largely controlling and protecting the disciplinary territory. This is not the most mature type of activity nor that which is most laudatory or characteristic of the best in professional people. It is, however, an expedient measure that accommodates personality variations that otherwise might make programming very difficult. It has merits as the substitute for better professionalism.

There also are occasions, particularly in the complex hospital operations, when the multidisciplinary approach is valuable. For example, there are times when the department of pediatrics needs information from the electroencephalographic unit or from the department of pathology. There is no reason why these three disciplines should not work independently and be able to funnel information to a single point. However, there are reasons why different departments might find it more beneficial to work closely together.

The multidisciplinary approach is the most typical of several intervention techniques. Many people erroneously believe that in multidisciplinary activities they are accomplishing an interdisciplinary thrust. It is important to stress that the multidisciplinary approach is unique, and its uniqueness should be understood by all participants in order to avoid confusion and at the same time to allow the best in professional operations. Too frequently we talk "multidisciplinary," but think we are speaking of "interdisciplinary" actions.

Interdisciplinary Action. Although interdisciplinary programs are much more difficult to operate successfully than multidisciplinary arrangements, the effort is worthwhile in the end. Interdisciplinary is just what the word implies: activities carried on between or among disciplines.

All of the positive personality traits previously mentioned are absolute requisites for the successful operation of this plan. All disciplines are equals among equals. Each discipline must be viewed as having a significant contribution to make, and each team member must be fully accepted by the others. An atmosphere of esprit de corps must surround all team discussions and operations. There will be times when individual disciplines, because of the nature of their contributions, may work independently, but ultimately their findings and conclusions will be returned to the team for discussion, evaluation, critique, and integration into the thinking of the whole group.

The interdisciplinary team chairperson should be evenhanded with team members. This prevents the chairperson from playing favorites with the disciplinary representatives. It is easy to establish a policy allowing the chairperson's position to rotate alphabetically among the members on a time-oriented, client-need basis. This procedure allows individual leadership potential to be fully exploited and prevents anyone from being slighted.

The concept of disciplinary equality is easier said than done. Nurses, who are historically subservient to physicians, often are uncomfortable when they assume team leadership roles in the presence of a physician. Over a period of time, however, these feelings of professional inferiority erode. The same situation often exists between special educators and psychologists, the former deferring to the latter. The professional "pecking order" is a binding thing, and many times it prevents provision of the best services to the client. The concept of "getting to know you" is a valid one—getting to know and to understand the personalities on the team, the valid contributions that each discipline can make to the understanding of a complex clinical problem, and an understanding of the professional overlapping that may occur. When these issues are successfully acknowledged, then any type of interdisciplinary team will succeed.

With reference to nursing, another matter comes to mind. It is absolutely essential that in any interdisciplinary activity each discipline be able to define its role, function, and specific place in the interdisciplinary milieu. Unless each team member knows these things with respect to the other colleagues, not only is much time wasted, but also it becomes more difficult to accomplish good professional actions. In a recent interdisciplinary activity I directed, nursing personnel were included on the staff. These people continually referred to the "extended role of nursing." In their effort to distinguish between bedside nursing and other nursing specialties this phrase occurred often. However, neither our nursing staff members nor their colleagues in the University of Michigan School of Nursing were able to provide the other staffers with a definition of "extended role." We watched our nursing colleagues' performance very closely to try to determine what this phrase meant. We saw them attempt a bit of assessment, particularly with young handicapped children, using many of the procedures an occupational therapist would normally utilize. We also saw them engage in counseling as a psychologist or psychiatrist would do. We observed them as they examined children utilizing pediatric techniques. They also employed physical therapy techniques, and sometimes even special education procedures. In all of this we asked what was meant by "extended role?" Never, as long as they were staff members, were we able to get a definition of the extended role of nursing in the interdisciplinary team. This failure placed all staff members on the defensive with nursing personnel; the nursing function of the interdisciplinary team simply was not understood and could not be defined for us.

There can be too many individuals on a team, which need not be comprised of all disciplines. I believe that every essential discipline for the specific task at hand should be included on any team. An *early intervention task force* could, for example, contain an occupational therapist, a person skilled in language development, a special educator, a pediatrician, and possibly a nurse. Here, disciplinary skills and knowledge are part of the basis of an organization.

A team concerned with the preparation of *human sexuality trainers* could be organized around other characteristics, including chronological maturity and sexual preferences, (i.e., male and female homosexuality, heterosexual life patterns, married and single persons). The earlier statement regarding equals among equals applies in this situation as well, but there should be more of a conscious effort to select persons for this team who represent well-developed levels of emotional security and self-acceptance. A team focused on the *severely and multiply handicapped* preschool child could be comprised of a nurse, a special educator, a language specialist, an occupational therapist, a physical therapist, and either a pediatrician or other medical specialists as consultants. The composition varies with the team focus and responsibilities.

In the institute to which I have made earlier reference we had numerous teams in operation, often with an individual of a given discipline being a member of more than one team at a time, i.e., the three teams already mentioned, a team on geriatrics and aging for the developmentally disabled, a continuing education unit, a dentistry unit for the handicapped team, a vocational adjustment team, a team on religious instruction and the handicapped for the clergy, and a large number of other topically related teams. In addition to these interdisciplinary efforts, multidisciplinary activities were carried on simultaneously. It is possible for all types of service-delivery arrangements in a given agency to function simultaneously on an equal basis. The key to success is that all staff members of an agency understand what role model is being followed for a specific function in a given time frame. Flexibility is an important characteristic of personnel who work in an organization where various models are being employed in an appropriate manner.

Transdisciplinary Action. In this model for either service delivery or training purposes, persons from one discipline perform duties normally assigned to another discipline. Transdisciplinary action is the least used and most difficult model, undoubtedly because there are many hazards present. First, it requires very secure professional people who are not made uneasy when they hear of or directly see a colleague performing functions that are normally reserved for another. Second, all staff members who assume another's role (never fully, but partially) must have an extensive knowledge of the related disciplines. Last, when a staff from discipline A moves to function as far as possible in discipline B, the personnel in discipline B must be informed of this in advance. To a large extent the success of transdisciplinary action depends on interpersonal confidence and trust.

Obviously, there are areas of disciplinary knowledge that cannot be assumed by individuals of other disciplines. In medicine, the responsibilities for medication cannot be shared with other disciplines any more than the responsibility for educational and psychological assessment can be shared appropriately with medical personnel. Logic must rule in the transdisciplinary approach.

Nearly the same results can be obtained for clients if the interdisciplinary procedures can be extended to include transdisciplinary activities. The best of both worlds is accomplished, and indeed good interdisciplinary practice contains most of the transdisciplinary advantages.

Regardless of which approach is utilized in a given program, all service-delivery procedures are founded on the human equation. The extent to which well-adjusted persons are brought into the professional fields, the extent to which egotistical disciplinary presumptions can be replaced with a concept of disciplinary equality, and the extent to which persons with encompassing and compassionate administrative skills are placed in leadership roles will be basic to the quality of clinical services rendered to clients and to students.

References and Related Readings

Brackbill, Y., McManus, K., and Woodward, L. *Medication and Maternity.* Ann Arbor: University of Michigan Press, 1985.

Cruickshank, W. M. "Definition: A Major Issue in the Field of Learning Disabilities." *Journal of Rehabilitation* 50, no. 2 (April-June, 1984): 7–18.

————. "A New Perspective in Teacher Education: The Neuroeducator." *Journal of Learning Disabilities* 14, no. 6 (June/July, 1981), 337–41.

Ellison, H. E., and Kopp, C. B. "A Note on Interdisciplinary Research in Developmental/Behavioral Pediatrics/Psychology." *Pediatrics* 75, no. 5 (May, 1985): 883–86.

Hobbs, N., ed. *Issues in the Classification of Children.* Vols. 1 and 2. San Francisco: Jossey-Bass, 1975.

Levine, M. D., and Satz, P. *Middle Childhood: Development and Dysfunction.* Baltimore: University Park Press, 1984.

Sweeney, D. P., and Wilson, T. Y. *Double Jeopardy: The Plight of Aging and Aged Developmentally Disabled Persons in Mid-America.* Institute for the Study of Mental Retardation and Related Disabilities. Ann Arbor: University of Michigan, 1979.

Chapter 9

Children with Retarded
Mental Development

I propose here to examine the concept of normalization of children with retarded mental development and, more specifically, normalization of those retarded children who are characterized as *educable*. By educable, I mean retarded children and youth whose accurately measured intelligence generally is found to be between an intelligence quotient of 55 and 80. In no way will I attempt to cover the total field of mental retardation, which complete books have addressed. Rather, I shall deal with issues that appear very significant to me and on which there is less than unanimous agreement.

This chapter will deal only with the endogenous type of retarded individual as opposed to the exogenous or mixed types whose learning problems, in addition to retardation per se, are characterized by perceptual processing deficits, which also are found in children with learning disabilities. Endogenous retarded children are those whose case histories have no evidence of brain dysfunction due to accident, illness, disease, or injuries, but whose histories show evidence of hereditary, familial, or genetic factors in the primary family group that may have caused the retardation. By definition, "primary" is considered to include the child's own generation (siblings or cousins), the parents' generation (aunts, uncles), and the generation of both maternal and paternal grandparents. Thus, if there is no evidence of exogenous factors in the child's history but there is evidence of retardation in the father, for example, or in a maternal sister, aunt, or cousin, retardation in the individual under consideration is assumed to be hereditary. Obviously, chromosomal studies, karyotyping, and related genetic studies are utilized as well. (Other familial factors have also been found to be related to retardation, such as epilepsy, alcoholism, schizophrenia, etc.) This is the "garden variety" of mental retardation, the *primary type* as designated by Seymour Sarason and others. From the viewpoint of learning, endogenous children function and apparently learn as do intellectually normal children of the same mental age (as opposed to the unique processing problems of the exogenous type children). An early study reported that endogenous children, when carefully matched by mental age with intellectually normal children, sometimes excelled over the latter insofar as certain psychological processes in arithmetic are concerned. It must be kept in mind, however, that the stress is on mental age matching, which means that retarded children with mental ages of ten and IQs of 75 would be approximately thirteen years of age chronologically. If their normal matched partners have IQs of 100 and are ten years of age chronologically, the mental ages also would be ten. The retarded children are more than three years older chronologically than their partners, and maturity may well account for their superior achievement in some of the most simple arithmetical operations studied.

Normalization

Let us consider the retarded children briefly described here. Assume that they have had optimal family experiences to date. In the light of mainstreaming, one needs to question where these children are to be placed in school. Remember their mental ages are ten and achievement levels, if optimal teaching has been experienced, will be approximately at the fourth grade level. But the chronological ages are thirteen. It would be a difficult decision, nearly impossible for the conscientious, to determine in which grade a child should be placed, what courses to take, what individualization of instruction will be required, what level of teaching materials will be needed, what training the teacher will need in order to individualize teaching so that success experiences will be ensured. Another tough decision is what prevocational training the school must provide retarded youths in order to prepare them for the work world when they graduate. There is something about exceptional children that prevents them from easily fitting into the educational molds that are more or less appropriate for all normal children. There are significant differences that those who believe in mainstreaming have forgotten or intentionally overlooked. The chronological-mental age discrepancy is one of these. The above-mentioned example is based upon the rarely obtained *optimal* home and school learning experiences. The problem worsens when considering less than optimal conditions.

Another alternative—placement in a school classroom according to mental age—means that a thirteen-year-old boy appears in the fourth or fifth grade. He is completely out of balance physically and socially with the nine- or ten-year-old children who are included appropriately in this grade placement.

A third alternative—the resource room—is also a possibility. However, resource rooms in the 1980s leave much to be desired. They either have become dumping grounds or have a teacher-pupil ratio so greatly in disfavor of successful achievement that they are essentially worthless. I have seen examples of resource rooms where the group composition of pupils changed completely every twenty-two minutes, and others where the teacher has had as many as sixty different children in the course of a single day—sixty children with sixty different educational, social, emotional, or other types of problems. In the dozens of resource rooms that I have visited in the United States and Canada, I have seen only a handful that come even close to accomplishing their purpose or in which there is a professionally contented teacher. These alternatives generally are not the answer to good education for retarded children. No homogeneity exists.

Advocates of normalization have another solution, namely, to place the child reasonably close to his mental-age peers, and then to integrate him selectively into various classes (gymnasium activities, art, music, and certain manual skills classes such as woodworking). It is assumed, of course, that the gym teacher, the art or music teachers, will be sophisticated regarding the retarded youth and respond to him or her appropriately in terms of mental age. Most teachers of manual arts have even higher standards of pupil achievement than do those of the more traditional "academic" subjects. This type of school readjustment often is not fair to the retarded students. It is more than questionable and is in no way a total solution.

As a matter of historical fact, mainstreaming, if carried on at all, antedated special education. The 1980s represent the completion of a circle. If retarded pupils were anywhere in the school system in the 1920s, they were struggling in the regular grades, and they were failing. As an elementary school child in the 1920s, I can remember retarded boys and girls in my classes. One boy followed us along until the then legal school-leaving age of fourteen years, when he dropped out of school. That was mainstreaming sixty or so years before the first Deans' Project (see chap. 7). There is nothing new about it, although the proponents would lead one to believe that a great new idea had just been discovered. One can justifiably ask what the difference is between integration efforts in the 1920s and in the 1980s. Integration failed once; it is failing again for these children.

Special education made its appearance in community education in the early 1930s. The negative attitudes of general educators toward special education quickly came to the surface and greatly hindered special education's chance to succeed. One's self-concept is not enhanced by being referred to as the "mentally retarded teacher" or the "blind teacher." Interestingly, few if any teachers of special groups of gifted children were ever called "gifted teachers."

It took a state department of education regulation in New York State to get classes for retarded children placed at ground level or above. The basement was the customary location, with classrooms for retarded children neatly snuggled up against the boiler room. These actions were not limited to New York.

Teacher preparation in special education was deficient and added to the poor reputation of the field. Adequate college professors seldom were to be found to teach special education teachers. In one eastern state, a teacher with minimal elementary certification could extend that to the teaching of retarded children by completing twelve extra college units of training: six in handicrafts and six in practice teaching. This was as late as the 1950s.

Diagnostic services and well-prepared psychological personnel essentially were unavailable. All of these factors combined to give special education an extremely unsavory and lasting reputation. Each of these factors was remedied in large measure during the period of 1960–75, but general educators at all levels kept up their attacks on special education. At the very least, they temporarily won the battle with the passage of Public Law 94-142. Normalization as it is known now as a program began in about 1975 despite general community unreadiness.

Whether people will admit it or not, financial considerations also contributed to the antagonism between special and general educators. Low special education teacher-pupil ratio is another, but finance was the major factor. With the passage of the so-called Kennedy legislation in 1960, the cornucopia flowed with funds for special education at all levels. At Syracuse University, I once announced to the faculty the award of more than a half-million dollars for a demonstration study of brain-injured children and their education, and there was a dull silence from my general educator colleagues. Funds raised at the same university for a new building for the Division of Special Education and Rehabilitation, funds for additional faculty members, fourteen research projects awarded to the division on the same date—each and together produced intracollege jealousies that were deep-seated. Similar experiences were reported across the nation by many of the leading special educators of that time.

Curriculum

Educators, both special and general, had a very hazy notion of what an adequate curriculum for retarded children should be. Good teaching materials with high interest levels and low vocabulary levels did not exist. Handicrafts were emphasized, and these had little relevance to children's needs. Remediation was the watchword. Repeating "grades" was a frequent occurrence. We have never had anything like a universally agreed upon curriculum for mentally retarded pupils. Rather, education for children with retarded mental development has been a hodgepodge of watered-down academic work sometimes combined with vocational education. We have throughout the special education history consciously or unconsciously infantilized the mentally retarded. There are bona fide reasons why parents, general educators, and even many special educators were not proud of nor satisfied with what retarded children received educationally. The stage was set for parents to demand that their retarded children be educated. Normalization and mainstreaming had healthy sounds to those who were discouraged by even the best of special education. It must also be kept in mind that those pressures for change in special education occurred at the same time as the national unrest by young people toward all things labeled status quo. On a different level the civil rights movement was contagious. The national concern over the Vietnam war, Watergate scandals, higher education sit-ins, protests against nuclear power plants, marches in Washington, protest vigils, and general agitation for change throughout our social system coincided with and supported parental agitation for change in the special education systems. It is not unreasonable that in this climate, parents sought changes for their retarded children.

I think it is important that a review is made of an educational philosophy and curriculum that, if it had been allowed to continue and to demonstrate its worth, may have enhanced positively the status of special education and rendered needless expense, frustration, and the too often failure of normalization programs. I refer to the philosophy of Occupational Education for Children with Retarded Mental Development that was, though short-lived and attacked by politically motivated and shortsighted special educators, the most creative curriculum concept ever developed for retarded youth.

Richard Hungerford, a supervisor of classes for retarded children, began the program in the Detroit public school system. His success in this endeavor led to his selection as the director of the Bureau for Children with Retarded Mental Development in the New York City public schools. He moved into a unique hotbed of political maneuvering. Mr. Hungerford inherited three assistant directors in the bureau, long a part of the city's educational system, each of whom in various ways and for various reasons took a position of opposition to Mr. Hungerford. These persons could not be removed, and retirement, except for one, was a long way off.

Mr. Hungerford was mild mannered on the surface, but had an uncontrolled temper when crossed. He was inventive and could challenge the few intimates who surrounded him, but he did not have the personality nor the force to move the gargantuan bureaucracy of his office, which serviced twenty-five thousand diagnosed retarded children in the school system at the time. Mr. Hungerford was political, but, on at least one occasion, was inept in his political decisions. He was open to attack by his opponents, and did not have a sufficient number of supporting professional allies to beat the system of appointment, tenure, and open warfare that so characterized the New York City educational system. He was a nice guy but not a warrior trained in educational infighting. At first all went well, but in a relatively short time he was defeated and left the system. No strong leadership has ever replaced him, and what could have been a remarkable educational program was dissolved; old guard educators again took over with outmoded antique programs. Once again, the easy way out took precedence over quality.

Hungerford's enemies need no mention. They are known. His supporters were many, but not enough. Included among this latter was a group of courageous educators: Chris de Prospo, Louis Rosenzweig, Winifred Femiani, Irving Goldstein, Frank Borreca, Leo Shainman, Stella Cohen, and many others whose excellent writings filled many issues of the *American Journal of Mental Deficiency* in the later 1940s and the 1950s. These people were dedicated, enthusiastic, and committed educators. They were intelligent and supportive of Hungerford, but they were not a large enough group. When Hungerford left the system, many of these remarkable people also left, finding positions in New York City colleges and universities, retiring, or accepting positions outside the city.

The special education world was ready for what Hungerford

had to offer. Unfortunately, his personality and his political naiveté resulted in his downfall. His efforts were too short-lived to have any lasting curricular impact. The special education world lost a major opportunity to gain its rightful place in the sun.

Occupational Education failed essentially because it was innovative and edge cutting, but most important because, as a new concept, it required *work* on the part of already overloaded special educators: teachers, supervisors, and administrators. The workload and demands for extraordinary initial efforts to get the program started could have been the single most significant factor in its demise, notwithstanding the antagonism and negative leadership of the three assistant directors of the bureau and their coteries.

Occupational Education was a curriculum based on the developing needs of retarded children and, in particular, on their need to enter successfully the world of work as retarded adults. Eight core areas of curricular emphases were conceptualized, each of which was related intimately to two initial, time-consuming steps: a survey of jobs in the community that were open to retarded adults, and an extraordinarily detailed analysis of each identified job. All eight core areas were dependent upon these first two steps.

Complicating issues were inherent in the curricular concept itself. Retarded children living on Staten Island, for example, would have some different job possibilities from those living in South Bronx or Manhattan. On a national basis, the vocational opportunities for retarded youth in Dade County, Florida, would in general be different from those in Manhattan. Curriculums had to be specific; few generalities were possible. Hence, while the philosophical structure might remain the same nationally, the curricular details would have to change with the geographical locality. A study of certain subway workers' jobs would be appropriate in New York City but would hardly be related to a curriculum in Los Angeles, even though both were large cities. Similarly, jobs in the cigar industry of Jacksonville, Florida, would not be appropriate to the curriculum of Rochester, New York. These requirements for local job surveys and job analyses were significant elements in the Occupational Education curriculum, for all else depended on their adequacy and completeness. To make an adequate survey and to make a detailed analysis of any job required understanding personnel, who were too often lacking.

Restricting this discussion just to New York City and to Hungerford's efforts, several job areas were identified that were appropriate generally to the city and contained jobs open to mentally retarded adults. These included, among others:

- Food trades
- Building maintenance trades
- Hospital related jobs
- Garment trades
- Transportation trades

Within each of these trade areas, the selected jobs were analyzed in detail to include, as a partial list, the following:

- Does the job require a written application form to be completed, an interview, dress or uniform requirement;
- Does the job require strength, standing, sitting, lifting, walking, etc.;
- What about withholding tax, social security benefits, health insurance deductions, pension deductions, other fringe benefits;
- Is there close supervision for workers;
- Does the worker need to know about use of the telephone, punching a time clock, transportation routes, changing work shifts, holiday and vacation opportunities?

These few items consist of a selected list from many others, characteristic of every job identified as appropriate for curricular inclusion. It was a time consuming but significant task, and it was important because all reading materials, social skills materials, arithmetic, writing, and spelling materials were teacher made and were based on these analyses.

As stated earlier, eight core areas of a developmental nature were identified as the curricular ladder; also included was an emphasis on preschool training for retarded young children:

Core I   The home
Core II   The neighborhood
Core III   The city
Core IV   The next larger logical geographical area.
           (Core IV provided some flexibility from community to community and might even under certain circumstances be focused on the state or the nation.)
Core V   A study of job areas

Core VI   Choosing, getting, and holding a job
Core VII   Ways of spending one's income
Core VIII The citizen as a worker and social being.

Each core area might be studied from one to two years.

Consider Core I—the home—as an example. During this core for six- to eight-year-old retarded children, the emphasis, among other things, would be on the mother's and the father's jobs both in and out of the home, children's jobs in the home, the changing nature of jobs during holidays, variations in seasons, etc. The emphasis throughout is on jobs and occupations. Core V is particularly significant, for here pupil guidance and counseling—emphasized at all levels, of course—were involved. It pits personal characteristics, strengths, and skills against job requirements that came from the original survey and analysis. Occupational Education, criticized by the unwilling and the advocates of the status quo, was—and still is—a forward-looking curriculum based on an honest assessment of personal characteristics of the retarded individual and an accurate understanding of his or her future work opportunities. It brings to mind the movie *To Sir with Love,* about tough kids in a city school who are taught by a teacher how to survive rather than where Mauritania is located on a map, and when the French Revolution began, and the difference between present and past imperfect tenses. Music, art, manual skills, and simple drama can be interwoven at all times as appropriate.

Back when it was begun, Occupational Education was certainly not a sterile curriculum. Its potential was unlimited. It was a tragedy that some shortsighted special educators made successful efforts to scuttle a heroic educational concept. If this philosophic and curricular concept here only briefly described could have succeeded nationally (and there was an initial readiness for this to happen), special education would have been revolutionized. Parents of retarded youth would have been content. Retarded young people would have been prepared in a preliminary manner for entrance into the work arena, and general educators would have seen honesty in an individualized curriculum that was different in terms of the differing needs of the retarded pupils in differing geographic localities. A significant educational opportunity was lost because of factors over which no one had any control. Occupational Education was no total panacea, but it was a dynamic concept requiring strongly motivated special educators who were committed to their profession. There were these, but in too small a number to ensure success.

Retardation and Readiness

Advocates of normalization of education for mentally retarded youth have never considered responsibly several essential characteristics of retardation in their haste to respond to pressure for mainstreaming.

Readiness to Learn. One issue is that of *readiness*. Although some advocate teaching children to read at the age of three, educators and psychologists usually take a saner position, along with the great mass of children, and view readiness to be in the neighborhood of six years both chronologically and mentally.

The human organism reaches several significant maturational growth stages at about the chronological age of six. Carpal and metacarpal bones in the hands and feet reach a more adult formation stage at about this age. The various structures of the eye—the consistency of the aqueous and vitreous humors, the function of the ciliary muscles controlling the lens, the maturity of the cornea, among other things attain a new maturational level at this age. Aurally, the organ of Corti and its cilia in the inner ear and the cochlea develop new and more mature responsiveness to auditory stimuli.

Furthermore, the life experiences and mental age of about six years are significant in the ability of a child to respond to abstract concepts involved in learning to read, to function with arithmetical processes, and to remember or recall in spelling and arithmetic. The normal child enters the first grade at about the chronological age of six. If he or she has an IQ of 100, the child will also have a mental age of six and will be ready for abstract learning. On the other hand, retarded children of six years, with IQs of 50, will have mental ages approximately of three years; if they have IQs of 75, they have mental ages of three to four years. These latter two examples show children who are between one-and-one-half years and three years away from the mental age of six, which is that presumed to be optimal for learning how to read. Normalization does not handle this problem adequately and does not provide success experiences for the retarded children. Intragroup comparisons in regular grades are not prevented.

Readiness and Achievement. Once a readiness level has been attained by retarded children, a second issue must be fairly faced. Mental age growth rates get no better in retarded children as chronological age growth continues. A normal child, for example, (with IQ 100) has a chronological age of twelve and is in the sixth grade. The child has an assumed (or measured) mental age of 12-0 years. Retarded children of the same chronological age and with IQs of 50 have mental ages of 6-0 years; ones with IQs of 75, mental ages of approximately 9-0 years. Retarded children never catch up with their chronological-aged peers. If the example is carried out to a conclusion insofar as achievement is concerned, the child with an IQ of 50 in the sixth grade will have an achievement age of the first grade; the one with an IQ of 75, an achievement age of about the third grade, if optimal teaching throughout has been experienced. These differences cannot assure peer-related success experiences and cannot adequately be rationalized by advocates of normalization of education for this group of exceptional children.

It is astounding to me how quickly significant studies are overlooked by educators. Research-supported findings do not need to be reaffirmed every decade for them to remain pertinent and current. However, too many professionals discount research that is not of a current date. Ruth Melcher Patterson (1939, 1940) reported in the 1940s that children in the 50 to 75 intelligence range progressed as far as achievement in school subjects is concerned at a rate of about 0.4 grades per year in contrast to the grade level achievement of 1.0 grades per year anticipated for intellectually normal children. The achievement age disparities do not go away because no new research has disputed it. The disparities will not go away by ignoring them, nor by wishful thinking. Normalization cannot handle properly the continuing and increasing chronological-age–achievement-age disparities.

Under good teaching, normal children at a chronological age of about seventeen years will have attained a twelfth grade level of achievement. Under similar circumstances according to Patterson (1939, 1940) retarded children will have attained a high fourth grade or a low fifth grade level of achievement. It must be emphasized that these conclusions are based on teaching of the highest quality throughout the school years. This probably is wishful thinking, so that I write about levels of achievement for the retarded youths that are themselves likely to be unrealistic.

Until the advocates of normalization can meet these realities and at the same time can ensure success experiences for retarded children, I shall continue to be skeptical about their promises. I personally doubt that the limitations mentioned here can be overcome successfully or minimized in a typical program of mainstreaming or normalization.

I reflect back on the brief discussion of Occupational Education. Within the various chronological age groups and their corresponding core area emphases, it was still necessary to individualize instruction. For example, in preparing reading material about a hospital worker's job in Core V, the teacher would write the same story or reading lesson at three different vocabulary levels; for low-achieving readers, a middle group of achievers, and an "advanced" group who might be reading at a high second grade or low third grade level. The same differentiation would be found in arithmetic or spelling, or indeed in any learning situation involving abstract concepts. This is individualization of instruction to a degree and is about as far as a good teacher can go in a self-contained educational program. But it is nevertheless individualization of instruction.

In colleges and universities, there is endless talk by professors regarding the merits of individualization, but never are students really taught how to do this, nor are they given supervised practicum experiences in doing it. Individual differences are stressed and understood by most people as a concept, but just how to modify basic texts, workbooks, or other teaching materials to meet individual differences in children in a typical grade group is seldom a reality. When general elementary teachers confront educable mentally retarded children in their classes, individualization is forgotten, eyes roll, and hope is expressed that the year will pass quickly and social promotions will take place.

Prolonged Preacademic Training and Early Intervention

It generally has become recognized that with all children, there are significant benefits from programs of early stimulation if the programs are handled logically in the home or in day-care centers. Again, Ruth Melcher Patterson (1939, 1940) long ago wrote of prolonged preacademic training, and suggested that, depending upon the intelligence quotient, such a program of enrichment could continue until the child reached a chronological age of seven or eight, sometimes longer, and certainly it would continue until a mental age of six had been achieved. The Occupational Education program and curriculum was based on these findings of Patterson. Core I was conceptualized for retarded children of seven or eight chronological years. Core I, concerned with the home, nevertheless contained many readiness activities as well, to prepare the students for good assimilation of abstract materials of reading and number concepts.

Samuel A. Kirk (1958), in the best-conceptualized longitudinal study of retarded preschool children that is found in English literature, demonstrates the value of early identification and training of mentally handicapped children. Those mentally handicapped children whose exposure by the chronological age of two to a well-planned program of early stimulation progressed much more evenly so far as the acquisition of mental age and its related areas of achievement were concerned than did a control group of similar children deprived of early stimulation. Similar evenness in the acquisition of skills and related learning was observed and traced directly to the early education program. Further, there were differences insofar as lasting effects were concerned after the program was discontinued.

Early intervention programs were sponsored for a number of years at the Institute for the Study of Mental Retardation and Related Disabilities at the University of Michigan. The personnel working in the program primarily came from the disciplines of occupational therapy, nutrition, special education, nursing, and psychology, although other disciplines were available and could be called upon as needed.

Mothers, and often fathers, accompanied their children to the institute and watched the program through windows, while a professional member of the team explained what was happening so that similar activities could be replicated in the home. Home teaching also took place. Often the father alternated work shifts with the mother, and it was possible for the visiting professional person to have sufficient time with both parents on an individual basis to conclude good home teaching. Multiply handicapped children, as well as those with mental retardation only, were included in the program. Clinically, numerous records maintained over several years indicate that the early intervention program resulted in easier assimilation of our "graduates" into nursery schools intended mostly for normal children. These same children later could be integrated into the regular kindergartens of public schools. How long this initial normalization could have been continued is questionable, because the rate of achievement and the time of readiness for abstract work would soon become evident and differences would become too great for successful handling by the regular grade teachers. However, as with Melcher's and Kirk's works, the significant values of prolonged preacademic readiness experiences were evident. This is not to say that these kinds of programs do not exist in many communities in the United States and elsewhere. That of the Evaluation Center in Children's Hospital in Birmingham, England, is noteworthy as a single example. However, these programs exist in insufficient numbers even in those states that have mandated them for preschool children. Michigan, for example, by law requires that all handicapped children be served between the ages of birth and twenty-six years. Many states require that programs begin by the age of three years. Even when such laws or state department of education regulations exist, too few early intervention programs are to be found, and many handicapped children of whatever clinical type slip through unnoticed. The maturational significance of prolonged preacademic programs and early intervention experiences can no longer be overlooked. They are an essential ingredient of a good total community program for all types of exceptional children, but in particular, for those with retarded mental development.

The Retarded Person and Sexuality

There was a time, within the years of my professional life, when the solution to all of the preconceived social problems related to the mentally retarded person was to have been "solved" by sterilization. Ultimately, the fallacy of this program and concept was understood, and the effort was concluded. It is an idea, however, that still has its advocates. It would be interesting to consider the magnitude of the cost to a state, community, agency, or physician if a class action suit on behalf of all those mentally retarded individuals who had been sterilized against their wills were undertaken, including not only prohibitions against such future actions, but dollar damages in behalf of those sterilized. Undoubtedly, the plaintiffs would win the case, and the financial awards could be tremendous.

Mentally retarded individuals have the same rights to participate in the sexual activities of their choice that all other human beings have. There can be no reasonable argument against this position, whether from the point of view of physiology, law, psychology, sociology, or mental hygiene. The issue is basically one of human right and not mental retardation. The latter is confused with the former in the minds of many.

A variety of myths pertain to this problem. It is assumed that the retarded adult will flagrantly violate the rules of society, rules that in large measure are puritanical in their controls of sexual behavior. It is assumed that retarded persons will not be able to learn how to use contraceptives and will, thus, populate the world with more mentally retarded children. Neither are true. Contraception can be taught to the retarded with effective results, and two mentally retarded adults or a couple in which there is only one retarded adult, do not necessarily produce retarded offspring. Further, the retarded individual often *chooses* to be sterilized, but even when this happens, many in the community frown on marriage involving one or two retarded persons. Living centers for retarded adults have been characterized by a great deal of community protest. One citizen said once in an open public hearing that "it will be nothing but a constant orgy." As if group sex never took place in WASP homes, and one wonders why he is so preoccupied with sex anyway! The fact of the matter is, however, that as a custom, orgies do not take place in community living centers, and the behavior of most residents who live in group homes is the height of decorum.

I do not wish to make light of the matter of sexual behavior for the mentally retarded adult, just as it would not be considered inconsequential for any person. The implications and economics of sex are too great to dismiss the issue without thought. Retarded youths and adults, however, have the inalienable right to participate privately in sexual activities of their choice, whether heterosexual, homosexual, or alone in terms of masturbatory behavior. Regardless of the attitudes of society in general, choice in sex is a private decision. With the retarded individual, as with young normal adults, the primary issue is to prevent sexual exploitation of whatsoever type.

Retarded adults can be taught and can learn what appropriate behavior is between and among persons in heterosexual groups. They can learn the appropriate, public "touching behavior." They can and do learn what appropriate speech and language is between men and women in public places. They can be taught where sexual activities should be practiced, and they can be taught the importance of privacy in sexual relationships. They can be taught the significance of sex, its hygiene, and its variations. The assumption that these things cannot be learned by retarded adults is a myth held by those who have had no experience with retarded persons or who are bound by outmoded and controlling ideas.

Society has a long way to go in the development of positive attitudes toward many aspects of the life and living of handicapped persons. Many professional persons likewise are less than completely understanding. A woman resident of a community residential home became pregnant by a man in another residential home when one was visiting another. The directors of the woman's home were in the process of handling the matter responsibly by a court-approved and parent-approved abortion, when the officials of the state department of mental health learned of the details. At that point an explosion took place; the directors were discharged, the woman was moved to another center, an abortion was not approved by the state department officials (until the court intervened), the newspapers became involved for several days in exploitive journalism, and directives were issued by the state that were in a major degree seen as threatening to all community home supervisors. Issues of extramarital and premarital relationships, abortion, and mental retardation are inherent in this example, each of which must be rationalized by families, neighbors, and by society in general. Each is a sensitive issue, but each must be resolved by the community in a positive manner and to a degree that the civil rights of the retarded individual are not violated.

Marriage is a civil right also. Retarded individuals, particularly those judged to be able to live independent lives in the community, have the right to marry and should if that is their choice and if the economics of marriage permit this action. Obviously, the retarded individual or couple, if vasectomy is not effected, for example, must be counseled regarding the issues of childbirth, the costs of child care, and must determine with assistance their capacity to care for a future child. These are significant issues, but if they can be handled, there is no reason at all to prevent marriage from taking place.

There is a set of circumstances that warrants serious consideration. Two sets of parents and the marriage of their children: a young man with a measured IQ of 55, and a young woman whose IQ was recorded as 50. The parents established them in an apartment, generally provided supervision, and established a trust to provide for them when the parents were no longer able. Marriage was performed. A vasectomy was performed on the young man, although there was medical evidence that he would probably not be able to father a child under any circumstance. An ethical question is raised by this action to sterilize. An equally significant question also arises pertaining to the level of mental retardation when marriage would be recommended or made possible.

It is likely that the issue of mental level is not an appropriate measure of the social adaption that leads to sexual success. Undoubtedly, a more significant issue is whether or not by the age when marriage would be appropriate the retarded individual has developed the social skills, the abilities to hold at least an unskilled job, and the abilities to manage one's self in the community and in the home with prudence, safety, and with a minimum of supervision. Perhaps, fortuitously from society's point of view, with the exception of masturbatory behavior, the drive to consummate the sex act appears to decrease as the intelligence level decreases within the levels of severe and profound retardation. It is in the range of educable mental retardation that the fears society displays are significant and must be considered. While one cannot place the total onus of responsibility on education, social education, training in good male-female relationships, and sound human sexuality education repeated on a developmental continuum will accomplish much to provide the retarded adult with healthy sexual experiences and to relieve communities of anxieties and fears that are all too prevalent. While the philosophy of Occupational Education mentioned earlier in this chapter could not solve all of the adult problems of retarded individuals, it could have gone a long way to accomplish that end. It was a concept that saw the long-term, adult adjustment of the retarded person as its goal, and it contained the elements by which this could be accomplished. It was the shortsightedness of a limited number of special educators plus the lack of dynamic and aggressive leadership in the bureau director that brought this remarkable concept to an abrupt halt. Someday one who knew this program better than I will write its history and give it visibility in the annals of special education.

Summary

Not all has been said here that could be written about mental retardation. We have consciously omitted the trainable child and youth and his or her problems of training and preparation for adult life and living. Space limitations must be recognized. I have stressed the need for a dynamic philosophy of education for educable retarded children and youth. This is so important a problem in American society that it cannot be left to chance nor ignored. I have suggested that special educators take a careful look at the philosophy of Occupational Education, which appeared to be a remarkable concept and one that would not only challenge the retarded individual, but would be satisfactory to parents as well. It would certainly place a greater responsibility on the teachers and the college professors to prepare teachers, for experience has demonstrated that it is not an easy task to accomplish. It is a dynamic and professionally honest point of view and program, and one that should, years after its initiation, be given a rebirth and a chance to demonstrate its worth.

I have singled out the issue of the sexuality of the mentally retarded, not because this is necessarily the most important aspect of the life of these people, but because it is so warped in the minds of many community leaders and because so much community education is needed regarding it.

The whole issue of job placement and supervision should have attention. Do these individuals work well on an assembly line in an automobile plant? Not in my experience. Textbooks do not treat this issue or some others. Do they need closer relationships with foremen and supervisors than other workers? Can they participate in labor unions? Can they obtain drivers' licenses? Can they vote? These and other questions need consideration and can be answered for the most part in the positive.

Individuals with retarded mental development have the unique characteristics of blending into society as they become adults. Are they lost? Do they die? What happens to them? Research of a longitudinal nature is needed on this topic. For the most part, I suspect that they do actually adjust to society, learn a trade or a job skill, and as reasonably well-adjusted adults do blend into society as do most of the other millions of citizens in the United States. Do we have evidence that the crime rate is higher among retarded adults? I think not. Do we have evidence that they are a community burden in any manner as adults? The evidence is not there, if they are, except for those of more severe mental retardation for whom community living centers and group homes may at least be a partial solution. The retarded person is an integral part of the community in which he lives. It is the responsibility of the intellectually normal citizens to reach out at least 51 percent of the way and meet him or her as a citizen with equality.

References and Related Reading

Baroff, G. S. *Mental Retardation: Nature, Cause, and Management.* Washington, D.C.: Hemisphere, 1974.

Baumeister, A. A., ed. *Mental Retardation: Appraisal, Education, and Rehabilitation.* Chicago: Aldine, 1967.

Chinn, P. C., Drews, D. J., and Logan, D. R. *Mental Retardation: A Life Cycle Approach.* St. Louis: C. V. Mosby, 1979.

Cleland, C. C. *Mental Retardation: A Developmental Approach.* Englewood Cliffs, N.J.: Prentice-Hall, 1978.

Dickerson, M. U. *Our Four Boys.* Syracuse: Syracuse University Press, 1980.

Gearheart, B., and Litton, F. *The Trainable Mentally Retarded: A Foundations Approach.* St. Louis: C. V. Mosby, 1975.

Kirk, S. A. *Early Education of the Mentally Retarded.* Urbana: University of Illinois Press, 1958.

Neisworth, J. T. *Retardation: Issues, Assessment, and Intervention.* New York: McGraw-Hill, 1978.

Patterson, R. T. Melcher. "A Program of Prolonged Pre-Academic Training for the Young Mentally Handicapped Child." *Proceedings from the American Association on Mental Deficiency* 44 (1939): 202–15.

————. "Developmental Progress in Young Mentally Handicapped Children Who Receive Prolonged Pre-Academic Training." *American Journal of Mental Deficiency* 45 (1940): 265–73.

Robinson, N. H., and Robinson, H. B. *The Mentally Retarded Child: A Psychological Approach.* 2d ed. New York: McGraw-Hill, 1976.

Chapter 10

Young People with Superior Mental Development

For many years the general public and indeed professional educators have considered exceptional children to refer only to the gifted and talented. Special educators utilize the term *exceptional* to include all those who by reason of an intellectual or physical disability are not able to profit from the educational services of the community without the intervention of specialists of one discipline or another. It is logical that misunderstandings occur when the term *exceptional* is used in a generic sense, for indeed it is often synonymous with other words such as exclusive, extraordinary, notable, wonderful, and others of similar implications. Be that as it may, within the concept of exceptionality in children, in addition to the gifted are to be found all of the other clinical categories mentioned in this book, i.e., blind, deaf, cerebral-palsied, speech disabled, and others through a long and almost never ending list of clinical problems that affect children. There is nothing wonderful about being deaf; there is little notable in the fact that a child has epilepsy. The term, however, is with us, and its use will undoubtedly continue for many decades into the future. The gifted and talented young person is one to whom the term definitely applies. These children are truly exceptional in one or more areas of their lives. These children also have been among the most neglected of all categories of child deviance at least insofar as the schools of the United States are concerned.

I have stated earlier in these essays that it is only the occasional public school that has a full program for gifted children. It is unusual in most school systems for there even to be one or two classes in the community set aside for gifted children, and when this occurs it is rare that a truly unique curriculum is available to the pupils involved. It is remarkable that in a country such as the United States that places its emphasis on invention, on music and art, and on its early history of leadership in politics and religion, that so little concern is expressed in the twentieth century for its gifted and truly talented children and youth. Political leadership has given way to mediocrity, and the result is that little is done for this group of future leaders. At the federal level it was decades before there was any representation for the gifted in the former U.S. Office of Education, and then until about 1950, the representation was by one person, albeit in the person of Dr. Elise Martens, an extraordinary leader. The present U.S. Department of Education exerts little leadership for schools in this field of special education. Although not all university students are gifted by any means in the sense that I write here, universities have probably done more in the United States for the cause of educating gifted and talented young people than any other level of education. The Harvards, Cornells, Michigans, Californias (Berkeley in particular), the Ivy League colleges and universities have always maintained a reputation of catering to the most able students. Indeed their ratings have attested to this fact, and their faculties in general are outstanding. However, in a democracy, criticism is extended to public schools at least when isolation of gifted youth into separate facilities is undertaken.

In contrast, while we may not agree with the methods utilized in educating their children, one must certainly recognize the almost hallowed position accorded educational leadership, intellectually talented, and gifted persons in Japan. There is a very small group of approximately fifty men and women in Japan known as "Living Treasures." These are the elite of the gifted among the gifted. They usually represent a single individual from a given field in the arts, namely, the ceramist, the maker of indigo cloth, the weaver, the sword maker, the bell maker, the puppeteer, the teacher of antique musical instruments, the Kabuki dramatist, and others. These outstanding individuals, some more than ninety years of age, are indeed hallowed, and serve as examples to the nation's young people of a degree of accomplishment to be desired in the advance and growth of their nation. A national stamp of approval is placed on talent and great intelligence.

We in the United States have also done some extraordinarily foolish thinking and planning regarding gifted children. In 1957 the Russians sent aloft their *Sputnik*. This caused a frantic effort throughout the United States immediately to put into place educational programs, particularly in the sciences, for the gifted. Some truly extreme examples of hasty thinking became evident. In one community of approximately three thousand persons the board of education authorized the expenditure of more than three million dollars for an addition to the high school—an addition to be solely devoted to physics and chemistry. This school system appeared to be out to save the nation. Other school systems made decisions that were almost as extreme. However, sadly, even the good programs initiated after the Russians' remarkable undertaking did not last long, and within a decade any strong national interest in this phase of child development and education essentially disappeared, and school curricula were back to where they had been. The average child and his or her needs again dictated the education for all children, and so it is as this is written. Education for the gifted has been a waxing and waning affair—opportunistic for the moment.

Who Is the Gifted Child?

It would be easier to state what a gifted child *is not* than to describe what he is. There are so many misconceptions about these young people. They are not for instance bookworms, although most enjoy reading. They are not recluses, although many enjoy the quiet of individually motivated library or laboratory research. They are not social isolates; many of them have a full social calendar and are popular with a variety of friends of all ages. They are not paragons of virtue; there have been examples of gifted young people who have performed notorious crimes. They are not docile; many enjoy contact sports of soccer, football, basketball, and noncontact sports of baseball and swimming—both boys and girls. They are not a lot of things, but simultaneously they comprise a group of children and young people who are one of the greatest resources of the nation and whose skills, talents, and abilities should be curried to the maximum in order that they may be able to take their appropriate leadership roles in the life of a society.

If one believes in the concept of the normal curve and applies this to intelligence per se, then these young people comprise the upper 2 to 4 percent of the population depending upon what cutoff point is used. On the basis of intelligence quotient only, superior intelligence is normally defined as in advance of an IQ of 120. The youth about whom I write here are those with quotients above 140, often reaching 175, 180, or higher. Sometimes they go off the scale. They are at the opposite end of the normal curve in relationship to mental retardation and comprise about the same percentage of the population as the lower group does. In contrast, however, these are the Ozawas, the Previns, the Bernsteins, the Gabrilovitches of the conducting field; the Chagalls, the Wyeths, the Degas of painting; the Fords, the Edisons, the Fultons of the mechanical engineering arena; the Menuhins, the Kreislers, the Perlmans of the violin; the

Wagners, the Beethovens, and Mozarts of the opera and composi-
tional fields—these are the unique, unusual, and significant individuals in whatsoever field of human endeavor whose efforts are
long lasting and tend toward a universal effect. Victor Hugo in
literature, Christopher Wren in architecture, Albert Einstein in
physics each represents others in other fields. No field, in reality
lacks the gifted: anatomy, biology, mathematics, chemistry, neurology, psychology, or the theater, et alia.

Three in a Family

I am aware of a family of five persons, including three children, who
are gifted intellectually. Their parents are likewise gifted, both
holding doctoral degrees in highly scientific fields. The family lives
in a suburb of Boston, the elder son was born in Cambridge. During
the preparation of this chapter, I conducted extensive and intensive
interviews with Marc, nineteen years old; Jon, just turned eighteen;
and Donna, fourteen. Marc is to be a junior in the university he
attends where he is following a rather unique program that he
describes. Jon is to enter another university that is geographically
close to Marc's. Donna is in junior high school. Her interview will be
omitted from this narrative for several reasons. As an adolescent
and the follower of two significantly gifted brothers, Donna at this
age did not have the opportunity to verbally express her brilliance
in the same open manner as the other two. Furthermore, as a young
lady being interviewed by a strange male adult she did not feel as
open and free as the other two particularly in the face of questions
that were intimate and highly personal. Gifted though she is, it
seems the better part of wisdom not to include her interview in this
discussion. However, these three young people possess many of the
positive personal characteristics I have earlier mentioned. They are
not wallflowers, but active, aggressive persons in the best sense of
these words. As a mountain climber and rock climber, Jon is hardly
reclusive. (During his eighteenth summer, Jon was one of two in his
group of six friends who climbed to the top of Mount Rainier, Washington!) When he was a sixteen-year-old employee and supervisor of
others in a commercial firm, Marc was not seen as an isolate. As a
swimmer and musician, and socially popular girl within her circle of
friends, Donna is not characterized as a bookworm, although she
loves to read. Three well-adjusted gifted young people are present,
and two of them speak for themselves.

While brothers and sister, nevertheless they also exemplify the often quoted truisms of nature and nurture. Reared from the same genetic background and in the same home environment, each youth has assimilated his parental guidance, religious heredity, school opportunities, and social life in three markedly different ways. At fourteen Donna, the sister, illustrates a quiet and retiring—often almost nonverbal sister of two intellectually active and outgoing older brothers. While not dominant in a negative sense, the boys' intellectual and social aggressiveness together with age differences, place Donna comparatively in a somewhat unfavorable position. Jon basks in the backlash of Marc's accomplishments, and at times one feels from his comments a rebelliousness against his brother, although in the last year he recognizes the origins of these feelings, and the youths have drawn closer together.

As Jon will say, one of his great sources of fun and satisfaction is in rock climbing. He is proud of the fact that he has gotten Marc to become interested in the sport. This is one time when his interests have superimposed themselves on his brother, and a great deal of satisfaction is derived from this. Marc is taking none of the credit from Jon. From my point of view this demonstrates an increase in maturity in both boys.

Obviously there will be some duplication in the comments of the two boys. I shall attempt to remove certain of these points by discussion here. One of the questions which was asked each of the youths pertained to their knowledge of their intelligence levels. Each was asked if he (or she) knew their quotient. Each answered "no," because their parents had not permitted them to take such tests. In discussing this later with the older brothers, it appeared that the parents did not want the children labeled on the basis of an IQ score. There is logic to this from the point of view of many educators. Better that children be considered on the basis of their production, not on the basis of a test that may have questionable standardization and be unreliable in other ways. Irrespective of parental reasoning no one of the children as children experienced intelligence tests, although they did respond to achievement tests and scholastic university admissions tests as those times approached later.

Another item which was omitted from these interviews related to the experiences which each had in the Hebrew school operated by their synagogue. Each had experiences pretty much similar to the other two. All had an exposure to the Hebrew language, but none sufficient to be proficient in the language as adolescents. Marc indicates that he can struggle through some newspaper reports in Hebrew, but this is a struggle.

The interviews that follow will take the form of uninterrupted questions from the interviewer and answers from one or the other of the brothers. I shall start with *Marc.*

Q. *Marc, how old are you?*
A. Nineteen.
Q. *Essentially you went into the sophomore year when you began studying at the university, correct?*
A. Well, in a sense. The program that I'm in is a bit different. I had enough credits after a quarter to go in as a sophomore. The program I'm in is a special medical program, and a class ranking really doesn't mean anything since you're guaranteed admission in the medical school and know you'll be accepted assuming you don't flunk out after so many years. What they do is to get freshman standing the first quarter, then the second quarter sophomore standing, then I registered as a junior for the next year (and my last year I register as a senior) even though I officially won't have the credits to be a junior I think until the middle of next year. I do three years of undergraduate work, four years of medical school.
Q. *It really isn't a matter of skipping or advanced placement. This is just a policy of the university, correct?*
A. With respect to this program, yes.
Q. *But all the students that are in this program have the same experience?*
A. Yes. In fact, most of them only stay for two years at the undergraduate level. I'm taking a biomedical engineering degree, so I'll spend an extra year doing undergraduate work.
Q. *What is your goal now? In bioengineering?*
A. Yeah. Well, at the moment, I don't know if that's possible, but what I'm shooting for now is to become a surgeon and researcher at the same time. It's been my experience with the limited research that I've done and the interaction that I've had with people who are both engineers and physicians and those who do both engineering and practice medicine, that there is a real lack of clinical people who can define a problem in clinical terms, and, while they won't do a great deal of the research, they are sort of a liaison between the clinical world and the research world.
Q. *That's the role now you hope to play?*

A. Yeah, eventually I can see myself directing a large-size research program, doing a little toward the administration.

Q. *In all of the things you did in high school that brought you so much notoriety, positive notoriety, did you ever have people working under you, assisting you?*

A. Well in the research that I did myself, in some peripheral ways, yes. Toward my senior year when things got pretty complicated, I had a machinist build some of the equipment for me, and I had the photography that I had previously done myself done by a friend of mine; some of it by a friend of mine who is a professional photographer and other parts of it by professional people. I think my earliest experience having people work under me was when I was working as a computer programmer for a local company.

Q. *How old were you then?*

A. I started when I was fifteen, that would be at the end of tenth grade, my sophomore year.

Q. *About how many people were involved in that experience?*

A. Of my age? [No, that were working under you?] Well, it was a very funny situation—working for any bureaucracy, one of the characteristics, if your bread and butter depends on the paycheck, sometimes you don't want to take controversial responsibility, and so one of the things I found there where I worked is if you're bright and if you're there for the summer, they hand you these things nobody else wants. The particular conflict here was the regional office wanted my division to buy a particular type of word processing equipment. The person I was working for wanted a different type so I was given the responsibility of evaluating both pieces of equipment and making a recommendation. It turned out that there was a hundred thousand dollars worth of word processing equipment. So in the initial phase of the project, I had one of the computer programmers who was I guess ten years older than I was working under me doing some other things and a couple of secretaries, one doing typing for me, and another one coming out with me to look at these things.

Q. *In these kinds of experiences did you ever have antagonism directed toward you that you felt came because you were younger?*

A. All the time.

Q. *How did this antagonism, if that is the proper word, get expressed?*

A. Well, it depends. In school among my teachers I got some of that. Well, people would talk to me and some of the teachers would be upset because I was doing most of my research outside of school, and in fact the school itself made no effort to support it. I had a friend in Marblehead who had the same problem. But that was really of no consequence—the fact that I would not give the school any credit for things that I was doing outside of school bothered them. A lot of people also felt threatened because I was doing things that many people don't do until they're out of college, especially supervising people that were a lot older than I.

Q. *Those people, the ones that were a lot older than you, how did they take being supervised by somebody ten years younger than they were?*

A. Well, there were really two attitudes that I found, and it's funny because they're like black and white. One type of person really doesn't care how old you are, just as long as you're competent enough to do the job, and who is willing to help out a person who's young in the sense that maybe the younger person is very capable, but they lack certain experience that you would only gain by being around putting in the time. Those types of people I had fun working with. The other type was very antagonistic. They were trying, not usually openly, but they were trying to hinder what I did by talking to my boss and saying "Well he's really very young to be doing this sort of thing," or going over my head. They never really saw me as a supervisor, just somebody put there in a controversial spot, and therefore they didn't feel they were responsible to me.

Q. *I wanted to ask you whether or not you felt that any of the antagonism that might have been directed to you as a supervisor were really anti-Semitic expressions that were directed at you because you were a young Jewish man, not because of your youth.*

A. I don't think so. I've encountered anti-Semitism on and off in the public school system, but it's never been a real problem in any important area that I've had.

Q. *That's good. Now, I'd like to back up, first. Have you ever been submitted to an intelligence test? Do you know what your IQ is?*

A. I have no idea. [Note: School authorities who knew Marc *estimate* that his IQ would be between 150 and 200.]

Q. *Have you ever taken an intelligence test that you can recall?*

A. Well maybe in first or second grade. I remember my mother once saying that if I ever took an intelligence test she wouldn't tell me the results of it.

Q. *Probably a wise decision to make. I was asking to see if you knew and how you felt about it. [I have no idea.] That's perfectly all right. You've taken achievement tests, such as the SAT?*

A. Yes.

Q. *How did you do on your SAT exams?*

A. Not really outstanding. I don't do well on standardized tests. I've really never considered those type of tests indicative of anything other than you were really good at taking an SAT test.

Q. *Have you had any tests of any sort where you were given your score in terms of percentile ranks?*

A. All the standard college tests give percentile scores.

Q. *And where did you fall percentile-wise?*

A. Always above the 95th, to the best of my knowledge.

Q. *Go way back now, how old were you when you started elementary school?*

A. I was older than everybody else in the class because the cutoff date for entrance was December 1, and so I missed it by fourteen days.

Q. *Did you go to nursery school before you went to kindergarten?*

A. Yes, I did.

Q. *Do you know when that started?*

A. Five or six, I'm not really sure.

Q. *Was this a private nursery school, or was it operated by the synagogue?*

A. It was the synagogue nursery school. All of us went there.

Q. *How long did you attend the synagogue nursery school?*

A. At least a year.

Q. *Did you learn Hebrew enough so that you remember any of it now?*

A. Not through that. I went to Hebrew school until I worked.

Q. *Do you have command of any other language?*

A. Spanish.

Q. *How much Spanish have you had?*

A. Five years of Spanish, and I haven't done any classroom work in Spanish in two years, but I've kept it up a little bit. I can understand spoken Spanish on news broadcasts. I listen to the Spanish radio every once in a while. I can read it very easily. Sometimes I get caught in the grammar like the tenses or something.

Q. *Can you remember when you were in elementary school you sensed that things began to be very easy for you, and when you realized that perhaps you were intellectually different than the other kids in the school?*

A. I can remember that very easily. It was in kindergarten when I was put into a special reading group with the first graders, and I was doing work with three or four other children who were taken out of various kindergarten classes, doing special work with other children, also the mathematics.

Q. *Could you guess now at what level of reading or what level of mathematics you were doing in that special group?*

A. The level of reading was probably second grade. By the time I was in third grade, no I was I think in fourth grade, I had adult privileges from the public library. I read voraciously, anything I could possibly get my hands on, quite rapidly.

Q. *Can you think of other things in elementary school, or in high school that happened to you as a kid that impressed upon you that you were more capable than most of the kids in school?*

A. Most of the work was very, very easy. I was able, well until high school, to breeze through it. In mathematics I was maybe one or two grades ahead of everybody else, and in reading I was far ahead.

Q. *Did it bother you that you weren't allowed to skip a grade and get up to someplace where things might be more challenging to you?*

A. I never thought about skipping a grade, but it always bothered me that once I got through with everything, that there was some formal structure to what everybody else was doing, but nothing else for me to do. I got bored very quickly, and even got bored with some of the regular work, because I knew after I'd finish there would be nothing for me to do so there didn't seem to be any point to it.

Q. *Do you have criticism of your teachers because they didn't individualize sufficiently to keep you hopping all the time?*

A. Yes. Well there were a few teachers in elementary school that actually held me back that said, no, you have to go at this pace with the rest of the class. I don't think they gave me reasons at that time. I was always very outspoken when I had criticisms of my teachers, and that got me into trouble because they didn't appreciate it. I always did much better when I was left to my own devices and they said, "Learn what you can, and we'll use this method to test what you learn."

Q. *Did you ever run into a teacher that agreed with you and allowed you to function in that way?*

A. None until high school. Well, in junior high they still had those formalized programs where you went on your own. They were a little bit more challenging and they were much longer so that you never ran out of stuff to do, but they were pretty easy. And initiative, self-initiative, beyond programs like that was never really encouraged. I really wish I'd had somebody who'd instilled some sense of discipline in me, because when things are that easy, then you get bored. You really don't learn discipline, and you're not pushed to your limits. I think because of that I'm not a very good student today. The only discipline that I have is in things that I do myself, and it's just recently that I've been able to transfer that over into school.

Q. *Just the fact that you have this self-insight, though, is important, because you could and can transfer or develop discipline in yourself if you aren't too lazy. Discipline requires energy output.*

A. Yeah, well one of the things that people have always said that they admired in me, in the things that I did outside of school, was that I always kept going, and it's a thing that I've noticed in myself. When I do something I don't think about failing at all. It's not like I ignore or put it out of my mind, it just doesn't occur to me.

Q. *Have you ever failed in anything?*

A. Oh, yeah, a couple of times.

Q. *Such as?*

A. One time when I guess I was in junior high I was helping a friend of mine rebuild his bicycle and we got it all apart and cleaned it. I couldn't get some parts of it back together again, and I think that was the first time that I ever really failed.

Q. *How did you feel about that experience, do you remember?*

A. It was really annoying. It was very embarrassing. I think more of the embarrassment came from the fact that I felt embarrassed that I couldn't do it. I've failed; I've done very poorly on examinations in school and things like that.

Q. *You actually failed examinations in school?*

A. I've come pretty close, I've never really failed an exam. When you do a lot of the things that I've done, people put you up on a pedestal and they expect that you're tops in everything. I made no secret that I was not an outstanding student in school. People ignored that, it makes you seem, well, it makes it easier for them to put distance between you and themselves if they feel threatened, or it makes it easier for them to critiize you. My teachers all recognized it; that I didn't put in as much as I was capable of into my schoolwork.

Q. *But the report cards that you carried home, how did they look?*

A. They weren't outstanding. Occasionally I got comments from my teachers that I was not putting in the effort that I should be. I never really distinguished myself in school. It was all fairly easy, and it was easy for me to retain a fairly good grade point average without doing much work. I went about high school and junior high even more so, in sort of a "well, I'll do what I can to maintain a decent grade average, but school is secondary to the other things in life."

Q. *Can you recall all of the science fair kind of things that you have won in the course of your junior and senior high experience? [Yeah.] Could you just list them off to me—what are they?*

A. I started out in eighth grade when I entered the Newton junior high school and also entered a project in the science fair where I built a calculatorlike device that could add two numbers in binary—as long as they were in base 2 and less than 16, and I won awards from two national associations. Then next year I entered the science fair with an engineering project on how plastics shattered and played with different types of plastics, and I won second place at the New England Science Fair. I won second place in the engineering category as well, and an award from the professional association that entailed the second place in a regional science fair. For that I was awarded an all-expense paid trip to the international fair, which was in Anaheim, California. That was for a week, and I didn't win anything there. It wasn't important at that time. I just had an incredible experience. I met a lot of people; it was an awakening in the sense that I met 480 people that were interested in the same thing that I was and my own age. After that, I won the local science fair again. I took first place this time with another engineering project involving mapping stresses in plastic using polarized light, and first place in physics and engineering category and some associational awards again. I went to the international fair in San Antonio, Texas, that time, and I placed first in the engineering category in the fair. I also won the Kodak award and an engineering award, then the year after that I took first place again at the regional science fair.

Q. *You're now what—in the tenth grade?*

A. No, this would be in my junior year, and I received first place in the fair in my category, and the Air Force Award and some other association awards, photography awards, then I took first place at the international fair held in St. Paul, Minnesota, in medicine and health, switched from the categories and three other association awards. Then in my senior year, I was in the honors group of the Westinghouse Science Talent search for the orthopedics project I had the previous year, and I placed first in the New England regional science fair again, with a category award and more association awards, and then I went to the international fair, and in addition to receiving association awards and placing first in medicine and health, I received the highest honor of the thing that was called the Nobel prize visit award, which was an all-expense paid trip to the Nobel prize ceremonies in Stockholm.

Q. *We mentioned teachers, did teachers out of a sense of jealousy because you were better than they intellectually, ever bear down on you in an unfortunate fashion?*

A. In a number of times that happened.

Q. *Have you one or two examples of when that took place?*

A. Well, in my ninth grade science class, this was related to the science fair business, the teacher gave me permission to turn in half of the manuscript that I was going to submit to the science fair as an independent project he required of all the students, and I turned it in and I got a B− on the project and the comments that I shouldn't enter it into the science fair. He didn't think that I'd win anything, and I was pretty upset because the type of things that I was doing at that point I thought were over his head. Well, they may or may not have been, but I thought they were, and so I didn't pay any attention and I did it on my own. What really incensed me was that after I received all those awards that year he would talk to people and the conversation made you believe that he was responsible for my great success. Meanwhile, I still got a lousy grade in the class. That really bothered me.

Q. *Did you ever discuss it with him?*

A. Yeah, I did it on the last day of school. [The last day of my ninth grade.] I had gotten in trouble before for correcting teachers in class and saying that I felt they were wrong, even though I felt in this case I was clearly right. My parents said well, no hold off, wait. Well, they didn't even want me to talk to him. But I did anyway, and he was sort of embarrassed about the whole thing and made me believe that the incident with the paper never happened.

The other incident was with a mathematics teacher, and initially at the beginning he was a man of very strong opinions. He used the classroom as a forum for expressing these opinions. At one point he was telling a class how the mileage on cars was computed at the agency I worked for. I had written a program to do it, and he was very wrong. It had to do with a problem in the class or something. Everybody in the class knew that I worked there and knew what I had done and were all looking at me. I could never stand to see somebody teach something that was incorrect whether it was trivial or not. And so I raised my hand and I said that's wrong, and he was furious because he realized what was going on. I never got along with him at all, and he would, I guess you could call it petty harrassment, take off points on my test for things that I did where somebody else who did the same thing didn't have points taken off. We never really got along very well.

Q. *In your high school years is there a teacher who stands out as an extraordinary valuable person in your life? Or does it all kind of blend into a mine-run of educators?*

A. No, there were a couple—my sophomore English teacher was a very good teacher. I consider a very good teacher someone who uses the classroom as a format for students expressing their ideas and who encourages, not only creativity, but independence. We had classroom debates about controversial current issues where we would all sit in a circle, and she would say "Well, what do you all think about this?" and we would take turns in some organized fashion arguing about it, and she would sort of mediate the discussion but not control it. Then there was . . .

Q. *For you personally, did this teacher in some way push you along because of her recognition of the really great mind that was in her class?*

A. Yes, she did. In fact it usually ended up, well I love to argue, and it ended up by our mutual conniving that we always ended up on opposite sides of the issue whether or not I agreed with the stand I was taking.

Q. *How did the other kids take that? In respect to you?*

A. None of them thought that I dominated the conversation. Well, the fact was and sort of continues to be that in many discussion groups people just don't want to speak out. When somebody does speak out, then they're upset because their time is being taken away even though they wouldn't use it. And before that actually my biology teacher in ninth grade was probably the best teacher I've had even to college. I was a pretty exceptional student in that class; I think it was the one time where I really loved what I was doing and I was pushed. Her exams were very difficult. This was ninth grade and we had 100 multiple-choice questions and five short answer questions and a big essay, and boy did I enjoy that class. I studied really hard for it, I knew the material, I went into the test with the attitude, "well, let's see if you can stump me," and she enjoyed that. I'd go back and talk to her all the time.

Q. *Were the standards that she set for you any different than for the other kids in her room?*

A. No, I don't think they were. She pushed everybody. In my first year of college whether it was a freshman seminar or graduate level class that I took, my performance in the class grade-wise, if you want to use that as an indicator of my interest, was always higher when I was challenged no matter what the level of the class. If I'm not challenged by a class I'll do about a B maybe a B−, and it doesn't matter what the level of the class is. In my senior year I had a couple challenging teachers in my humanities program, which was really outstanding, and then in college I had this year two outstanding teachers, one in chemistry and one in a graduate level philosophy class last quarter.

Q. *Did you have any trouble getting into the graduate course?*

A. No.

Q. *Did they know you were an undergraduate?*

A. Yes. The chairman of the department taught an introductory level class that I took the first quarter. There were 180 people in it, and the nice thing about that class at the end was I got very involved. I would come every week to office hours and talk with him. At the end of the class I got a letter from him saying that my performance in the class, along with that of three others in the class, was outstanding, and if he could do anything to further my education in philosophy even though he knew what program I was in, I shouldn't hesitate to ask him. So I went over and talked to him about course selections and things like that. I had no problem.

Q. *If you could somehow lump all of your junior and senior high school teachers together, what grade would you give them?*

A. Probably a B−. Even though I thought I received a much better education than a lot of the people around me.

Q. *Because you were initiating things yourself on the outside?*

A. To a certain extent, yes. Right now, I'm speaking just in the sense of academic education, excluding anything I did outside. I don't really consider that I had teachers in the conventional sense for the things that I've done outside. That's something that is totally separate from any sort of any academic format. But I think just in terms of academic preparation for college, as an indicator, that speaking with the people around me (and the university is a fairly decent school) that I received a much better education in high school and in junior high than most of the people, but I would give my teachers a B and B− as a whole. I would hate to think what these other people have for teachers.

Q. *Jon is a pretty good student, too. How did you feel when your younger brother came home with a better record than you had? How did you react?*

A. Maybe, my first immediate reaction was just a tiny bit of jealousy and after that it really didn't matter. I've never cared very much for comparisons in the sense that they don't mean anything to me. There were people in my classes around me who were much better students than I was.

Q. *I can understand about other students and friends, but a brother is a little different.*

A. It bothered me a little bit. Jon and I for a while had a pretty strong sibling rivalry, and over the petty things that you quarrel with your brother about when you're little, but ever since high school we've been reasonably close and I can think of only one or two incidents in the past four years that we've had any really serious differences.

Q. *Jon thinks very well of you.*

A. I think very well of Jon.

Q. *I think you do. He has a warm feeling toward you. He's a wonderful young fellow.*

A. He's a great guy.

Q. *And your little sister looks up to both of you. I felt when talking to her that she's a little concerned about the fact that she won't have either of her brothers as a stability factor this coming year at a time when she needs stability.*

A. She'll be going to high school the year after, and I'm sure that she's worried about that. She's just starting to get into the world of work and I think the idea of being at home, and there won't be the kind of hectic exciting things at home, I think she's going to miss that. Jon ran a marathon once.

Q. *Are you interested in sports?*

A. Not the way Jon is. I weight lift. Recently, Jon's gotten me interested in climbing—rock climbing. I went out with a couple of his friends the first weekend I was back from school. I came home Saturday evening and Sunday morning I went rock climbing with Jon. And I survived. And I'm hooked, I've been climbing every weekend.

Q. *That had your mother's attention and concern?*

A. Well, I think anything that we do that she perceives as being a little bit risky adds to her attention and concern. That's her function and I understand that as much as I can.

Q. *How do you perceive your parents? And how do you get along with them?*

A. I get along with both of them very well. There was a point, I guess during my junior year, when we were really at odds over a number of issues.

Q. *The issues were not such that you felt that they couldn't be solved?*

A. Either solved or I could ignore them and go on or ignore the way my parents dealt with them and go on with my life.

Q. *What part does religion play in your family's life?*

A. In the sense of cultural heritage that comes with the Jewish religion, I think that's distinct from the religious part and is a very strong part. The tradition value system I think is valid because I think you'll find in most Jewish homes that's been translated to us as value for education, value for family, value for friends and good standard of living, and the good idea to treat your teachers with respect and also the idea that your children should be a little better off than you were.

Q. *Are Friday nights, Friday evening dinners, celebrated as a religious experience in your home?*

A. Lately not often. I think when beginning, I guess with my first year in high school, tenth grade, when we all started doing different things, it became increasingly difficult to get everybody in one place on Friday night. When I started going out and dating, Friday night was a time to go out. My mother would like that to be in the more religious sense. We go to synagogue infrequently but not rarely. My parents have started going more often and bring my sister. I've gone at school on my own, and we go for all the major holidays.

Q. *At school has your Jewishness ever been perceived by you as a hindrance, as a disadvantage?*

A. No, I never really thought of it as a disadvantage.

Q. *Do you have friends that are both Christian and Jewish at the university?*

A. Yes.

Q. *Do you live in a dormitory?*

A. Well, this year I lived in a dormitory, next year I'll be living in a fraternity.

Q. *Is that made up of both Jews and Christians?*

A. Yes.

Q. *You mentioned dating, when did that begin?*
A. My sophomore year in high school.
Q. *Did that create any problem at home?*
A. Yeah.
Q. *How did you handle that?*
A. By ignoring it.
Q. *If your mother and father said no, not this Friday night, or I'll drive the car, how would you handle it?*
A. It never really came up.
Q. *What came up that you ignored?*
A. They didn't like the girl I was going out with. I went out with her for about a year and a half, and she was too bold, too bohemian for my mother, and my mother thought I was getting far more involved than she would like.
Q. *Were you?*
A. Yeah. They weren't very comfortable at all with the relationship.
Q. *I'm going to get personal now. Were you getting involved sexually with her?*
A. Yes.
Q. *And that you had sexual relationships with her? Actual relationships?*
A. Yes.
Q. *How old were you the first time you had sexual relationships?*
A. Sixteen.

[Is Marc unusual in relation to the onset of his heterosexual activity insofar as age is concerned? The answer is a flat "No." Utilizing somewhat old data, Kinsey and his associates (Kinsey, Pomeroy, and Martin 1948, 316) indicate that 82.4 percent of their male population studied had had their first sexual intercourse at or prior to the age of fifteen years. Thirty-four of the 183 subjects studied at this chronological age had had no previous sexual experience of this nature. The age range of the fifteen-year-old males in this particular group was eight years through fifteen at the time of their first experience. Masturbation was reported in excess of 60 percent of sixteen-year-old youths, although this is believed to be much lower than reality. Nineteen eighty data from the United States Department of Health and Human Services (Chilman 1980, chap. 5) indicates a significant increase in heterosexual experiences among younger and older adolescents ". . . with a sharp increase from about 20 percent of females under the age of 19 or 20 from the late

1920's to the early 1960's, to 40 percent by the late 1960's, and perhaps, 70 percent or higher of college groups by the mid-1970's." Most individuals dealing with adolescents and preadolescent youths, estimate this to be a much higher percentage of the total youth population at present. Kinsey's data of 1948 is undoubtedly no less in 1986 and it is probably higher. Marc is certainly not unique among his age group.]

Q. *That was with this girl?*
A. Yes.
Q. *Where?*
A. Her house.
Q. *How much time did you spend with her—with her all night, or a short time?*
A. A short time.
Q. *Were you scared?*
A. No.
Q. *Where had you learned about sexual behavior before that experience?*
A. I can't really pinpoint one place; I had the traditional sex education classes in school.
Q. *Did you ever talk with your dad or mom about your own sexual development?*
A. No.
Q. *Not with your father?*
A. No. In fact, I think he sort of avoided the issue. No, not really.
Q. *How many times would you guess you had sex relations in the time you were going with that girl?*
A. Oh, boy.
Q. *Well, then don't guess the number, was it daily, or weekly?*
A. Weekly would probably be a good . . .
Q. *Always at her house?*
A. Yeah. I've never felt comfortable bringing any girlfriend or friend home. My parents tend to scrutinize.
Q. *So I take it that her parents weren't home during these periods?*
A. No.
Q. *Did you ever stay overnight with her?*
A. Yeah.
Q. *How about with other girls?*
A. Well, I've had relationships with other girls in the same interim.
Q. *And, have these continued into the university experience too?*
A. Yes. I had a girlfriend who is going to the university for part of

the year. There was nobody at my university that I was really interested in romantically or physically for a very long time.

Q. *So how did you take care of your sexual needs during that relatively long interval?*

A. I didn't.

Q. *Did you masturbate?*

A. Yes.

Q. *About how frequently?*

A. Twice a month, maybe.

Q. *Did that bother you in terms of thinking about it afterward?*

A. No. I've always been reasonably comfortable with my body, and nudity. Sexuality has never bothered me.

Q. *Was there ever another adult with whom you could discuss these matters, or did most of your education come from the locker room, or reading, or your friends?*

A. Most came from reading. My parents never limited what I read. In fact there was one incident where my father would rather have me reading *Playboy* than watching a violent show on TV. And so being the somewhat aggressive young person I was at the time, I called his bluff and promptly received that month's issue of *Playboy*.

Q. *That kind of relationship with your father is important too. How'd he take it? When* Playboy *comes rolling into the living room?*

A. It didn't come into the living room; my mother won't permit that.

Q. *How did he know you had it?*

A. He gave it to me.

Q. *That's wonderful—I thought you'd gone out and bought it.*

A. Too expensive. If he were going to buy it, why should I?

Q. *How would you feel about your own son that someday you may have, having sexual relationships during high school years?*

A. Well, I can understand and sympathize with my parents' viewpoint and probably would feel the same way, a little bit apprehensive.

Q. *Do you think you would talk with your son or would you take the same route that your dad did?*

A. I probably would talk with him about it, definitely.

Q. *How young would you begin that kind of conversation, do you think?*

A. Maybe ten, eleven or so.

Q. *Were you aware of the issues of contraception?*

A. Yes. I've never been one to take on calculated risks.

Q. *Did you use the contraceptive? Or did you get the girl to use it?*

A. Initially I did, but in any relationship that I've had that's continued, and all of them have, I've always insisted that we both use contraceptives, unless she were on the pill.

Q. *Did you have any embarrassment when you went to buy them yourself?*

A. I had a couple of amusing incidents—one that occurred recently when there was no price on the box of condoms I bought at the drug store and the woman called out for a price check. That was sort of funny. It wasn't that embarrassing; I was in a pretty good humor that day. But I remember plotting and scheming that I would go to the drug store and drive across town where I thought that nobody there would know me. That sort of thing I imagine is somewhat ritual for people that age.

Q. *It's too bad it has to be that way, don't you think?*

A. In a certain sense, I don't think so. I see parental guidance and guidance in that area, with a few qualifiers, as sort of an equilibrium. They pull a little bit farther to one side than they really genuinely feel, and the child pulls a little bit farther to the other side. If there has been an attitude of respect instilled in the child, a little guilt reflex doesn't hurt either. Then you reach some sort of equilibrium in the middle that nobody's really upset with, either party would like it a little bit more one side, but people can live with it, and I think making anything too easy for somebody, whether it be having sex, or learning something, you don't appreciate the value of it.

Q. *At the dormitory, did you bring girls into your room?*

A. Yes.

Q. *Would this be possible at the fraternity as well?*

A. Yes.

Q. *So it's generally accepted activity*

A. Yes.

Q. *that the members can bring girls in for the night, or whatever time they wish?*

A. Yes.

Q. *Do you have your own room, or do you share a room?*

A. I shared a room last year, and I'll be sharing one this year.

Q. *Does that make it difficult?*

A. It means that you have some understanding with your roommate, he lives there, too, and you're considerate of his wishes and nobody really likes to be kicked out of their own room for a weekend or an evening.

Q. *Did you ever have any difficulties with your roommate?*

A. No.

Q. *What kinds of things outside the physical activity arena do you like to do? Your sister plays an instrument, and Jon made reference to the fact that he enjoys singing at the religious services at the synagogue and enjoys plays. What things do you like?*

A. Academic activities until this year have always been sort of a minor part of my life, or that's what I considered them, even though they took a large amount of time. I read a lot, not as much as I would like to; I play golf, and I enjoyed that a great deal. I love to work with my hands, build furniture, repair things.

Q. *How about concerts?*

A. I love concerts.

Q. *Classical or jazz?*

A. Mostly classical, though I do enjoy jazz.

Q. *Do you go to the symphony?*

A. I go to the symphony, I went to lyric opera this year. I went too, when I was home. I think the concert selection here at home is much better than there. In my last two years in high school I spent forty dollars one year and fifty dollars in another year buying tickets to the concerts here, and I really enjoyed them.

Q. *Do you ever go to ballet?*

A. Yeah, I saw Baryshnikov the time before he injured his knee.

Q. *How about an art museum?*

A. I go there probably once every six weeks. Toward the end of the year I started going. They have a lot of nice private galleries, and on Friday afternoons they have openings. A friend of mine was going to the art galleries, so I would go some Friday afternoons with her and talk to the artists. They would serve wine and cheese and it was very enjoyable.

Q. *Do you have a rather steady, solidified, organized group that you pal around with other than the fraternity members, or even with the fraternity?*

A. Yes, well this year they were sort of divided into friends within the fraternity and friends outside of the fraternity. Fraternity relationships brought a different sort of meaning to friendships that would have been different without that relationship.

Q. *Both sexes, or essentially males?*

A. No, in fact, most of my very close friends are female, and that was true in high school, and it's true now to a lesser extent in college, but I think two of my closest friends in college out of the four people I would consider very close friends are women.

Q. *Older, or younger, or your own age, generally speaking?*

A. In high school, it was older. And now they're the same age.

Q. *Older by how many years?*

A. About a year.

Q. *In what areas does your reading carry you? Reading for pleasure?*

A. During most of high school, I enjoyed fiction, political fiction a great deal. I went through a science fiction binge at one time and then into suspense. I never really cared too much for love-story-type things, Westerns, and now I enjoy reading philosophy, reading that makes you think and short stories you read both for the pleasure of the story and the technical beauty of the writing.

Q. *Do you write at all?*

A. Yes, I do.

Q. *For publication, your own pleasure, or what?*

A. Well, both. I write, with my research it means I have to do technical writing.

Q. *Have you had some of your research papers published?*

A. I had an abstract published and I've got one paper that's now being reviewed for publication. By the end of the year I should have another abstract that's been submitted on another paper.

Q. *In the science field?*

A. In the science, in professional journals.

Q. *Do you keep a journal, or a diary?*

A. I keep a journal, infrequently whenever the urge strikes me.

Q. *When did you start that, how old were you?*

A. I was sixteen.

Q. *How did you get started?*

A. I thought it would be fun to write down stuff and then be able to look back.

Q. *It was self-prompted?*

A. A lot of my friends were doing the same thing; that probably influenced me.

Q. *Are the friends that you have about of your same estimated mental level?*

A. Some of them yes, some of them no.

Q. *The nos would be less capable than you intellectually?*

A. No. When you say intellectually I think of that, not only in terms of their thinking potential, but their motivation.

Q. *Fair enough. In terms of their thinking potential, would they be less capable than you?*

A. Some less, and some are the same, some I think weren't.

Q. *How did it happen that you chose certain people as friends? Can you see any reason for you having teamed up with someone?*

A. Sure. The fraternity people—I joined the fraternity because I made friends with a lot of people there and decided I'd like to live with them. When I went to college, I was attracted to a lot of people first quarter because they seemed so much more mature than I was in possessing some sort of wisdom that I didn't have and that I wanted to possess. That's how I became friends with three of the people of the fraternity. Some of the other people I met at parties, others I met through the program that I'm in. Everybody in the six-year medical program took the same physics class, and as a group we tended to be pretty close. So I've got a number of close friends within the group, and then at the dormitory.

Q. *Do you have among your friends one or two, or a dozen, but do you have one or two with whom you feel very close and from whom you have no secrets? Do you have a friend you would talk with and say last night I was out and had sexual relations?*

A. Yes. In fact, I'd say four of my close friends.

Q. *And they share with you their highly personal experiences of this sort?*

A. Yes.

Q. *Do they also share or do you also share theirs or your disappointments, your financial worries, your . . .*

A. Anything that comes up in conversation.

Q. *You feel very free with those guys, or do I sense that some are girls?*

A. Three of them are women and one of them is not.

Q. *That's interesting to me that you would share with the women as well as with the men.*

A. I really don't, you know, a person is a person.

Q. *You don't differentiate?*

A. And I'm not too embarrassed by it and they are not embarrassed by it. We could be talking about, well, not the gravity of what we're talking about, but in terms of the ease in which a conversation is carried and we'll be talking about the weather.

Q. *Do your parents have any sense that you're engaged in premarital behavior?*

A. I think pretty much the whole family knows. Well, after the incident with my first girlfriend, where I actually told my parents, well, they asked and I didn't deny it.

Q. *That took some guts.*

A. Yeah. And they didn't stop me from going out with her afterward.

Q. *Did they express concern?*

A. Yeah, they still continued to express concerned feelings, and I still continued to express mine. But they know that I'm sexually active.

Q. *You're pretty open with your dad and mom, or with your family as a whole, I take it.*

A. About some things.

Q. *Do you and Jon talk about your sexual experiences?*

A. A little bit, not in as much detail as I would talk about it with my friends. Jon doesn't approve; I don't know if he still does. I don't think he does, but he doesn't approve of that, and he didn't and he told me so when I was going out with Jan.

Q. *That was how many years ago?*

A. About my sophomore year.

Q. *High school. Times can change. People's attitudes, people's behavior.*

A. Jon's not too comfortable, at least that's the impression I get. I don't try and push my opinions on other people about that. I'll let them know what they are, but if that's the lifestyle that they've chosen, as long as it's not detrimental to me or the people around that I care about, then they have the right to do with their lives what they want, even if that unfortunately is self-destructive. If there's some way that I can help them, then I will, but I will never get involved unless I am asked.

Q. *Did you have opportunities in high school to get into the drug scene at all?*

A. Yeah, I did.

Q. *Have you ever tried marijuana?*

A. No. Never.

Q. *The fact that you didn't, did this have any negative effect on your friends' attitude toward you at all, in high school particularly. In college, I don't think it would have so much bearing?*

A. No, not my friends. There were other people that thought that was sort of ridiculous, but I was not very close to any of them.

Q. *Were there pushers in high school?*

A. Yes.

Q. *They were high school kids, or were they coming into the school, and didn't belong there?*

A. Well, they were pushers in the sense that they were a source of supply of drugs. They got them from somebody else who was off campus.

Q. *One other issue—as you see yourself and know yourself as a human being, where do you place yourself in terms of all other nineteen-year-old men in the United States?*

A. At least in the top 1 percent.

Q. *So you see yourself right at the top?*

A. More or less. I mean there are people that are above me, but I think that I'm in that group.

Q. *But how does it happen that with that understanding of yourself that you represent the highest level of achievement, the highest skills of young men and women of this country, that you are such a well-adjusted person?*

A. My parents had a great deal to do with it. I had a pretty large ego throughout a fair portion of high school due to all the honors, but I was getting a little bit arrogant about the whole thing.

Q. *You seem to have handled it.*

A. Yeah. I came to terms with it, and . . .

Q. *How did you come to terms with it? Talk it through with someone?*

A. Yeah. I knew I had that problem and my friends were quick to point it out in a healthy sort of way. I think it was only when I went to school and nobody knew who I was or what I had done that I worked it out.

Q. *At the university?*

A. Yes, and I was pretty reluctant to give out some of the information for a while. In fact, I think for about half of the first quarter, first month and half, not even my really close friends knew that I was going to the Nobel Prize ceremonies.

Q. *How did you tell them about that? How did the news leak out?*

A. We eventually got around to talking about it. I had some fairly unusual things going on at school; I spoke to the chairman of the Department of Orthopedic Surgery the first quarter I was there, and he took a personal interest in my career and doors opened for me at the school that didn't open for many other people there.

Q. *Through this gentleman?*

A. Well, not through him, no, although through him, but just because of the things I had done that people knew about or that I let them know about. And because I think I handle myself in a manner that suggests that I know what I'm doing.

Q. *What's your weakest point, personally? How do you see yourself?*

A. I have a tendency sometimes to let important things slide sometimes and procrastinate. Sometimes it's healthy procrastination, like reading a novel in the middle of final exams just to get rid of the pressure.

Q. *Do you think that's different than anybody else?*

A. No.

Q. *So that in a sense you're saying the one weak point that you sense in your life experience is typical of a lot of other people, not just Marc?*

A. Yeah, I look at it sort of differently. There's a lot of stuff that I like to do and I sometimes get upset with myself when I waste time, like I became, oh, semiaddicted to pinball, some of the electronic games. And you know, I knew that I had to do some studying or something like that, but nevertheless I would spend half an hour in the student union or an hour sometimes doing that sort of thing. And then instead of having a great deal of time to accomplish the things that I had to do, I would be under a little bit of pressure. I think I work better under pressure.

Q. *The converse, where is your greatest strength?*

A. Well, I think I've got two, one of which I've always had, and the other one has just come about recently. I can't really give a time, but I think somewhere after my first quarter in college my persistence, the fact the thought of failing at something I do doesn't even enter into my mind; the fact if I'm going to do something and it's important to me, I'm going to do it well. It doesn't matter, with some qualifiers, what the cost is in terms of my time or money, and it doesn't matter to me what the conventions are, even when things look like they're not going to succeed and they have at various points, I keep on going and keep on trying. My science fair endeavors, the last three, have been one hundred fifty to two hundred page papers, dissertation size. Last year I invested a year and a half and close to a thousand dollars, and I was working on the research exclusively forty hours a week in addition to school, a job, and debate. Even with my work when I'm employed, the fact that maybe I have to spend a little of my own money or use some of my own resources or contacts that one wouldn't consider normal in a job, it doesn't matter to me because I think what I'm doing is important and the ethics of doing it well.

Q. *You said that there was one characteristic that you've had all your life, and that's the one you're talking about now?*

A. Correct.

Q. *And then the one that you felt you'd developed more recently; I want to be sure I get these straight.*

A. The one that developed more recent, I've always been fairly tolerant, growing up here in Cambridge one can't help but be tolerant of varying life-styles and attitudes, and things like that, but it's only just recently that I've come to believe that everybody, no matter the person from the one that impresses me the most as an intellectual to somebody who you wouldn't consider doing an intellectual activity, every person that you speak to has some sort of wisdom that only they have in the form of the experiences they'd had. What they've been through is important, and that to hate somebody or to despise somebody doesn't make sense and that you get along a lot better in the world if you understand why people feel the way they do if you can see that you would feel the same way given those circumstances and if you can deal with them on a personal level knowing why they are the way they are and trying to work with that instead of clumping somebody into a label. Especially with my parents, I think the beginning of this transition was when I realized that my parents were people and not some demagogues handing down the law from the top of the mountain, and everybody has their own faults, well what they consider faults, desires, and neuroses, and idiosyncracies and that's what makes up a person. If you can understand that and deal with it then you realize that there aren't a lot of things in life that are worth getting upset about because when you understand them you deal with them instead of setting up a defense mechanism. People can get along fairly well.

Is Marc a typical gifted youth? Obviously these young people differ one from another as much and as frequently as do any other members of a group of youths of whatsoever intellectual ability. In my considered opinion and from observation and work with many gifted young people, Marc represents the best characteristics of many of his peers. There are some aspects of his life in which he may differ. Psychologists usually define giftedness, from at least a quantitative point of view, from the results of a standardized intelligence test to be those who achieve at a quotient higher than approximately 125. Marc differs from youths at this level if his teachers' estimates of his intelligence are correct and it is actually in the vicinity of 200. It is my feeling that this estimate is quite accurate, particularly in the light of his scores on college admissions tests and other achievement tests that he has taken and of which the results are known to him.

He is an active young man, reading much, but not defining himself as a bookworm. He is interested in sports, but not to the exclusion of other activities. One of his recreational activities, i.e., rock climbing, is just beginning, but may expand. His research activities, not necessarily typical of all gifted children in kind, still, however, represent out-of-school activities that characterize many gifted youth. As such Marc appears typical of many of his peers who are intellectually nearly equals. He is not a recluse. He is not an isolate. He is a social being with interests that are those of his age group of friends.

What about his sexual interests? Is this area of his life different or unusual in comparison to other eighteen- or nineteen-year-old young men? Studies which have been carefully undertaken and critiqued by competent persons indicate that well over 50 percent of adolescent males experience frequent heterosexual activities; nearly 50 percent of girls have similar experiences. Masturbation is a characteristic of nearly all adolescent males. Insofar as these two avenues of sexual and emotional release are concerned, Marc is typical. A healthy and significant element of this phase of Marc's life is that he does not keep it a secret from his parents even though they would prefer he not engage in these activities. Marc's openness about this aspect of his life is typical of the outgoing characteristic of his total life. He challenges adults when he knows he is correct. He delights in taking opposing sides of challenging arguments when his adversary understands the roles each is playing. He is openly outspoken regarding the incompetence of some of his teachers, but at the same time he knows that at his age he is probably not going to be able to change the situation very much. This doesn't provide him with satisfactions, however, for he is sufficiently capable to understand how much he is missing. This forces him to undertake his research interests outside of school, but it doesn't make him tolerant of those teachers who take credit for things they have had little influence in bringing to a successful conclusion.

My contacts with Marc both within the confines of the interview and elsewhere bring me to the conclusion that he is a very wholesome and relatively typical gifted youth. Would that all were like him.

Jon—Jon too submitted to an interview that was for all intents and purposes nearly identical to that of Marc. Jon, although slightly more than a year younger than his brother, is nevertheless a fully developed adolescent youth. He is a tall, blond young man, just slightly taller than Marc, and when he reaches his maturity he will undoubtedly be taller and heavier than his brother. He is quiet, perhaps more introspective than Marc. He is equally intelligent, but frequent comparisons of him to his brother by teachers and family members have caused him to be somewhat more withdrawn than one would like to see in a youth his age. This youth, appealing in almost all respects, can be compared to his brother and to himself more accurately after the interview.

Q. *Jon, tell me how old you are.*

A. I will be eighteen years old in a month.

Q. *You've just graduated from high school, seventeen, that's a little young, isn't it?*

A. I have a late birthday; I didn't skip a grade.

Q. *Did your parents try to get you skipped?*

A. Not in regular school, in Hebrew school they did, I was only seven, a grade ahead.

Q. *Do you sometimes wish they had? Was school sometimes a bore to you because it was too simple?*

A. I suppose there were times, but no, I don't wish they had pushed me ahead. It's hard to say. If I had, I probably would have accepted it, as something that happened.

Q. *You had a good time in school?*

A. Depends. In high school, there are a lot of things. Elementary school is much different than junior high and junior high different than high school, but overall I suppose I could say half and half.

Q. *Can you remember when things began to become very easy for you in school as compared to the rather tougher times that the other kids had?*

A. In kindergarten I was already reading. I learned Dick and Jane books in nursery school, so I used to read lots and the teacher liked that.

Q. *Did the teacher push you in reading?*

A. I would say she didn't push me too much; she let me go at my own pace, but I guess I was pretty eager.

Q. *Where had you learned to read?*

A. My parents.

Q. *Your mother or dad actually sat down with you to teach you words?*

A. Yeah. I don't know how long or just when.

Q. *Were there other books?*

A. Eventually it was the Golden Books, things like that. I can't remember too much. Dr. Seuss.

Q. *You read the Dr. Seuss books?*

A. Yeah.

Q. *Rather difficult for a kid of three or four.*

A. More like five or so.

Q. *Did you also write words at that time?*

A. I don't remember writing the words, mostly in first grade.

Q. *How about number concepts. How early do you think you might have started knowing what numbers and how to put them together?*

A. I think kindergarten.

Q. *Jon, I don't want to embarrass you in any way, but do you know, or has anybody ever told you or estimated what your IQ is?*

A. I've never had anybody estimate my IQ.

Q. *Why is that?*

A. I don't know—nobody ever asked me to and I guess I never thought much about myself as a very bright person. It might be interesting just to take one, but I guess I'm skeptical of how much it measures creativity or other things. I've never even seen one.

Q. *You've taken the SAT and probably other kinds of achievement tests? Do you know your scores on the SAT?*

A. My SAT scores were above average, but here too, there are still quite a number of other students who rate far above that. I think I work most of the time; I like to be methodical about what I do, and those contests have always gotten me apprehensive and tense. I felt they are mostly for getting into college.

Q. *Do you feel that your scores had any negative effect on your consideration for college entrance?*

A. No. I think the university for some years has had a certain stereotype, just like some Ivy League schools being a place where 4.0 kids go and all they do is read books, and all that kind of stuff. I consider myself very well rounded and very well educated and creative in many other aspects of life, and my schoolwork is really very important to me. I think that is what the university is looking for.

Q. *Have you taken any other kinds of tests for your scores that have been reported in percentile ranks?*

A. I scored in the 95th percentile, 90, 98 on various achievement tests. One time I took a math test in tenth grade, I went off the board.

Q. *Can you put a time during the years, perhaps in elementary school, when you began to realize that you were intellectually different than other kids?*

A. I suppose in kindergarten with the reading, but maybe in third grade.

Q. *Would you have any idea of what gave you that impression?*

A. In the third grade I had a very hard-nosed teacher, and she was very strict and pretty mean sometimes. We all resented her a great deal. I guess the thing was maybe in a way kind of a rebellion, or just getting back at her, saying "look I'm not stupid, you know." She was a very poor teacher.

Q. *Generally speaking, how do you feel about teachers that you had exclusive of this one?*

A. There was another one who was very, very poor—sixth grade teacher before I switched classes, but I believe with the others I felt very positive toward them.

Q. *Did you switch grades in the sixth grade—was that because your family considered this teacher to be poor?*

A. In the sixth grade, yes. He was a very extreme fellow. He had a great many odd habits, I remember, it was a combined fifth-sixth grade class, and pretty much individualized. In some ways it was kind of holding me back sometimes. He didn't like you to get ahead, even though individualized. There was a point where we had units on reading so many books, and I was just reading books and doing book reports, many, many more than expected, and he said I shouldn't be, but I guess the clincher was one time we were standing in line in gym to line up for a chorus, and I had my hands in my pockets and just standing there in line with the other kids and he came up to me and said that I shouldn't have my hands in my pockets, that people might think that I was picking at my testicles and so

Q. *Is that what he actually said?*

A. "scratching my testicles" is exactly what he said, and I really blew up inside. I didn't say anything.

Q. *Did the other kids hear him?*

A. Kids were right around him, and I wasn't doing what he had said and I told some of my friends about it and we all put our hands in our pockets, and we got back at him. It was just the number of things; he was always yelling at me. One time I was just reading a book and he immediately blew up and asked me if I had all my work done. I had my math and all my other units done, and I shouldn't be reading unless I had. I worked ahead. He just blew up at me.

Q. *Do you think he blew up at you, or just treated you cruelly because of your brilliance? Because you were such a capable person, trying to put you down?*

A. I honestly think so. He had been a Boy Scout leader of mine for a while, that year in fact, and then I switched classes halfway through the year. It was interesting seeing how things went after that.

Q. *How'd they go?*

A. They went fairly easy, he wasn't necessarily as friendly; he was very superficial in the way he treated me.

Q. *How long were you in the scouts?*

A. In his particular group I was in the whole year.

Q. *Transfer to another troop?*

A. No. That was from Cub Scouts, and then the next year I went straight into Boy Scouts.

Q. *Other than this person, your elementary teachers apparently didn't treat you too much differently than the other kids in class? Or is that a wrong assumption?*

A. Maybe I was further ahead than some of the other students, but it helped me do more things. It was a matter of help, not criticism. Not putting me down.

Q. *Your brother was equally as good as you in school and he was ahead of you by a couple of years, wasn't he?*

A. He is a year and a half older than I am, a year ahead in school.

Q. *How did you feel about him and his successes? In junior high or senior high?*

A. In junior high I felt a great deal. I suppose it was at that time he was doing a lot of stuff in the science fair and doing well, and my parents pressured me a great deal into that track, but I think the more they talked about it, the more they tried to push me, the more I fought back. It was a bad thing to do. The fact is that I am interested a great deal in science, but I just didn't want to pursue that because it was putting a lot of pressure on me to enter the science fair. They might have said you can have all these things like Marc has, but they were saying in junior high and high school, maybe next year you can both go to the international fair, you can both win first and second place and it will be so neat.

Q. *Were you getting the same kind of pressure from both your Dad and Mom, or from one or the other?*

A. Both. My mother a bit more. Marc never gave me any pressure at all. In high school Marc and I became really close. Before that maybe not so close in junior high.

Q. *When you say close, what do you mean?*

A. Just talk to each other, and not yell at each other and all sorts of things. That was kind of different because I guess we were both getting a lot of pressure from our parents at the same time.

Q. *Do you think your parents realized the pressure that they were putting on you?*

A. No. Never.

Q. *Did you ever talk with them about it?*

A. Yes. And they'd always say no, we're not trying to do that.

Q. *When you were in high school, did you take a goodly number of elective courses?*

A. There were courses I didn't have to take, but I was more or less told what to take.

Q. *By whom? Your parents?*

A. By my parents, and mostly since Marc had, always since Marc did it.

Q. *Do I sense a note of antagonism here a little, "always since Marc did it?"*

A. Yeah.

Q. *Was that the way it was then?*

A. Through junior high and early high school, yes it was. They thought I should keep up with Marc then. I suppose if we were just person A and person B, we would keep up with each other and not always look at it as brother keeping with brother, but there was pressure.

Q. *Were there report cards that were compared? Every time they came out?*

A. Yeah, but mine came out better. Mine usually always came out better. I would always point that out to my parents.

Q. *How did your parents react when you pointed out your better scores?*

A. They would say, "Oh, yeah, we're proud of you," and all that, but they're still proud of Marc.

Q. *How do you really feel toward Marc today? You said you were on good terms and you talk together frequently.*

A. I have a great deal of respect for Marc. He works very hard at what he wants, he's very goal oriented, but at times I see him hurting people knowingly or unknowingly, and I'm not the only one who says this or sees it. I've had other relatives tell me, his friends, friends of mine. . . .

Q. *Have you ever talked with him about this?*

A. Not really.

Q. *Will you characterize your relationship with Marc on another plane as two brothers that genuinely love each other?*

A. Yes, definitely.

Q. *As you have been reared by your dad and mom, do you feel that you have been permitted to live independent lives pretty much, independent from one another, or have they been closely intertwined of necessity?*

A. I'd say, probably less intertwined, because we branched off more distinctly into different interests.

Q. *What are your primary interests?*

A. Like career goals? I would like to work in health related fields, work with people. Probably medicine; I've been thinking a great deal about medicine. Exactly what, I wouldn't want to say for sure.

Q. *Other than career goals, what are your interests?*

A. In school and out of school, I like to write. I like to write a great deal.

Q. *What kinds of things?*

A. Anything, essay, poetry, and I keep a writing journal.

Q. *What are some of the topics you or anybody might find in that writing journal?*

A. Feelings I have about people in general, maybe not one specific person, but the attitudes I see in people generally; or maybe some goals of mine, realistic or not; maybe moods that I may be in, or any number of things. It's not a diary by any means.

Q. *How often would you write in the journal?*

A. At least three times a week.

Q. *Is this something you share with your friends, or is it highly private?*

A. I've only shared it with one other person, and not because that person told me to do so, but out of my respect for him, and that was the person who encouraged me to keep the journal.

Q. *An adult?*

A. An adult, an English teacher of mine, who I look at not as a teacher any more, but more as a very, very close friend. I have a great many friends who are a great deal older than I am, and my parents appreciate that as much as I think they should, people who are twenty, thirty, forty years old who can be good and close friends.

Q. *What kind of activities do you get involved in with those older friends?*

A. Everything from discussions to going bicycle riding, and going camping, or this week I plan to go out to Washington and go mountain climbing on Mt. Rainier with some of them.

Q. *Will there be other young fellows, such as yourself?*

A. Oh, yes, there will be others. A group of six of us.

Q. *And how old are they?*

A. One is twenty-eight, the other is twenty-three, one is eighteen, one nineteen, and one is almost sixty. I don't know him very well, but he knows somebody else, and he just happened to go on the trip.

Q. *How did you happen to get in this interesting group for this kind of activity?*

A. I've always been interested in camping and the outdoors. I love being outside, this comes from Boy Scouts camping, and when I was in high school as a sophomore I also ran a great deal long distance. After cross-country season was over, I decided it was finally time to look for a job, and I decided to apply at the places I wanted to work at, not just McDonald's, and one of the places I applied to was a camping store in town. I also applied at one of the movie theaters, and got a call from the person who hired me at the movie theater one afternoon, and the same night I got a call from the person who was manager of the camping store. I took the job with the store.

Q. *How long will you be on this mountain climbing trip?*

A. We'll be on the trip for two and a half weeks; approximately ten days we'll be on the mountain itself.

Q. *How much weight will you be carrying on your back in the beginning?*

A. About fifty pounds.

Q. *What kind of food will you be taking with you?*

A. Mostly freeze-dried food, a great deal of fruits.

Q. *Army K-ration type of thing?*

A. No, freeze-dried, which I get discounted because of work. In planning for the trip, I wrote the company who made it and found out all sorts of information so that I could plan my diet around it. A great deal of care went into planning my diet.

Q. *What you eat will of necessity be somewhat different than the others won't it?*

A. Quite a bit. In fact, I'm carrying all my own food, so that I know every last detail of what is in my diet, so that I don't have to worry about it.

Q. *How long have you been a diabetic?*

A. Five years this fall.

Q. *Medically, is it considered to be under control?*

A. Yes, I would say it is.

Q. *One or two shots?*

A. Two a day.

Q. *Do you give them to yourself?*

A. Yes.

Q. *What sort of arrangements have you made for sterilization of needles while you are on your trip?*

A. I'll take disposable syringes, which come prepackaged and sterilized, but if need be, I will save all of them on the trip and resterilize the needles.

Q. *You mentioned the fact that you felt comfortable with older friends. Do you feel more comfortable with older ones than with younger?*

A. I would say about half and half. I have very close friends who are my own age. I would say the older friends I have listen to me and give me a lot of respect, and sometimes much more than they do people their own age. They tell me this, and it's kind of funny, well, funny is a poor word. At first it struck me as kind of odd, but then I realized that they share of lot of the same values that I do, and I think that that's probably the biggest drawing point. They don't know a great many people my own age who do all the things I do and have accomplished a great deal. I just hear a lot of praise.

Q. *I think there is another reason, and that is the fact that you appear to be a very secure young man, and not one that appears to be dependent or has a need for dependency on other people.*

A. That's a very bad habit to be caught up in, to be dependent upon others than yourself. You need to know yourself very well.

Q. *I did not get that impression at the house—you were very quiet. You were letting Marc and your parents take the lead conversationally. Tonight, it's a different Jon than I saw the other evening. I wondered as I left your house what kind of guy you were, because you appeared to be withdrawn and quiet and not as active intellectually as I had anticipated. When you function with other adults, you emanate security all over the place, and the other person is made to feel that he is talking with a very secure young man. I'm saying that as a compliment.*

A. You have to trust yourself a great deal all of the time.

Q. *Where did you learn this business of trusting yourself?*

A. I guess my parents come from really poor families in big cities, and they had to work a great deal when they were young and a lot of things were hard for them and they developed very strong self-support. It hasn't changed much. Even they don't appear as such. It's always negative talk about work, money. As a result I don't see them trying to make themselves happy as much as I think they might. I think they have been trying more recently to enjoy life. A lot of what I've seen just comes from trusting yourself. That's always kind of a favorite phrase of mine.

Q. *It's not an excuse for not doing anything?*

A. Exactly, it's not an excuse. It takes a lot of frustration out of unnecessary trial and error activity.

Q. *So that you feel that you have learned to understand yourself, and I presume that's an ever-developing experience essentially through reflection of the behavior, attitude, and conversation of your parents, is that correct?*

A. I think a great deal of it also goes to my writing, because I can look back on that and see where I was at this point in time and how I've changed from what I might have been thinking later on. Many different things.

Q. *So you do a lot of self-reflection? No psychiatric self-analysis, just individual cogitation.*

A. Yes, I do, and I think it's a good thing.

Q. *When you're bicycle riding?*

A. Sometimes when I'm out riding, because it's just a change of pace from home and school and work. It allows me to go out and in a way it's kind of an escapist thing. But often it helps me see something I might be thinking about a problem at home or school or something, see it in a different light.

Q. *I don't look upon that as escapist, Jon, if by escapist you mean something negative.*

A. Escapist was just the word I used.

Q. *I know your background is Jewish, have you experienced anti-Semitic attitudes that have been disturbing to you?*

A. Within the high school itself, practically nonexistent, I shouldn't say that, in tenth grade, I remember there were a lot of Palestinian kids, Arab kids with the Palestinian movement who would go around and paint things like PLO in the bathrooms and things like that. But most of the anti-Semitism I encountered was in elementary school, about fifth grade.

Q. *From kids, or from teachers?*

A. From kids.

Q. *How did you handle that?*

A. At first I was pretty quiet about it and just let it lay and didn't pay any attention, but then I got teased more and more by certain people and I got into a number of fights as a result.

Q. *Did the teachers intervene at all, or attempt to intervene, or do you think they knew?*

A. They knew.

Q. *Did you discuss it with your parents? Ever?*

A. Not much. Hardly ever.

Q. *So you tried to solve it by yourself?*

A. Yeah.

Q. *How about high school?*

A. Anti-Semitism, some.

Q. *You mentioned earlier that you enjoyed singing.*

A. Only in synagogue, I don't sing in a choral group or anything like that.

Q. *What is it about the music of the synagogue that attracts you?*

A. I feel my ties to being Jewish are cultural rather than simply religious and I separate the two, and part of that is the singing, the cultural part, and there's a tremendous bond for me.

Q. *You've told me that your friends, both older and younger, are mostly boys. Do you go out on dates?*

A. Yes. I have a lot of friends who are just boys, who are men who are older, but a great deal of women, too.

Q. *Are you comfortable with girls your own age?*

A. Not all of them, but in high school it's difficult or different because of the fact that there are just too many social cliques that kids are put into. I've never seen myself as belonging. I haven't gone out of my way to be distinctly different, but I have friends in all the groups that people would separate into jocks and preppies, just so many different groups. As far as girls, I go out fairly often.

Q. *Dances?*

A. Dances or high school parties, well just dancing at parties. Dancing is not as much a social thing to do as in the 1950s or 1960s.

Q. *Are any of the groups that you've been in involved with drug usage of any sort?*

A. A great many of my friends have tried it at one time or another, but none, maybe just a very few heavily at one time or another, but . . . .

Q. *Have you ever tried it?*

A. No.

Q. *Have you ever been kidded because you wouldn't? Or didn't?*

A. Not by friends, but I remember one time when I was little in elementary school, I was going to a swim club party down at the pool only a block away. There were some neighborhood kids who asked me if I wanted to buy some pot and dope, and that really had me frightened and there was a big uproar. Oh, I was really scared and I called my parents and it caused a big feud between the families whose kids were known for dealing with drugs.

Q. *Do you feel personally at ease when you're out on a date with a girl?*

A. Depends, depends on who it is.

Q. *Can I get really personal now?*

A. Sure.

Q. *Have you ever had sexual relationships with a girl?*

A. As far as like sleeping with someone, no, although that's something that I talk about with people.

Q. *Have you had an opportunity?*

A. Yes, the opportunity, mutual agreement, somebody older, but those were strange circumstances. I've had the opportunity, but both later on mutually declined.

Q. *When you say both later on, do you mean both people or both decided that it wasn't the wise thing to do?*

A. Right. The latter.

Q. *And this was with an older woman?*

A. Yes it was.

Q. *Have you attempted to or have kids you know had sexual relations?*

A. That's not the kind of things, that's not the kind of friends I have. It's not to say that my friends haven't, I mean a great lot of them have had pretty intense sexual relationships.

Q. *But you haven't? [No.] Have you felt a need for it?*

A. At certain times I would say yes.

Q. *Do you and Marc ever talk about this matter, this issue?*

A. Yes, we have, but not often.

Q. *How do you handle your own sex drives, is masturbation an important issue to you?*

A. Once in a while, yes. A lot of kids my own age who think of sex as a very witty kind of thing. I'm not saying that just because you have sex with someone you're committing yourself to marriage or anything like that. I think it's a very naive view a lot of kids who have that view. But I would not marry someone that I'd never slept with.

Q. *So that you would see the importance of having sexual relationships with a girl before you would marry her?*

A. Yes, I'd not want to spend the rest of my life, yes, with someone I didn't feel very comfortable with sexually.

Q. *Where did you learn about sex?*

A. Probably from friends—talking with them, a little sex education that's first introduced in the fifth grade, or at least when I was in school. But before that kids would talk, and Father always had *Playboy* for years around the house, but he stopped buying them a few years ago.

Q. *Did he ever talk with you, I don't mean formally, in the sense of birds and bees in a lecture, but did he ever just talk with you informally about sex, girls, sexual development, sexual relationships.*

A. Never. Well, one time I remember, it's really funny, coming home from Scout meeting one time talking with other kids and the word prostitute came up. I was already about 13 or 14 or so, 12 or 13. When I got home I mentioned the word prostitute in discussion and he said quite frankly "Do you know about those things?" and I said "Yes." "Those things" that he was referring to, I assumed were just sexual relations in general.

Q. *Have you ever been sorry that you didn't have an opportunity to more closely talk with him about this phase of your development, or have you always felt pretty secure about it?*

A. I felt pretty secure.

Q. *And most of it has come from the sex education course or from talk with kids?*

A. No, that's initial, but a lot of it later is reading. I read a great deal and all sorts of things, everything from *Psychology Today*.

Q. *Have you gone out of your way to get books that are sexually oriented?*

A. No.

Q. *Now let's switch topics. If you were to change your whole educational experience as it has occurred up to now, what would you change?*

A. First thing I'm thinking of is getting rid of my calculus teacher this year.

Q. *But you got an A in her course, I take it?*

A. No. I got a C in the course.

Q. *Really, how did that happen?*

A. Probably a lot of reasons. I would say it was earlier than that, but in high school my attitude toward math changed drastically. I had a string of poor teachers, and instead of rebelling, I'd try to forget about the teachers and the way they taught and just learn. It's very hard for me to associate to a teacher as a teacher, because I don't see a person as just somebody who knows math. I see a teacher as someone who deals with me as someone who's supposed to relate to others. A lot of different things go into being a teacher; more than just knowledge.

Q. *So if you were going to change at least one thing so far as your educational experience is concerned, you would be looking for teachers who had a more well-developed personality and greater acceptance of kids, is that what you're saying to me?*

A. Yes. In general, yes.

Q. *What else might you change?*

A. As far as just the educational process—can't change students. I mean, if somebody doesn't want to learn there is no way you're ever going to make a kid learn. I've always felt that way, and it can be hard. Probably more, much more parent involvement sometimes, although sometimes I feel it's been too much parent involvement, but a lot of parents just don't know what their kids are doing in school. I know many of my teachers, not only as teachers, but as friends—from teachers to administrators. I happen to be very, very good friends with the assistant principal of the high school who I got to know through work on a city bicycling committee. In fact, he invited me to serve on the committee. I just know a great many people in education, so I guess what I'm trying to say is that you're not only there to learn subjects from the teachers, but also how to think. Maybe differently about what your textbook says and how to think about math, but also how to think about how what your learning relates to what you're doing in life, and how to deal with people. High school really shows you how important it is to learn and how to deal with people.

Q. *But a lot of kids don't have that appreciation, or that point of view.*

A. Oh, yes, too many.

Q. *Do you think that kind of a quality, or that kind of an attitude can be learned, can be taught? How did you get that point of view?*

A. I can't really say. I think about ninth grade or so. At that point things began to change a great deal socially, and I think that at that point I felt that way about teachers and friends.

Q. *You write, and you imply that you read considerably. Into what areas does your reading carry you outside of school books?*

A. As far as magazines, I read the *New Yorker, Psychology Today* consistently; newspapers, I like to read the Sunday *New York Times*. It's nice to read it weekdays too; if I go away on a trip somewhere, that's one thing I try to do is buy a copy of the *New York Times*.

Q. *Books?*

A. Books, all sorts of things—different classics to Russian literature, Solzhenitsyn to . . . .

Q. *Are you a science fiction addict?*

A. No. I'm not a science freak or addict.

Q. *Novels, or biographies, or autobiographies?*

A. Novels, a great deal.

Q. *Historical things?*

A. Not a whole lot of historical stuff.

Q. *Political?*

A. Political, yeah, everything from Abbie Hoffman to . . . .

In retrospect, parents in particular frequently recognize things that they might have changed or done differently in the rearing of their children. While I have not discussed this with Marc's and Jon's parents, I suspect that this might have been the case here. Would the prohibition against advancing the children in school grades have been repeated? Would the comparisons of Jon's record against that of Marc's have been so frequent or so openly discussed—sufficient to the end that Jon withdrew considerably in nonverbalized competition? It was sufficient that Jon presented to his peers, some teachers, and initially to this writer, the appearance of a lack of personal direction and life goals. This was different, in large measure, as one compared him with the more aggressive firstborn son who appeared always to know the direction in which he was traveling.

Four years later, Marc's goals have changed only slightly from the time of the interview: from orthopedic surgery to a medical degree presently less well defined, but now coupled with a Ph.D. degree in cellular physics. The medical speciality will become apparent as he continues to achieve his combined, yet unified academic goals. He has no hesitation in knowing that his life goals will become apparent to him and to others.

Jon, on the other hand, has shifted his academic efforts considerably since the time of the high school interview to university graduation, which takes place in a few months. Finishing high school with interests in medicine, he moved in college toward law and ultimately to the broad field of political and social sciences. A senior paper required by his university is written in the area of terrorist movements and fundamentalism in the United States. He has moved swiftly through undergraduate university years, but as graduation approaches his graduate study goals are not defined. He has taken foreign service examinations among others as entrances to a career, but that career is still fleeting in his mind and he plans to take a year or so away from higher education before continuing. During his university years he has given a day a week to the Anti-Defamation League and to other similar significant social efforts. He is a thoughtful, astute, and socially minded person. He is a concerned person as is his brother Marc.

It is interesting, in visiting with the two brothers, to observe how Marc now often defers to Jon, recognizes Jon's values, and verbalizes Jon's skills and achievements. "Tell him, Jon . . ." is a phrase often heard now from Marc as the latter consciously pushes Jon into the center of a conversation and obviously recognizes the significant things Jon has accomplished and is doing. In Jon's interview his anticipation of a mountain-climbing experience yet to come was important. That now is a thing of the past, something of which Jon is exceedingly proud—as is Marc for Jon. Jon, Marc finally got him to relate to me, was one of two who made it to the top of Mt. Rainier. Jon's planning for proper food, weight of his load, medications, and all other details of the climb paid off in a success experience that will live with him always. The two brothers are "close" to one another now. Maturity has produced gains, and a close alliance between them apparently exists. This was not always the case as Jon's comments in his interview illustrate.

They have been separate in their university programs yet close enough to be together as they wish. Each has had problems which the other has helped to solve. Being in a community with five major universities and several smaller colleges, made it possible for each to live separately from his family and separately as brothers. Yet a telephone call made it possible for the two brothers to get together as often as it was wanted. This has happened, and it appears that space has made it possible for the two to see growth in one another and to observe values which could often be integrated into the life of the other. If prompted, they would say this directly. It is so obvious in their mutual behavior that prompting is not necessary. Two brilliant minds are supporting one another in a highly functional manner at their present stages of growth and development.

As I read and re-read the contents of the interviews, I am immediately aware that I am dealing with two independent thinkers and two young people who are able to analyze themselves as well as others. Jon, although he maintains a fully independent stance, looks to Marc in both positive and negative ways. He admires his achievements that are many and remarkable, but at the same time he resists comparisons to him. He seeks independence from his leadership, excellent as it is. The implications of these interviews, their ramifications for school programs, and their implications for home and personal relationships will be examined in the next chapter.

References and Related Readings

Barbe, W. B., and Renzulli, J. S., eds. *Psychology and Education of the Gifted.* New York: Irvington, 1981.

Chilman, C. S. "Toward a Reconceptualization of Adolescent Sexuality." Chap. 5 in C. S. Chilman, *Adolescent Pregnancy and Childbearing.* NIH Publication No. 81-2077. Washington, D.C.: U.S. Government Printing Office, 1980.

Gallagher, J. J. *Teaching the Gifted Child.* 2d ed. Boston: Allyn and Bacon, 1975.

Guilford, J. P. *The Nature of Human Intelligence.* New York: McGraw-Hill, 1967.

Kinsey, A. C., Pomeroy, W. B., and Martin, C. E. *Sexual Behavior in the Human Male.* Philadelphia: W. B. Saunders, 1948.

Martinson, R. A. *The Identification of the Gifted and Talented.* Reston, Va.: Council for Exceptional Children, 1975.

Miller, M. J., and Price, M. *The Gifted Child, His Family, and Community.* New York: Walker, 1981.

Chapter 11

Implications of Giftedness

The reader accurately may have come to the conclusion that I am fully in agreement that there is an appropriate place for the special class within the public school system—a special class for those pupils who on one basis or another exhaust the regular grade offerings. The gifted children of a community constitute one of these groups. I am well aware that there is not full agreement on this matter, and temporarily I may be in a minority. Issues of discrimination quickly come to the fore by some, the term "undemocratic" is pressed forward by others, and the argument that gifted youth of all the clinical categories in special education need experiences with those of lesser ability is strongly argued. The arguments supporting these points of view are more than unconvincing.

It is my long-time considered opinion that two things are in operation with gifted children and youth. First, they constitute a special clinical category of learners in the same magnitude as the mentally retarded, those with speech impairments, and other types of physical, emotional, or intellectual differences. They, the gifted, are unique, and their uniqueness quickly exhausts the teaching capacities of most educators. These children have the same needs for individualized instruction in groups as do those with retarded mental development. Second, the argument that these children need experiences with those of lesser ability may be quite true, but it is a superficial emphasis. There are dozens of ways in which this can be accomplished in the course of a normal day in school or in the neighborhood in post-school hours as Marc and Jon have expressed in the previous chapter. In addition, I am not advocating that gifted children be separated from their nongifted peers for a full day, any more than it is advocated that the resource room be utilized during the total day for services to other types of children with other types of learning difficulties. The gifted child, as Marc and Jon state, have learning needs that exhaust the regular classroom teacher's abilities, and these can best be handled in a special class situation. It is not undemocratic to meet the needs of children, and public schools have been doing this in varying ways for many years, i.e., special schools in the community, special classes, resource rooms, itinerant teachers, hospital and bedside teaching. It is no less undemocratic to meet the unique needs of the gifted children of a community in ways that will appropriately exploit their remarkable capacities to the benefit of the community, themselves, and indeed of the nation.

The United States is one of the countries of the world that makes little or sometimes no effort to cater to gifted youth. Germany has for generations utilized the *gymnasium* as its partial answer to the education of the gifted of that nation. The *école superior* has served this purpose in France. To a lesser extent the great public schools of the United Kingdom have provided educational opportunities for the future leadership of that set of countries. Japan, through a rigorous program of examinations (with which I do not agree) screens its best, and permits them to move upward into selected advanced schools culminating with the University of Tokyo, which is viewed as the outstanding institution of higher education in the country. Regardless of one's political philosophy, selected youth in the Union of Soviet Socialist Republics and in the People's Republic of China are screened into special schools for gifted youths and others into academies for those with great talents, e.g., music, art, ballet, and the sciences (the Leningrad Conservatory for Piano or the Mariinsky Theater for Drama and Ballet). Not so in the United States except for children of the affluent, some of whom have opportunities to attend certain schools that are not always geared to the needs of the gifted. The Julliard and Curtis institutes, both private, do serve talented musicians, although few young people can afford to attend. A few public schools such as the High School for the Performing Arts, the High School for Science, both in New York City, and a handful of similar secondary schools in other communities do serve gifted young people. Education in the United States is the great leveler, and more than one gifted child, discouraged by mediocre teachers and boredom, has either left school entirely or has achieved at levels much below his or her capacity. In the preceding chapter both Marc and Jon, but Marc in particular, expressed his discontent with most of his teachers throughout his school experience, and in reality has been challenged by only one or two of his first year university professors. This is outrageous when one considers the intellectual capacities of these two young men. The United States can ill afford to neglect this segment of its child population or wait to serve it only *after* something comparable to another *Sputnik* has occurred.

As one considers the teachers to whom Marc and Jon have been exposed during their educational lifetimes, one is impressed by the few whom these gifted young people regard as outstanding. Each can remember only one or two from kindergarten through high school. Marc gives his teachers a collective B− grade. As a matter of fact, each can recall teachers who literally discouraged learning. In a community such as these two gifted young people lived and which then were located five major universities and almost a dozen lesser ones, this situation is inexcusable. Perhaps it was wise for the parents to discourage skipping a grade or two to bring the children into competition with their intellectual peers. Perhaps on the other hand they should challenge the school system on this matter. I am aware of the arguments against this practice, and for the most part I would agree that it is better to have gifted children developing alongside their chronological-aged peers and developmentally with their social equals. On the other hand, if this be the path followed, then teachers must be available who know how to individualize the educational expectancies of their pupils. Teachers of these children must not be allowed to hide behind the excuse of their so-called large class enrollments. The problem is that teachers generally do not know how to individualize instruction for a class of children and many administrators are less knowledgeable. It is also easier to have everyone performing at the same rate on the same assignment, and in the same manner. I have often had undergraduate university class enrollments of two to three hundred students and have individualized. It is not difficult to do.

A professor of English once asked me as an undergraduate student to serve as a companion to his ten-year-old genius son, and to do anything he and I wished to do except schoolwork. At that time I was studying Greek in my undergraduate program, and the boy discovered this one day when he was going through my college texts. He asked if we could "talk Greek." That was beyond me at the time, but we did agree that we could put Greek names on most if not all of the things we saw and did together. That taxed the tutor-companion, but both learned much, and the child had an enormously enriching experience, not via the school unfortunately, but in an extracurricular sense. The child's schoolteacher, as a matter of fact, was infuriated that the child was spending his time on something that was of "no value" to the school work he was "supposed" to be doing—things he had long since completed. Jon had this same experience with an English teacher who criticized him for reading when he didn't have his "math" completed—which he did!

I put a very large blame on teacher education centers that do not give preservice teachers, or others for that matter, any real experience in the process of individualization. Students graduate without knowing how to enrich a curriculum for advanced pupils or to modify it appropriately for those who are slow learners. Teachers do not know how to allow certain students to explore areas tangential to that being emphasized for the group as a whole. What is appropriate enrichment? How far should the pupil go? Marc did all of his research "outside the school," and purposely failed to give the school credit for his efforts. I agree with his stand under the circumstances, but it certainly did not endear him to certain teachers. He found, as did I upon inquiry, that the schools were more than willing to take the credit for his outstanding achievements, but in reality they gave him little encouragement during the process of his remarkable efforts. The newspapers reporting on Marc's prizes always recognized the school in which he studied, but never mentioned that the school did little to encourage the young man. Marc's attitude, generous in the extreme it seems to me, was corroborated when I made personal inquiries to school personnel to ascertain the extent to which the school people provided guidance, encouragement, financial assistance, or other forms of leadership. He did what he did essentially in spite of the schools! One of Marc's teachers, in a conversation with me a year after Marc had graduated from high school, took full credit for Marc's science prizes, until I asked him about the project titles, the contents of the projects, and the relationship between Marc and this teacher as the projects progressed. When the teacher failed to respond, it was obvious to both of us that less than minimal guidance had come from the school for this outstanding student. Marc's statements were correct.

In approaching the matter of teacher interest as negatively as I have, it must be recognized that I also frequently see outstanding teachers at work with children, teachers who give their best and are valued by their students. I know many of these teachers, and they live and work in almost every community, large and small, in this country. But these are not enough. There are likewise those who do not go the last mile with children. I have been their pupil, on rare occasions, and so has Jon, for example. He had teachers, he tells me, who held him back, who never encouraged initiative, who rarely if ever complimented him, and who compared him with his older brother. As he grew older he developed the capacity to be selective, to selectively make judgments regarding his future teachers and to screen the poor from the good. His mother was effective also in assisting in this effort. Parental intervention does not come into the picture frequently enough. Jon, according to his story, essentially solved this issue himself, although while not verbalizing it, he apparently had the full support of his parents in the decisions he reached. In the ninth grade he had a biology teacher who was "good." This person pushed him to greater limits and held high standards, not only for him, but individually for the class as a whole. He also had an English teacher who urged him to begin to keep a journal, and who has subsequently become a close personal friend, the only one with whom he has shared the contents of his journal. This man has had an impact on the life of a gifted student. This teacher knows how to stimulate students, to appeal to their innermost feelings of personal responsibility, and to motivate them to enter into activities that will have a lasting effect on their lives. In doing so pupils become friends and are placed in a position where the teacher can be even more effective in their lives.

It is not merely the teachers on whom the onus of responsibility for a lack of interest in the gifted must be placed. It is the school systems themselves. At Syracuse University we had a splendid program of teacher education in the field of special education—in all areas except the gifted. I was determined to correct this situation, and, beginning with the summer programs, established workshops for teachers in this area including the provision of demonstration classes filled with gifted children and led by outstanding teachers. For the workshops the leaders in the field of the education of the gifted at that time were employed as visiting professors: Dr. Ruth Strang, Dr. Paul Witty, and others of similar stature. School superintendents were approached by personal letters and scholarships offered to them for selected teachers who ultimately would return to their localities and establish programs for gifted children and youth. The maximum number of students who ever enrolled in this extraordinarily extensive program of teacher preparation was eight! It was continued for several years, and then dropped because of lact of interest within the school systems. Until on a national basis the educational leadership of the United States sees the value in appropriately educating the most gifted of our children and youth, the country will continue to lose the extraordinary contributions of much leadership in many fields. Some young people will make their ways in spite of the schools, and ultimately many of these students will assume roles of national significance.

There are many misconceptions regarding gifted children and youth, and often thoughtful parents go to great lengths to protect their sons and daughters from having this label placed on them. If one reads carefully the interviews with the two young people in the preceding chapter, however, it will be seen that they who represent many such youth have interests that are typical of most children their ages. Jon is a rock and mountain climber and has gotten his older brother into this activity. Both were involved in Scouting. Both were active in selected youth activities in the synagogue. Both boys dated girls as adolescence took over, Marc heavily.

It is interesting to me that both boys have selected friends from a very wide age bracket, and in this they may be different from others of their age group. They are stimulated by conversations and friendships with older persons, both men and women. Undoubtedly, some of their interests in nonschool but cultural or intellectual activities stemmed from these contacts. Marc, for example, spent considerable amounts of his own money to purchase tickets to concerts and other related cultural activities. Neither parent is an artist; where did Marc's interest in art and his periodic visits to the art museums come from? Jon, although attending a different university, expects to meet Marc once in a while to visit an art institute. Marc's interest in this activity was not merely to view paintings, but to visit with the artists during a gallery opening and to experience the socialization of the occasion over wine and cheese. It is an intellectually expanding experience.

These are youths who are outspoken regarding those things in which they believe and about which they know. Teachers must understand this characteristic of gifted youths. Teachers do not have to be omnipotent in order to gain the admiration of their students. Students do have minds, and they should be allowed to express their opinions and to challenge. Marc and Jon have often done this and have experienced rebuff many times from insecure teachers. Recall the gasoline mileage topic which Marc reports, wherein the teacher made remarks which Marc, through his youthful employment with the ecology agency, knew were incorrect. When corrected by Marc, the teacher was not secure enough to admit a mistake or to acknowledge Marc's contribution. Since the entire class of students knew who was correct, the teacher lost face with the group as a whole. His effectiveness as a teacher was dulled, and no one really profited.

Teaching gifted children is different than teaching the intellectually normal child. Education with the gifted is more of a partnership between teacher and student; with the intellectually normal, the relationship is more of a leader and a follower. Cicero (*On the Character of the Orator*) provides one of the best descriptions of the characteristics of a teacher of the gifted to be found in the literature, and he speaks with force about such things as eloquence, wide knowledge of many subjects, style and the arrangement of words, a "thorough familiarity with all the feelings which nature has given to man," humor and wit, an acquaintance with history, and "a store of instances [examples]" with which he can impress a point upon his listeners. There are many more characteristics that Cicero lists, but these few are enough to raise the question: how many of today's teachers possess these traits so necessary in challenging the minds of the nation's future leaders? Sadly, too few, is my opinion.

The two youths interviewed in the previous chapter come from a family that places a premium on intellectual activities. The parents have obviously made many opportunities available for the expression of such interests, and the children have responded. I have stressed the importance of sex education in the lives of exceptional children, if not indeed for all children. This phase of these two youths' lives, important as it is, however, has not been as fully developed as others. Each has experienced a "class" in sex education in the latter part of the elementary school, and undoubtedly the topic was contained as a part of other classes from time to time. Each of the two youths, however, indicates that in one way or another this aspect of their development and "growing up" was minimized and indeed neglected. *Playboy* magazine is hardly a reasonable substitute for one of the most significant aspects of human development. There is nothing wrong with reading and using books on the topic of sex, but if these are to be the substitute for discussions and direct information, then such reading materials must be carefully selected and themselves be developmental in nature. Such written materials do exist, and these two youths rather wistfully express wishes that they had been available. The boys got some things on their own, but it would have been better if there had been guidance.

One boy is sexually active, and has been since he was sixteen years old. He had the courage to face his parents regarding his activities, and there was a difference of opinion expressed strongly. But, with due credit to the parents, prohibition was not invoked, and it is doubtful that this approach would have been effective if it had been. On the other hand, Marc needed good guidance and his story to me does not indicate that this was received.

Jon, likewise, although much more guarded about his relationship with an "older woman," lacked knowledge and basic information regarding this extraordinarily important aspect of adolescent development. While Jon's problem was solved in some manner, and he has maintained a virginal status until now, whatsoever information he has regarding human sexuality has essentially been self-gained. He has strong opinions of what his sexual relationship will be with a girl before he marries, but he must learn that sex per se is only a part of the marriage relationship. Somewhere along the developmental line, probably in an optimal program on a continuing basis as youths grow older, the totality of sexual interrelationships, broadly defined, needs to be the focus of either school or home or both. Gifted youth need this formalized as well as do others. Neither school nor home is doing the job well at the present time. Too often children are reticent about discussing this significant facet of human growth with their parents. I have seen the school's outline of this course, which the two youths experienced and it is indeed superficial, although in fairness it must be said that most aspects of human sexuality are included. Whether these are fully explored by teachers and students, is another question entirely. One does not carelessly point a finger of criticism at this family in relation to the sex education of the two children. This family is certainly not atypical of most families. I emphasize the lack of complete orientation to issues of human sexuality, both because they are so seldom handled adequately in the home or in the school, and because they probably constitute the single most important aspect of child growth and development. As such this phase of growth can hardly be ignored.

These youths have escaped the "drug scene," undoubtedly to the relief of their parents. They are aware; they know that drugs are pushed in their school and that their friends in some cases have used them. The fact that Marc and Jon particularly have not used drugs has not isolated them from their friends. I suspect that in part this is due, not just to the fact that they did not sample drugs or use them regularly, but because they are such fine persons, have good personalities, and can contribute something to practically any social group in which they find themselves. They are "well rounded." Their emphasis often in their interviews is on friends. Jon wishes to live in a dormitory during his first year in the university in order to "make friends." Marc has friends of both sexes both in and outside of his fraternity, and cultivates these relationships. Friends with like interests and with good minds have been more than reasonable substitutes for drugs. There has been no necessity to use drugs as a status symbol. Just where the two boys learned this or how they came to this conclusion is not obvious, but certainly the family aura would place human values elsewhere.

As Jon and Marc have grown older the brother-to-brother relationship has become deeper. Jon has felt deeply the comparison that has been made too often between him and Marc by both teachers and his parents, and he has resented this at times. He too is gifted, but he has consciously (or perhaps unconsciously) avoided those things which have brought Marc his reputation, because he wanted to be himself, not Marc's reflection. This issue has kept the two more separated than perhaps either wished to be. Both, however, express their high opinion of the other. I believe it is wise that they are to attend different universities. They will be close enough to visit one another as frequently as they wish, but far enough apart to be able to maintain a high degree of independence and privacy. They will grow together as maturity continues.

The children's relationships with their parents are warm, but objective. They each speak of the excitement of the dinner table and the discussions which take place there. The parents have been sources of security, and this is expressed in many ways. While they may not agree with the sexual life-style of Marc, they have never penalized him for it. They have expressed their opinions fully, but they have given him the support he needed while he worked through his own problem and ultimately solved it. Such would be the case with Jon as well, and support apparently was present in the single situation which Jon mentioned to me.

There is, however, a degree of separateness which exists between each member of the family and the others and among them all. Such is not to criticize, for every family must work out its own interrelationships. Such is to say, however, that in families where there are gifted youths, the relationship between parents and children must be as close as possible without overwhelming in order to provide every possible opportunity for development of remarkable young minds. Donna at fourteen is having this experience now through her father. The latter has obtained a nonpaying job for her in a university mental health research institute where after a few weeks of experience (after the interview) there is excitement in Donna's mind, and satisfaction with her accuracy and work skills on the part of her supervisor. A rich and possibly career-finding exploratory experience is in the making, and Donna recognizes the role which her father had in this opportunity. Would that every gifted youth had this type of opportunity and one in which the parent had participated to some degree. Donna's mother likewise entered into an enrichment experience with her daughter when Donna was in kindergarten or the first grade and when an opportunity was provided for an enriched reading experience which Donna might otherwise have missed. One of Donna's concerns at present is the "dull" life that may exist in the home when the two boys go off to college and take with them the excitement which they have always contributed to family living.

It is not easy to be the parents of gifted children. A ten-year-old boy who looks ten physically, may in reality be a fifteen- or sixteen-year-old person insofar as mental age is concerned. Misconceptions are bound to occur often. The young people who are the center of our discussion here are each among the top 1 percent of the child population in the United States and probably in the world. Fortunately these youths also had brilliant parents who are undoubtedly their children's mental equals. But what about the gifted child who comes from a family where the parents are not as intellectually superior as the child? This does happen, and it is a struggle to maintain communication and understanding of one another. What about the young person who lives in a rural community, and he or she alone in the whole school reaches this extraordinary level of accomplishment? Carl Sandburg in his book *Always the Young Strangers* expresses often the confusion that existed in his mind as he tried to rationalize his interests and capacities with a father whom he dearly loved, but who with his Swedish accent worked as a laborer in the railroad yard of Galesburg, Illinois. A gulf existed that nature produced, and that in turn caused confusion and often misunderstanding between the two.

The problem of a gulf is more pronounced, however, when the adult is not the parent, but is the teacher. While the teacher is responsible in many ways for the child and probably has an interest in children, the moral obligation for the child does not exist. Youths who do not conform or who challenge the established ways of doing things can be exploited, or at the least the blame for their behavior can be placed on "the parents" rather than on the teacher himself who fails to understand or seeks an excuse for his own failure.

It has been my experience in dealing with gifted children in school situations that one of the most helpful individuals on the faculty is often the school librarian. It does not take too long for this individual to sense, through requests made of her, that she is dealing with a student of notable intellectual capacity. Since there is no competition within the library situation, and since the librarian often can carry on with a student in a very informal manner, supporting and positive relationships can and often do develop between the two. This is a resource which gifted students soon recognize and learn to utilize to the fullest. Rarely is the corps of librarians given the recognition they deserve in the total educational process, to say nothing of their impact on the enrichment process with gifted youths.

Separate and Special

At the opening of this discussion I indicated my preference for a self-contained special class for gifted children and youth, and I indicated some reasons for this approach. As I then stated, I do not necessarily favor such an arrangement for the total school day, although logical reasons to support such a program could easily be made. I do believe, however, that a special class for gifted children by whatsoever name is more than appropriate for at least half of each school day. My reasons for this have been expressed before and by others as well, but they warrant a brief restatement at this point.

Children who are two to four standard deviations superior to others of similar chronological age are *different,* and there can be little argument to this position. To state that to have these children in the regular grade in order to motivate others is to put the responsibility for education on children when it ought to be placed squarely on the shoulders of the adults. Gifted children have responsibilities and obligations other than to motivate their classmates. This is not their role. We have stated that they are different. They are different, at least in the intellectual realm in practically every arena and on every topic that comes into the class conversation. Other pupils look to them for leadership, but that does not mean that these upper-level children need to be responsible for their less-endowed classmates. The life of the gifted child is not an easy one in the classroom. Often they are not understood by other children. They may be teased. As with Jon when he was coupled with some childhood anti-Semitism, he got into fights; something which was certainly not a generally ascribed personality characteristic of his. He found he had to stand up to others on two scores: his Jewishness and his brilliance. Children can be cruel, and particularly so when they do not understand the reason for differences. This aggressiveness frequently lessens as adolescence appears if the gifted child is relatively well adjusted. By that time prejudice on the basis of ability lessens as other children begin to recognize the inherent qualities of their classmate.

In the separate classroom the gifted children are together. They can compete with each other on more equal terms. They can learn to understand their differences, and to see themselves appropriately in comparison to their classmates who are also superior intellectually. Well-informed teachers, or sometimes parents, can lead discussions within the group dealing with their abilities and with their responsibilities as gifted youth to the school and later to society generally, and to the leadership role that in some form will eventually be thrust upon them in law, in medicine, in education, in architecture, in politics, in religion, in the arts, or in whatsoever endeavor they ultimately choose to follow as a life career. If the special class occupies only one-half of the child's daytime schedule, the balance of the day will be in appropriate activities with a heterogeneous mix of pupils of his or her own chronological age.

In this discussion I am not writing about the twelve- or thirteen-year-old boy who registers as a freshman in a major university. Such happenings are reported from time to time. This situation can be tragic, or it can be successful in the degree to which highly individualized attention is given to the child. Obviously such a youth is automatically excluded from many normal first-year university activities. These children usually are not candidates for fraternities or sororities. Rarely are they participants in either intramural sports or intercollegiate activities. I have known one who participated successfully in a university debate team. For the most part, however, socially and emotionally they are not ready for the university. Usually they live at home and attend a college or university within the community. The number of these highly gifted young people is small, statistically probably not more than 0.001 percent of the child population, and not much more than that of the gifted population itself. Jon, Marc, Donna, and others like them comprise about 1.00 to 0.05 percent of the total child population: gifted, yet at least chronologically able to participate socially and emotionally with their peers.

The Curriculum. In the separate and special self-contained class of gifted children, the curriculum can be as rich as the teacher, students, parents, and the school administration will permit or be able to conceptualize. There is no standard curriculum; there are many ideas, and these, of course depend upon the chronological age of the children involved. The basic contents of whatsoever chronological grade level the child represents will be covered by the teacher. If the child is a second grade pupil, concepts of addition and subtraction will definitely be learned. Spelling and reading will be firmly established. Gifted children often tend to be careless. From that point on, the extent to which the child is permitted to pursue academic interests is relatively limitless. The separate and special class permits exploration and enrichment beyond anything possible in a heterogeneous situation. Obviously the teacher is the keystone to the success of the total venture. Some examples, in addition to the basic skills instruction I have just mentioned, may be in order.

In one elementary school class for the gifted that was comprised of children of the third through fifth grades, reading skills had been thoroughly established. At that point all reading of standard materials was done in French. French became the second language for these pupils. Correspondence in French was established with pupils in Rouen, France, schools; ours in French, theirs in English. Pupils corrected each other's grammar and spelling and returned it. The American children wrote and performed a play in French for the whole school, a play whose actions made the experience understandable to those who did not know French. During the second year, this group visited the city of Quebec in Canada, and lived with a French-speaking family for a week. The possibilities of a second language in situations such as this are not limited. In one large community where many minority families had immigrated, gifted children studied the languages of others represented in their classes, visited their homes, ate their foods, lived together for a short time, had parents come to the class to discuss native customs, and in other ways made differences come alive and be meaningful.

In an elementary school located across the road from a community college, a combined self-contained classroom of fifth and sixth grade pupils spent three mornings a week in the community college. Here they engaged in exactly the same computer programming class as did first year college students. Furthermore, through funds available from local industries, home computer terminals were installed in each child's home permitting intraclass computer conversation, problem solving, and experimentation. Mathematics teachers from the local high school cooperated in guiding the program, and the teacher of the gifted children, already one who was interested in computers, was given a scholarship the summer before the program began in order for her to take an intensive university course in a nearby university. She has now completed a master's degree in this field. The other two half-days per week were spent by the gifted children in ascertaining that they maintained their skills in fifth or sixth grade reading, spelling, social studies, and the other things expected of their normal peers.

There is a school system in the wine-growing country of the southern tier of upper New York State counties where a group of gifted junior high school students with the cooperation of a local winery are studying intensively the wine-growing industry. They follow and participate in the program completely beginning with the development of new plants, planting, studying the soil composition, daily amounts of sun light, care of vines, general environmental conditions for this crop, harvesting, preparing the grapes, and so on through barrel storage and ultimate bottling. Some of the older pupils are involved in the business office where again the computerization of the industry is available, and where they are able to follow the product into retail stores and to the hands of buyers. The minimum (which is a poor word for this group of students) requirements in all basic junior high school classes are met, and this group of students annually stands in the top 10 percent of their respective classes in all subjects.

In a western community twelve gifted pupils of high school age spent the fall and much of the winter studying the Alaskan pipe line, which was then under construction. In late winter, in order that they could sense the severity of the conditions under which men were working, they visited Fairbanks first, and then in small planes made prearranged trips to the construction sites. Mathematics suddenly became alive. Geology and geography about which they had been reading at home took on new meaning. Each student had an opportunity to do some welding under the watchful eye of skilled workmen. Social problems of the working force who were living in isolation were discussed directly. The students who were permitted to remain at the work site for a two-night period, put on a party for the crew, both boys and girls doing the cooking. Friendships developed that were lasting for a period of time after the pupils returned. One boy with an interest in photography took 8 mm motion pictures of as much of the experience as he could afford, and upon return shared these with social studies classes throughout the community. An enriched learning experience was obviously the result of this community-school-sponsored project. Such an experience could not be repeated annually for obvious reasons, but other group activities, which while based upon the school's curriculum went far beyond it, have been planned and executed.

A final example will illustrate a different type of experience for children obtained through a half-day self-contained class. A high school teacher with a responsibility for twenty highly gifted students (average IQ 153) carried his program into the summer. The winter instructional days were spent in intense preparation for the highly individualized summer program. Basic classes required for graduation and college entrance were all achieved. In addition, however, on the basis of individual student interest, this teacher was successful in obtaining a job for each of the twenty students. One accompanied an archaeological dig in the southwestern United States; another joined a large lumbering firm in the northwest, and was engaged for ten weeks in the reforestation and ecological program. A third was apprenticed to a cardiologist and moved upon graduation into a medical program comparable to that which Marc experiences. Another pupil worked in a large law office and on the side took training as a legal aide in a local community college. One pupil, through a relative, was interested in railroad operations. He was assimilated into the office of the Canadian organization comparable to Amtrack (VIA). His buddy, hoping to devote his life to the production of educational films, was able to associate himself with a professional photographer who under contract was engaged in making a film of the history of the Canadian National Railway. And so it continued through twenty exciting and appropriate learning experiences. The teacher through funds made available from the board of education and to some extent by the cooperating businesses was paid a salary and visited each pupil one time during the summer to ascertain what was happening educationally, to determine how the winter program could be improved, and to insure that the contribution of the young people was sufficient that the cooperating businessmen would be willing to consider it for a future activity. This is enrichment. This is the adaptation of education to the nature and needs of children. This could be the way all children learn irrespective of the level of intelligence—including high-grade mentally retarded children as is so well proven by the U.S. Armed Forces Dependents School in the European Area (USDSEA). Here mentally retarded children of United States servicemen, through their dependent schools program, go, for example, to Switzerland for a period each winter, live with a Swiss family, and learn to ski while they also continue their studies. But we speak of the children at the other end of the intellectual spectrum at the moment.

It is possible to individualize instruction to the point where significant contributions are made to the lives of gifted children. These few examples illustrate some ways in which this can be done. I have mentioned the Armed Forces Dependent Schools program in the European Area. While what I am about to describe is not solely for gifted youths in those schools and certainly this example could not be replicated in many schools of the United States, the USDSEA program utilizes the countries in which the children are temporarily living and does so to the fullest. Enrichment may be somewhat easier both for pupils and parents when the history of Europe is directly at hand, and when Berlin, Paris, Copenhagen, the Rhine River, Amsterdam, and all of western Europe and the United Kingdom could become the classroom. In the European Area this program is under the direction of the United States Army; in the Pacific and Atlantic areas, by other military services.

One annual experience is significant to report. Social studies classes board a ship in the Mediterranean, and for a lengthy period of time sail around the sea with their teachers and visiting lecturers, stopping at major ports, visiting places pupils have studied, and continuing their educational experiences in classes on shipboard. How enriched an experience can one provide for students? This may be the extreme, and it is not just for gifted youth. The other examples, some of them more modest, have been conceptualized for gifted children of a community.

One wonders what the impact of such creative education might have been on Marc and Jon—brilliant, but not fully challenged by the programs offered in their schools. Every school in the nation has the capacity to challenge gifted youth to the utmost. At the least this must be done, for indeed the future of the country depends upon the development of creative leadership in every aspect of American life. When we see the difficult task of finding leaders to stand for election at the various levels of our government and the extraordinarily poor results from whatsoever efforts are made, it becomes obvious that the United States cannot be other than challenged by other countries of the world. Leadership in all fields must be developed based on the innate capacities of a small percentage of our youth. For too many years the gifted youth of this nation have not been challenged by schools, and the nation can ill afford that this resource be left to develop by chance.

References and Related Readings

Heimbeiger, M. J. *Teaching the Gifted and Talented in the Elementary Classroom.* Washington, D.C.: National Education Association, 1980.

Karnes, F. A., and Collins, E. C. *Handbook of Instructional Resources and References for Teaching the Gifted.* Boston: Allyn and Bacon, 1980.

Povey, R., ed. *Educating the Gifted Child.* New York: Harper and Row, 1980.

Roedell, W. C., Jackson, N. E., and Robinson, H. B. *Gifted Young Children.* New York: Teachers College Press, 1980.

Sellin, D. F., and Birch, J. W. *Educating Gifted and Talented Learners*. Rockville, Md.: Aspen Systems, 1980.

Tuttle, F. B., and Becker, L. A. *Program Design and Development for Gifted and Talented Students*. Washington, D.C.: National Education Association, 1980.

Ziv, A. *Counseling the Intellectually Gifted Child*. Toronto: Guidance Center, Faculty of Education, University of Toronto, 1977.

Chapter 12

Disability and Sexuality

It is disconcerting, if not tragic, that one of the most fundamental aspects of human growth and development—sexual growth—has been ignored and even denied to the disabled for so many ages by actions of physically normal individuals. There is no other single area of human life surrounded with such taboos, myths, strictures, and illogical prohibitions as that of sex. Despite all of the openness regarding sex—even pornography, communal living, gay life—it has still not alleviated the problems. Also, with the relatively easy access to contraceptives, the problem of the care of offspring could be eliminated in large measures. There are now new conditions to be considered. Sex still is couched in secrecy, fear, and guilt even in its broadest interpretations. An experience that should be immersed in joy, fun, and deep emotion is trapped in historical bigotry that at one time led to death and still is the basis of great sorrow, misunderstanding, and frustration. For disabled adults it has been worse. Until they began advocating for their own sexuality, no one else did. The clergy, as spokespersons for society, hid behind sanctimonious robes and denied this right.

Over the years I have heard dozens of sermons, many dealing with aspects of sex. "Companion at marriage" was decried. The sexual freedom of the 1960s was a shock. Coed dormitories, long a practice within most European universities, had American community clergyman and legislators up in arms. At no time did I ever hear a call, even among the Catholic hierarchy, for sexual relations within marriage for the disabled, even though such couplings might have resulted in the creation of added faithful. This is part of the hypocrisy that young people abhor. This is sexual cowardliness and blatant thoughtlessness. At the least, it is a lack of social realism.

Apparently, the issue of a sex life for the handicapped was too close to open nerves to be acknowledged. Sociologists, educators, psychologists, and the social leadership of the community generally denied the existence of a sexual need among the handicapped. Certain groups of handicapped people, it was whispered, should never be permitted the satisfaction of sexual intercourse, particularly by those with epilepsy, mental retardation, or cerebral palsy because society would surely be burdened economically by the dependent offspring that would result. In the minds of many, sexual expression and procreation are not separated.

The sexual rights of the handicapped persons have been ignored even among the intellectual leadership of developed societies: the professors and teachers, psychologists and psychiatrists, social workers and intelligent businessmen and politicians. Essentially, all leadership has remained quiet and hidden behind a Puritan ethic or an unsupported ecclesiastic dogma.

Persons in Confinement

While not in the same category as the disabled persons about whom I write, the social attitudes toward sex and sexual relations for those committed to prisons reflect society's rejection and intolerance of such a deep need. The media's reports of frequent homosexual behavior, said to be daily occurrences for both men and women as well as for young boys and girls who are incarcerated, reflect how appalled communities are by this behavior. There probably isn't a single area of human life that can create the outspoken cries of indignation as that of sex. The individual's own sexual fantasies and ensuing guilt feelings get in the way of logic, and outspoken protest is the result. I can remember during my childhood how enraged my neighbors became when a boy of six years became engaged in infrequent sex play with friends. Parents en mass held protest meetings, called the boy's father, and threatened the imposition of "federal" law on the child! What accounted for the blatant, unintelligent, and erroneous hostility illustrated in this neighborhood fiasco? There are answers, but these are often as threatening to the individual who holds them as is the overt behavior itself. It is likely that the attitude of protest is embedded in another facet. The profound nature of having offspring—its meaning to humankind—is a part of this most meaningful experience and must be protected. It is better that compassion rather than anger is a more appropriate explanation for the adult behavior I have described.

Shortly after World War II, I was invited by members of a committee of the Michigan legislature to assume a temporary position to assist in the reorganization of the Michigan Boys' Vocational School (no longer in existence), which housed some five hundred adjudged delinquent youths between the ages of twelve and eighteen years. Many of these street-wise adolescent boys were at the peak of their sexual interest and activity.

Upon arrival at the school, I found two things among many that needed attention. First, the youths were not segregated according to chronological age within the living quarters, and this resulted in diverse delinquent sexual behavior: sodomy, fellatio, group sex, and "gang bangs." On some occasions, younger boys served as the sexual slaves of the older ones. It was a miserably unhealthy situation, to say the least, with all problems essentially based on a lack of consistent information and knowledge, intensified by the limits of confinement and inadequate supervision.

Second, the so-called cottage parents, most of whom were far from being adequately prepared or selected for their jobs, frequently utilized the boys for their own sexual satisfactions. Protected by civil service and their own employee coterie, it was nearly impossible in the absence of complaints and witnesses to remove them from their positions, and they knew it. Returning to the institution late one night, I noticed a light on the third floor that had not been on earlier. I went to the light source—a "solitary confinement" cell—and found a male employee sodomizing a thirteen-year-old resident. I had no witness except the child, and no medical personnel were available on this late Sunday night to examine the youth. The employee went free for the moment, but on a similar charge a few days later with witnesses available, he was discharged on the spot and turned over to police authorities. Although I have no adequate data, I suspect that this type of behavior in these locations is still at about this level and that society in reality has been able to do very little about it.

It is not entirely this type of sexuality that I am addressing here or advocating against, though it does indicate what often happens when sexually active individuals are denied appropriate outlets and when ineffective employment and personnel policies are set in place. This is also what happens when society places such an extremely negative value on sex, yet ignores the consequences and assumes a "holier-than-thou" attitude toward any evidence of sexuality. All of the data regarding incest and teenage pregnancy also corroborate the basic point I make here, namely, there will be sex of some kind. Also there exists a "society" that persists at this level.

The teenage pregnancy issue of our society is a case in point, and those who oppose the legalization of contraception and abortion add to the social problem in a magnitude that we see in the perpetuation of social catastrophe. Who is responsible for the tragedy of the teenaged pregnancy: the adolescent couple, their parents, or the conservative social groups that prevent an honorable solution, and that thoughtlessly use the resulting pregnancy as punishment?

The protests made here and elaborated on further are written, not to minimize the psychopathic and premeditated sex crimes against which society must take a strong stand and aggressive attitude. The imposition of sexual behavior on an unwilling partner is a crime not to be condoned. In this chapter I am concerned about the reverse social crime, namely, the denial of the disabled person's right to experience fully the sexual expression of his or her choice.

Social Attitudes

Historically, society has relegated sexual behavior to the privacy of locked doors. Myths regarding the birth of children abound in otherwise enlightened families (cf. Sandburg 1952). Embarrassment often is observed in conjunction with naive verbalized sexual references of small children. Children quickly learn that sex is not to be mentioned, not even to parents. One of my students cannot recall that there was a single sexual reference made in his home all during his childhood and adolescence. Much healthier attitudes toward the physical self, initiation to adulthood, circumcision, and the physical manifestations of the sexual experience exist in so-called primitive or underdeveloped cultures. The hypocrisy, unctuousness, and sanctimony that surrounds the sexual life of human beings in the United States as voiced by pietistical church and social "leaders" is in a large sense the issue that has driven thousands of young people from the churches and toward forms of personal living characterized by realistic principles, guiltlessness, and candid truth. It has caused suicide in some youths and adults. Too many guilt-ridden people of all ages are seen in psychological clinics not to be able to recognize the unfortunate truths of these statements. In clinical practice and in counseling students, I have seen too many warped lives and threatened suicides. These have stemmed from conflicts between current sexual deportment and attitudes and the oppressive guilt-creating controls of the Catholic, Dutch Reform, Christian, and other heavily conservative religious groups that outwardly control, but that within the privacy of closed bedrooms condone almost limitless behavior.

Given such controlling attitudes toward sex for "normal" people, how much more devastating are they in relationship to those with handicaps? While the literature is full of examples, it is not necessary to go further than one's clinical practice to verify the state of affairs.

Some years ago my wife and I, in connection with an entirely different activity, entertained in our home six teenaged youths, each of whom had epilepsy. Among them was Mike, a handsome, intelligent, and appealing young man of sixteen years. Conversations ranged over many topics during those four or five days—boyfriends and girlfriends among them. On one occasion, Mike remarked that his mother would not let him ride his bike, and the thought of him driving a car or even enrolling in a driver education class provoked all sorts of acrimonious discussions at home. "You're an epileptic, Mike," reminded his mother, "and you can't do these things." Mike said that every time he would ask a girl for a date his mother would call the girl's mother and tell her he was an epileptic. "She upsets every date I have ever tried to get. How am I going to test myself with girls? I guess I'll go to a whorehouse and see if she calls there first!" Mike had actually been free of seizures for more than two years. His mother's apparent smothering of him proved to be more significant than the epilepsy per se. She allegedly stultified his normal adolescent behavior and warped his wholesome development and attitudes. As discussed in relation to the paradigm that follows, Mike's mother failed to serve in any positive degree as an external support system to Mike as he sought to move through adolescence, to deal with his legitimate sexuality, and to maintain as positive a self-concept as possible as a boy with epilepsy, which he didn't understand.

It should be made clear that sex per se and procreation are not considered synonymous. In this situation and others like these the youth is entitled to genetic counseling as well as to good sexuality education. The parents likewise obviously need assistance. I do not advocate promiscuity, but I do advocate rational approaches to one of life's most significant elements.

Consider Thomas as a second example. Tom was also a student of sixteen years who had both severe learning disabilities and social insecurities in many areas. As a nonreader, his therapist read to him on each occasion from Sol Gordon's excellent book, *You* (Gordon 1981). After an appropriate period of reading, the two would discuss what had been read, relating the content insofar as possible to Tom. Ultimately, the reading involved adolescent sexual development and specifically dealt with masturbation during one appointment. "That doesn't apply to me," related Tom. "My Dad would kick me around the block if he ever caught me doing that." "There are a lot of words and meanings for masturbation," said the counselor, "are you sure you know them?" "Yeah, I do, but maybe you should remind me." The therapist did. "Wow, does it mean all that," Tom whispered to himself.

"Tom look at me," demanded the counselor. "You trust me and I trust you. Why did you whisper to yourself just now? Do you know what these words I have just told you involve?" "Yeah, I guess so, but for gosh sake, don't tell anybody that I do." "I won't, but why are you so frightened? Shouldn't we talk about it? You can make your own decision then. I'll tell you the truth to every question you ask me."

It turned out that Tom's father had caught the youth masturbating. He told the youth that masturbation would cause learning disabilities, and that if he were caught doing it again, the father would not only tell Tom's mother, but also would carry the tale to the school teacher and to the principal. A considerable threat was embodied in bringing normal adolescent behavior to the attention of school officials because Tom attended a parochial all-boys' high school. For a youth already overwhelmed by inherent learning disabilities, the added pressure regarding his sexuality and the lack of any external support system was almost a burden too great to bear. This issue will be examined in greater detail in the following section of this chapter.

Sexual growth in all young people is spontaneous, predictable, and unavoidable. Schools, churches, parents, and other adults, for the most part, impose their own fears, misconceptions and falsehoods on a child's growth process. As a result, children and youth are caught in a vicelike grip and quandary irrespective of what they do—paralyzed by fearful parents on the one hand or ridiculed by peers when evidence of "knowledge" and "sexuality" unintentionally or inadvertently becomes apparent. The presence of a disability complicates what under the best of circumstances is often an unholy adolescent dilemma.

Sex and Life Span

In 1980, one of my former students, Dr. Lawrence J. Lewandowski, conceptualized a schema (see the figure) that is significant at this point (Lewandowski and Cruickshank 1980, 346–47). The schema and some of Lewandowski's comments regarding it follow.

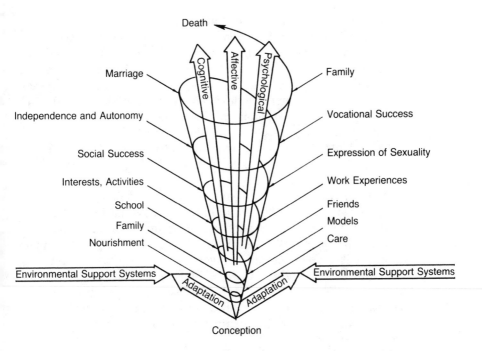

[This figure] is a hypothetical visual representation of the developmental process. Although it is a simplified schematic, it warrants some explanation. The figure is a three-dimensional cone intended to depict the development of an individual from conception to death. The outer wall of the cone serves to differentiate the organism from the rest of the environment. Within this outer wall extend three developmental lines—cognitive, affective and psychological—which represent the dimensions of the overall development. The spiral inside of the cone represents the synthesizing function of the organism throughout the development—illustrating isomorphically the autonomy and interdependency of the three developmental dimensions. Outside there are some examples of environmental support systems that are necessary in human development. The arrows pointing toward the cone signify environmental forces that are available for the individual to adapt to. The quantity and quality (strength) of these forces will have a dictatorial effect on the way a person actualizes his potential. The arrows extending from inside the cone reflect the internal forces of the individual as proportional to that person's ability to adapt to the environment. When the two arrows meet head on, this dictates equilibrium between the mutual influences of internal and external stimuli. This makes for successful adaptation and development favorable to the ego. For example, if an individual has one or more developmental lines attenuated (such as the atypical physiological development of a dwarf), is lacking support systems, or is unable to utilize the environment in an adaptive way, then such an individual will be prone to delayed or maladaptive development.

"Expression of sexuality" appears as one of the major environmental support systems in the individual, involving not just sex per se, but love, caring, economics, and all of the facets in a complete and complex relationship. While this is reflected as a single element in the figure, it is obviously interwoven with other systems involving the "Family," "Friends," "Care," "Marriage," "Independence and Autonomy," "Nourishment," and in effect probably all of the systems noted in the figure as well as others. Recognizing this, however, I choose to deal with sexuality individually and in a relatively narrow sense.

From conception to death expressions of sexuality make themselves vital forces in the lives of every human being. The "sex drive" is considered basic with many ramifications. Thus the sex drive or its absence is a force to be reckoned with and remains as such throughout the entire life span of the individual starting prebirth! There is evidence through fluoroscopic studies of pregnant women that the fetus may frequently evidence masturbatory behavior during the third trimester. If one wishes to consider these primitive, but repetitious physical efforts at self-stimulation during prenatal life as an aspect of the sex drive, then the concept of "expression of sex" as developed in Lewandowski's figure may indeed begin before birth. Masturbatory behavior is observed frequently as the infant gains coordination of the upper extremities. Depending on the attitudes of the parents toward the behavior, the child will learn early that it is a satisfying behavior appropriately employed, or that it is a behavior frought with imagined dangers and containing socially disapproved attitudes. It is hoped that the former will prevail. The issue of genetic influences versus acquired learning in the heterosexual-homosexual arguments, are, of course, not solely related to the primitive sexual explorations that are typical of infants. But certainly the emotional attitudes that are exhibited by others around such behavior serve to reinforce whatever "internal forces" may exist for the individual within the paradigm presented. The attitudes exhibited by the adults do not permit the arrows to meet "head on," and disequilibrium is the result, making unsatisfactory adaptation and development unfavorable to the developing ego, a factor that will have significance throughout the remainder of the individual's life. This is the situation for the "normal" infant; that of the disabled person is different.

When we state there there are differences insofar as the disabled infant is concerned, we must first realize that essentially the differences exist for all chronological ages within the disabled population, and, second, the differences apply primarily to those with upper-extremity disabilities. The normal individual is able to participate in sexual activities utilizing the entire body. The disabled person essentially utilizes only those portions of the body that are unaffected by the diseases (i.e., cerebral palsy, multiple sclerosis, progressive muscular dystrophy, congenital amputations of the upper extremities, and many others).

Masturbation and Disability. In masturbation, the individual learns about the way in which his or her body functions. In a marked sense the youth tests the limits of his body through masturbation, and in doing so, experiences physical satisfactions that are positive in terms of future sexual relationships involving two persons. The emotional components of sex are almost limitless. In a major degree, it is this limitless aspect of the sexual experience that makes it both so attractive and so guilt producing to people. Whereas the physically normal child or youth can explore his or her body with complete freedom because hands and fingers are physically helpful, the physically handicapped youth with upper extremity disabilities does not have this same freedom, and is helpless insofar as self is concerned. Many times, young people with cerebral palsy have asked me, as well as aides, nurses, and physicians, what it feels like to masturbate. "Why do my friends talk about it all the time—the normal ones? It must be really something!" A cerebral-palsied young man can report that he often has nocturnal emissions—"wet dreams." This not only brings expressions of disgust from his mother when it is discovered, but also is not as satisfying as he thinks it must be for his normal friends because he is not conscious when it happens, and he cannot experience what ejaculations must be like when fully awake.

Masturbation is such a normal function, practiced by such a

large percentage of boys and girls, men and women, that it is difficult to understand why it continues to receive such an odious reputation. A medical resident of the adolescent floor of a local hospital reported that he was recently asked by a fourteen-year-old patient what the word masturbation meant. Because he was too embarrassed to reply, the young physician tossed a dictionary to the boy on his next trip by the room. Later the resident was called into the room by the youth and asked what "self-pollution" meant. Curious as to the reason for the question, the boy told the resident that this was a definition the dictionary gave for masturbation. Unbelieving, the resident looked up the word and found that self-pollution was the only definitional term included for the word in question in a copy of *Webster's Collegiate Dictionary!* At this point the resident felt he had better act responsibly. He told the youth in carefully worded, honest statements, what normal masturbatory behavior really was. One of the most normal of all developmental processes in human beings is filled with so much misinformation, so many old-wives' tales, so many archaic legalisms that it is a wonder young people achieve any degree of decent mental health regarding it. The unfortunate issue is that many of them don't. Disabled youth need all the information they can get regarding their physical and sexual development, and what they receive must be accurate, explicitly stated, and developmentally appropriate. It must not be assumed from this chapter's emphasis on sex, that this is the only thing disabled young people think about. Sexual growth and activities do, however, constitute a major portion of the conversation and thought of all growing children, particularly adolescents. The disabled youth are not different. Likewise, adults need only think of the tremendous emphasis on sex, insofar as conversation, thoughts, jokes, TV, literature, movies, and actual sexual activities are concerned, to recognize its place in a total life experience. This too is not different for the disabled individual, except for the fact that thinking is not acting, and for the disabled individual not capable of having sexual relationships, thinking is too often a poor substitute for reality.

"Why did this have to happen to me," asks a boy following a waterskiing accident. He is now a lifelong quadriplegic. "What do I do for sex?" queries a "new" paraplegic teenager after a motorcycle accident. "All around me I hear my friends talking about jacking off. It must be great. But do you know how to go about it when you have no arms?" This question from a seventeen-year-old youth with double upper-extremity congenital deformities. "A prosthesis is a good thing, but not for everything!" Even a sense of humor covers up a large degree of pathos. "I wonder if gals have the same problems as guys?" asks a seriously disabled youth of his hospital resident when he and his roommate were once talking with the young physician.

Information and Misinformation. Some years ago I had the pleasure of following up on a group of children—now adults—whom I had had as pupils in some experimental programs for learning disabilities. Then seven through nine years of age, the young men were at the time of follow-up nineteen through twenty-four years old. After locating each person, a two-hour videotaped interview was held between each young man and me. These conversations covered a wide range of activities in which the young men were or had been involved after they left the clinical teaching programs. Among the topics discussed were family relationships, drug and substance abuse, sexual growth, jobs, high school experiences, automobiles, and a variety of other personal and developmental problems.

With reference to the men's sexual growth and experiences, one question, among others, pertained to the source of the individuals' sexual information. The responses generally were from "the gutter," "the locker room," "my friends," "a book my friend gave me—a dirty book," "my Dad when I was eight years old (never again)," and a variety of similar responses. Never once was consistent and logical information provided to the group.

This series of responses disturbed me—responses from a group of young men whom I had known as children and whose backgrounds were so filled with failure experiences that certainly within this vital area of human life, if in no other, they needed accuracy and positive points of view. I decided to look into the matter further.

As it happens, I often speak to groups of teachers and other professionals about the problems of those with learning disabilities. During the course of a two-day workshop I usually arrange to have six to eight people brought into the program with whom I can demonstrate certain diagnostic procedures. These adolescents are usually between the ages of thirteen and nineteen years. With appropriate permission, I have recently arranged to meet with the young people, both boys and girls, prior to the actual demonstration. In private and in confidence, I have asked them to explore much sexual information with me, I usually have another adult present.

Two lists of words were given orally to each student: one a list of sexual terms that are accurate scientific words; the other, a list of similar terms but related to slang and "the gutter." Each word was read out loud to the group, with each person indicating his or her knowledge of the term with a plus or a minus sign. The youth was then asked to write its meaning using any spelling or symbol or synonym the person wanted in order to convey the meaning to me. The list of terms of a scientific nature included the following:

1. penis
2. vagina
3. sexual intercourse
4. masturbate
5. nocturnal emission
6. sperm
7. ova or ovum
8. clitoris
9. womb
10. cervix
11. placenta
12. climax
13. birth control techniques
14. the Pill
15. breasts
16. scrotum
17. testicles

The list of slang terms included the following:

1. cock
2. dick
3. prick
4. cunt
5. screw
6. fuck
7. wet dreams
8. jerk or jack off
9. clit
10. afterbirth
11. knock up
12. rubber
13. boobs
14. balls
15. nuts
16. laid
17. make out
18. sleep together

The results of this informal survey of sexually relevant information on the part of adolescents with learning disabilities are not encouraging. Eighty-nine youths took part (eighty boys and nine girls). No attempt to analyze the data by sex was made. With a group of this size, 1,513 responses to scientific terms were possible. Eighty-seven percent of the responses were either wrong or answered as "I don't know." Of this latter percentage, answers were in addition given, but 63 percent were wrong. The general information that learning disabled adolescents have regarding sex information presented in socially acceptable ways is disappointingly poor and inefficient. Knowing that they do not have the proper vocabulary, some of the youths told us they didn't ever ask adults questions about sex because they were embarrassed that they didn't know "the right words." The opposite side of the picture is even more discouraging.

In the second aspect of this task, the reader will recall that young people were asked to respond to other words meaning the same thing or to define (with their own brand of spelling) sexually oriented slang words. Again, eighty-nine youths participated, but this time, each responded to eighteen terms. A total of 1,602 responses was received. Only 6 percent were wrong or "don't know"; 94 percent of the words had a correct response (by correct is meant another slang synonym or a correctly defined, if incorrectly spelled, response). A correct response might be, "Cock, the thing you put in a cunt, I think." The word most often unknown was "afterbirth."

It is obvious from these informal data that these learning disabled adolescents have a very poor basis for understanding one of the most significant aspects of their adult lives, an aspect of human living that in the minds of most adolescents is synonymous with adulthood. All of these eighty-nine pupils were in junior and senior high schools located in relatively large middle-class communities. Not one of them was a student in a human biology or sex education class. Their lack of language skills kept them out of the biology classes and may have been the reason for their absence from sex education programs. In some few instances, they were not participants because of religious reasons or parental concern.

Like social dancing, driving a car, or getting a job, sex—both narrowly perceived and broadly defined—is equated in the minds of youth with adult status. If most of their information regarding this important area of life is coming from friends, locker room talk or behavior, or pornographic literature, how indeed can those youth with learning disabilities be provided with success experiences that will carry them into adult living with healthy assurance and security? There obviously are exceptions to the examples illustrated here. It is assumed, however, that the experiences reported are very typical of those held by the great majority of learning disabled young people, if not the majority of all disabled youths. A final note is important, it appears to me, insofar as this group of eighty-nine adolescents is concerned. Fifty-three of the young people reported they had already had sexual relations: two of eleven thirteen-year-old boys; four of the nine girls; and all of the sixteen- through nineteen-year-old group (thirty-four boys). Three of the boys were involved in repeated street-oriented homosexual experiences for which they all received money. A large percentage of the children, already in jeopardy insofar as general social and educational achievements are concerned, are likewise in need of sound information regarding facts and practice in what many consider to be the central core of human life. That they do not have this information constitutes another significant aspect of a life failure experience. Trial and error behavior, the basic operational mode in many aspects of the life of the learning disabled child, is accentuated in the sexual aspect of their life. They want to be adults; they do not have the needed information to be such; they operate as they think adults do; they make mistakes. Although it is a guess at best, three of the boys in the above-mentioned group of adolescents "think" that they are fathers. I have no corroboration of this volunteered information, and the question was never asked of the entire group.

The Physically Handicapped. In another chapter I have written of the sexual rights of mentally retarded persons. The sexual sophistication of learning disabled pupils is a matter of considerable difference when compared with physically handicapped youth and adults. The individuals who are either blind or deaf in no way experience the limitations to their sexual life as do those with orthopedic or neurological handicaps. Although the former groups, often living in residential schools for the blind, are reputed to engage in homosexual activities in greater frequency than other adolescents, no well-developed studies have been conducted on these issues. Thus, it must be assumed that the issue is no greater than that reported in residential schools for normal youth and possibly is less.

For the orthopedically and neurologically handicapped individuals, however, there are many more significant problems due to the nature of their physical limitations. Sex acts in any form require physical activity, generally of the total body. Under almost any circumstances the physically handicapped are limited in their movement, particularly those with severe forms of disabilities such as those affecting the neurological system, amputations, and in particular, pelvic and lower extremity disabilities.

Sex and Realism

This chapter has not been intended to shock; it is a chapter intended to face realistically an aspect of life in which the physically handicapped individual is also sexually handicapped. The handicapped are not asexual. The sexual limitations that the individual experiences are real. The need for sexual release is often paramount; the need for experimentation in the young person is as great as with any physically normal adolescent. The failure to be able to consummate sexual acts leaves the individual frustrated and often extremely angry. I discussed earlier in the chapter the limitations of masturbation for individuals with upper extremity handicaps. The issue is more significant for those with lower extremity disabilities, particularly neurological problems, when the complete sex act is attempted. Often with this latter group, males can have neither erections nor ejaculations.

Among my friends in the psychology and psychiatry fields, and within my own professional experience with handicapped persons, numerous avenues are reported and are followed to permit the individuals to experience at least semisatisfactory sexual lives. Obviously, because human sexuality is such a private aspect of one's life, attempts are first made to handle the issue on an individual basis or, at most, on the basis of a joint physical activity between a man and a woman or between two members of the same sex depending on individual choices. There is, however, the frequent situation where it is physically impossible for an individual to masturbate. Some courageous parents or close friends have provided this service to their sons, daughters, or close friends without entering into the emotional aspects of sexuality or sexual relationships. They have simply brought the handicapped individual to a state of climax and have provided temporary relief. This and other arrangements I will mention take courage on the part of both persons, but it is possible.

A young physically handicapped man of twenty-two, who was sexually active for several years before a motorcycle accident, frequently employs a prostitute to have sexual relations with him. A similar arrangement is provided to a young man by his parents, who leave the house for a weekend when these arrangements are made. Still a third situation involves a couple, both of whom are physically handicapped, and both needing assistance to complete the sex act. The couple is left alone for a period of presexual activity, and when they are ready for the final phase of sexuality, a very close male friend who has been waiting in another room comes into the bedroom to assist the two people in completing the coupling. The friend actually inserts the penis into the vagina and helps to establish a satisfactory rhythm (cf. Lewandowski and Cruickshank 1980, 363–68). Mechanical devices for both men and women have been devised that, although requiring the assistance of a second person, provide autostimulation, which has proven to be a satisfaction to some handicapped persons. The number of inventive solutions to this highly personal activity is just about as great as there are physically handicapped adults who need repetitive sexual outlets. The tragedy of this is the need of assistance in order to complete what is normally considered to be the essence of privacy. Sex has both its public and private aspects for normal individuals, as well as for those with severe disabilities. However, the final physical act of human sexuality is normally a private experience. To have to share such privacy with even the closest of friends places sexuality in a different type of arena and imposes public knowledge of an individual's behavior on something that should have the value of privacy. It may be helpful to point out that few sex therapists are prepared to help out in these matters. The greatest source of help is an individual, man or woman, in whom the disabled person(s) feels complete trust and confidence, and in whom there is a recognized level of high personal confidentiality and acceptance.

I have made a number of points in this brief discussion of a very significant aspect of life. First, all handicapped people have a right to have sexual relationships, the nature of which is of their own choosing (i.e., heterosexual or homosexual). Sexual testing of oneself is important and significant to marriage and lifelong experiences. Who, in the absence of experience, is wise enough to think that two can enter into the complications of marriage as virgins? And why in the face of modern psychology and psychiatry is virginity valued in such a hollow and hypocritical manner? The answers to these two questions will undoubtedly place this book on the Index. Regardless, mental health, logic, and personal freedom in our society recommend sexual freedom that does not impose responsibilities by others onto those who wish to engage in them. For the handicapped, this is at the very least as significant an aspect of personal growth and development as any other. Sex in marriage implies responsibility. Sex out of marriage by two responsible young people—physically normal or handicapped, involves pleasure, the testing of oneself and a partner. Testing of self and exploration ultimately lead to mate finding and satisfactions in life. While what I say here may be considered anticlerical, it is psychologically healthy. Normative sexual growth needs the sponsorship of healthy parents and professionals, and through these efforts, provides healthy growth and increases "in wisdom and stature" to young people who earnestly seek information and experience significant to their development.

References and Related Readings

Gordon, S. *Living Fully: A Guide for Young People with a Handicap, Their Parents, Their Teachers, and Professionals.* New York: John Day, 1975.

———. *You.* 2d ed. New York: Quadrangle Press/New York Times, 1981.

Heslinga, K. *I Am Not Made of Stone: The Sexual Problems of Handicapped People.* Springfield, Ill.: Thomas, 1974.

Johnson, W. *Sex Education and Counseling of Special Groups: The Mentally and Physically Handicapped, Ill, and Elderly.* Springfield, Ill.: Thomas, 1974.

Kempton, W. *Guideline for Planning a Training Course on the Subject of Human Sexuality and the Retarded.* Philadelphia: Planned Parenthood Association of Southern Pennsylvania, 1973.

———. *Sex Education for Persons with Disabilities That Hinder Learning: A Teacher's Guide.* North Scituate, Mass.: Duxbury Press, 1975.

Lewandowski, L. J., and Cruickshank, W. M. "Psychological Development of Crippled Children and Youth." In *Psychology of Exceptional Children and Youth,* 3d ed., ed. W. M. Cruickshank, pp. 363–68. Englewood Cliffs, N.J.: Prentice-Hall, 1980.

Robmault, I. P. *Sex, Society, and the Disabled: A Developmental Inquiry into Roles, Reactions, and Responsibilities.* New York: Harper and Row, 1978.

Sandburg, Carl. *Always the Young Strangers.* New York: Harcourt, Brace, and Co., 1952.

Chapter 13

Students: The Reason for It All

As I stated in the preface of this book, students have had a tremendous influence on my thinking throughout my career, and I hope I have had a similar influence on theirs. I am always appalled when I hear faculty members say that the university would be a great place to work if it were not for student interruptions. Without students, the university would be a meaningless place. There certainly would not be any need for professors; who would they teach?

It appears that negative comments about students are repeated by those who are not in the applied field of learning. As an undergraduate, I can remember a professor of Greek who stimulated my curiosity endlessly, beyond anything she realized at the time. In her class, Xenophon did more than march us around the Mediterranean Sea; he and others marched straight into my mind in strange symbols and with new and challenging ideas. Professors I have had as both an undergraduate and graduate student have influenced my thinking, practice, and life experiences.

I have no idea how many undergraduates I have taught. In more than four decades of teaching, I suspect that number runs well over ten thousand. There have been times when I have been able to dip into the undergraduate crowd, syphon off a brilliant young mind, proselytize it, and turn that individual in the direction of special education. Dr. William Meyers, presently of the University of Texas-Austin, is a good example of this. While he did not earn his doctoral degree with me, Bill was influenced as an undergraduate to pursue a career in special education. Dr. Joseph Cunningham of Vanderbilt University began his graduate work in special education at the University of Illinois after he had many very informal conversations with me during his undergraduate years at Syracuse University. There are many others.

Former Syracuse University Chancellor Dr. William P. Tolley used to caution his faculty against recognizing individuals during a banquet for fear of omitting someone significant. He then proceeded to do exactly that and identify many, and I suppose, omitted many as well. I will follow his example in this section and leave out a large number of names in this recital—a large number of students who have taken their places in positions of professional responsibility throughout the world. I shall limit my comments essentially to doctoral students, with whom a faculty member has an opportunity for a much greater in-depth relationship over the period of four to five years that the graduate student will study. This group consists of nearly one hundred and fifty carefully selected individuals, most of whom have become very successful in their chosen fields. I shall not follow all of them here.

During my career I have chosen to seek out graduate students rather than merely accepting those who applied to study with me. With few exceptions, I do not rely on pencil and paper applications from unknown individuals. I prefer to have a student in a class or two, become acquainted with him or her, make judgments regarding abilities and personality, and then suggest to the student that I would be pleased to serve as an advisor if desired. Only twice in my career have I ever regretted having a student study with me, and other than these two I have never been embarrassed recommending my doctoral students to others for employment.

In recruiting doctoral students, my colleagues and I have, at times, invited the individual to visit the university, to live at our homes, and then to go through a series of interviews as rigorous as if we were screening a faculty member. This procedure has had good results, and I recommend it highly. In fact, I have made more mistakes in faculty employment than in the selection of doctoral students.

My first doctoral student was Dr. Jane Dolphin-Courtney (Syracuse University). She is a brilliant individual. Her dissertation, replicating with intellectually normal cerebral-palsied children the earlier work of Strauss and Werner on exogenous mentally retarded subjects, was significant and resulted in several publications. Her work also supported and expanded my own career interests. Here, once again, is an example of a student having a powerful impact on a professor. Now the head of an important school in Florida for physically handicapped children, Dr. Dolphin-Courtney has made significant contributions to the field for many years and also has raised a family.

I recall her doctoral oral examination, for it was my first as well. Without question, I was as nervous as she as I stood in the presence of my faculty peers showing what I, as a new young professor, had produced. She passed, and apparently, so did I.

For some reason, women doctoral students have not been as

plentiful as men. Edith Romano (Syracuse), Elfreda Sprague (Syracuse), Mary Marshall Grube (Michigan), and Mollie Romer-Whitten (Michigan) were some. Dr. Jean Hebeler (Syracuse) of the University of Maryland has made a significant reputation for herself and has enhanced mine in the process. Her work has been outstanding as a professor, a department chairperson, and as an official for the national Council for Exceptional Children. Once more, a student challenged a professor and made him grow. Her dissertation dealing with the structure of family attitudes toward mentally retarded children, employed such a volume of statistical procedures that the advisor had to run to keep up. But isn't this the function of a graduate school; students teaching faculty members and professors teaching students?

Dr. Judith Weiner (Michigan), by now a member of the faculty at two Ontario universities, is a more recent doctoral graduate whose dissertation subject expanded my thinking in the direction of social adjustment of children with learning disabilities. There are other outstanding students with whom I have been associated. Ellen Quart-Montgomery (Michigan), brilliant and a hard worker, discovered a heretofore unsuspected relationship between learning disabilities and Reye's syndrome, which is being pursued on a postdoctoral basis.

Graduate students have been found in unusual places. Three such individuals, who have equaled or outshown their professor, are: Dr. Norris G. Haring (Syracuse), University of Washington; Dr. James L. Paul (Syracuse), University of North Carolina; and Dr. Daniel P. Hallahan (Michigan), University of Virginia. Haring was discovered operating a mimeograph machine during a national conference in Omaha, Nebraska. Portions of his published doctoral dissertation (1957) still are often requested. Paul was eating breakfast alone in a hotel, again at a national conference, and appeared in need of a doctoral advisor! Fortunately for the two of us, immediate diagnostic decisions are easy to come by when one has dealt with hundreds of students! Hallahan came to my attention as a graduate student working in the Institute for the Study of Mental Retardation and Related Disabilities at the University of Michigan. He was ultimately persuaded to pursue a career in learning disabilities. Hallahan is a strong individual who didn't always buy his professor's teachings, yet continues to earn the latter's respect. How long that will last is unknown to me, but meanwhile in Virginia, he has helped build one of the most outstanding special education preparation centers in the United States. These three individuals have had a significant impact on my life.

The Lutz Street Gang of Ann Arbor was another facet of graduate learning and professional concerns. How these four disreputable individuals merged together to form a wonderful quartet of doctoral students is beyond me. Yet Dr. Lawrence Lewandowski, now of Syracuse University; Dr. Terry Goldberg, of the National Institutes of Health; Dr. Jeffery Stone, in clinical practice in New York City; and Dr. Douglas Buyer, a school psychologist on Long Island; became a big part of both my wife's and my life in a variety of ways. With this crew we lived through beards, long hair, home-cooked dinners, baseball and basketball games, sprained ankles, girlfriends and marriage, children, and often their families. Professors need to enter into the lives of students in order to be of real service to them. In this case, the four have had a lasting influence on our lives. It is my belief that a professor-student relationship is only as good as the capacity of one to vicariously become a part of the other. This can often be accomplished, and with these four, very completely. Lewandowski, his wife, children, family, and their families have had a particularly close relationship with us, including several jointly authored publications.

Matthew J. Trippe (Syracuse), now retired from the University of Michigan, has made a significant contribution, or series of contributions, in the fields of the emotionally disturbed child, in the area of human sexuality for the disabled, and in the field of cerebral palsy, which was the subject of his dissertation. Other Syracuse doctorates, included Howard Norris, now of Queens University; Harry Novak of Rhode Island State University; and Merville Shaw of Chico State University in California.

Sometimes professors make mistakes, and they should rue that day. Such was the case with one student, a longtime head of an education program for exceptional children. Accepted as a doctoral candidate, and studying part-time, usually in the summers, he was confronted by university regulations that I felt he could not and should not attempt to circumnavigate. He persisted, however, in effect saying to me: "Let me at least try to prove you wrong." He did and has performed at a very high professional level and made several significant contributions to the public domain. I only feel fortunate that he disregarded my advice. The best admission policy standards and quality assessment by a graduate faculty advisor are often wrong. For these reasons, I have subsequently become very cautious

244 / Disputable Decisions in Special Education

not to make the same recommendations ever again. Students have a way, when they are motivated, of overcoming the seemingly greatest financial, family, and university hurdles in order to accomplish their goals. This student typifies the observation; he taught me an important lesson.

There are others, of course, who have contributed vitally to my professional life. Among them are Dr. Steven Russell (Michigan) of Bowling Green State University; Dr. Michael Eastman (Michigan), now of California, whose work in human sexuality and the disabled will one day be nationally recognized; Dr. Charles McNelly, a quiet, self-effacing faculty member formerly at the University of Maryland; Dr. Paul Gerber, an important faculty member and associate dean at the University of New Orleans; Dr. Donald Blodgett, now of the U.S. Department of Education, who, while Director of Special Education for the city of Milwaukee, produced an outstanding public school program; and Dr. Andrew Shotick of the University of Georgia.

Then there were those who were the students of faculty colleagues yet crept into my life in many ways. Dr. John Junkala of Boston College was at one time a vital colleague when we worked together on a curriculum development program for the Armed Forces Dependent Schools in the European Area. Dr. A. J. Pappanikou of the University of Connecticut was another Syracuse student who has made significant contributions through his teaching and writing.

I do not think that all universities should attempt to be all things in special education. We practiced this philosophy at Syracuse University, often loaning faculty members to other universities until the latter formalized their own special direction. Many times we received students officially enrolled at other schools that could not provide a complete curriculum for the student. This was true of Dr. Jack Cawley of the University of Connecticut now of the University of New Orleans. He was sent to us for most of his special education preparation. This is also true, for somewhat the same reasons, of Dr. Alec Peck now an associate dean of Boston College and then a student of Pennsylvania State University. Each of these people in his own way has enriched my life and has provided new horizons for my professional experience.

There are others, not always my students, whom I have helped. In the future, watch for Herrn Dr. Gunther Opp, who was a graduate student at the University of Munich in the Republic of West Germany. I was impressed with him at a Kephart Memorial Seminar in Aspen, Colorado, some time ago. I was privileged to be on the doctoral committee of Dr. Francisco Alberto Chueca y Mora (Frank Hewett) while a visiting professor at the University of California, Los Angeles. Alberto, a professor now at the University of Deusto, Bilbao, Spain, is one to watch as in the years ahead he, with Ministry of Education and university support, molds a strong teacher education program for his country.

Dr. Lester Baker (Michigan) will one day make his contribution to the knowledge of the young adolescent. Other Michigan doctorates with whom I shared direction of their dissertation research as a cochairman included Steven Timmermans (with W. C. Morse), Terry Braciszeski (with Clement Johnson), Frances Berg (with W. C. Morse), and Jackson Roush (with Charles Tait). Each of these faculty members has a reputation on the Michigan campus of being as deeply involved with their students as I usually am, and this is much to their credit.

And so it goes—a chain of professor-student relationships that began with Socrates, or earlier, highlighted by Mark Hopkins on one end of the log and a student on the other, by Mark Van Doren, by the Trappist monk Thomas Merton, and hundreds of other significant scholars who have invested deeply in students. For Picasso, it is said, bullfights were the link between his life and students in France and in Spain. For concerned faculty, students are the link between the abstract concepts of the university and the human equation of the broad community.

I believe that the number of student advisees a faculty member has at one time should be very limited. I once declined a deanship at a major university when I discovered that several faculty members had as many as forty doctoral students at one time. At Syracuse University in the Division of Special Education and Rehabilitation, we urged faculty members never to accept more than five doctoral students simultaneously and only four if one were at the dissertation-completion stage. Only in this manner can quality and humaneness be insured.

In students one can find a reflection of one's own ego. I do not apologize at all for bragging about past and present students who have been and are a part of my professional responsibility. *Professional* and *responsibility* are, I am sure, the key words. Heaven help the student who has fallen into the hands of a disinterested faculty member. The latter can make life miserable for the student, though at times unintentionally. One of the characteristics of a good university employment policy is being able to assess a potential faculty member's warmth and wholesomeness in his relationships with students. I cannot understand how university faculty members, including researchers, have the gall to accept an appointment if they plan to isolate themselves from students, place publishing as a higher priority than guiding and counseling students, refuse to answer telephone calls, and even behave sadistically toward students. Referring again to W. P. Tolley's statement, "a university is a farm for growing people," meaning the total university population of students, I see this particularly in a relationship that, when permitted, is engendered between a graduate student and his advisor. Anything less than this concept is unworthy on the part of the faculty member. Conversely, no faculty member should smother a student with guidance and advice. Students must practice the art of finding themselves. At the same time, the student must be related to a behavioral model that permits him or her to function in the future as a wise professor or in other positive ways to further the careers of those who are still younger. The chain continues to unwind and advance.

There are good professors who are well qualified and concerned about their students, and there are poor professors, who are more interested in writing and expanding their own careers than the primary goal of a university—perpetuating the brilliance of the student population. Within the academic community these two groups of professor-colleagues become known rather quickly. When I think of professors who have shown a great concern for their students, an economics professor at the University of Michigan comes to mind. This faculty member has held the highest responsibilities in the United States government, in addition to holding a number of ambassadorships. He has represented his government abroad not so much for his ability as a politician, but for his skills as an economist. Yet each semester, this remarkable professor teaches at least one undergraduate course because, in his own words, "I enjoy young minds and ones which are not solidified in a given point of view—mine or others." Graduate students flock to his courses, even though they are geared toward undergraduates.

In my opinion, an academic advisor's responsibility is to direct students into the classes of able faculty members, while steering students away from professors who show little interest in students. How can one make these judgments? Obviously, one can make errors, but over the years, I have found that by lunching with a new faculty acquaintance, I can learn of his or her interests, appraise his or her personality, and learn of joint ventures undertaken with or involving students. This practice provides a relatively accurate forum in which to make judgments. These appraisals can later be verified in more traditional ways to the end that an advisor can eventually make appropriate recommendations to a student. I am concerned when I overhear a student in a cafeteria line remarking to a friend that he or she has averaged only one good professor per semester. What makes it worse is that the student or his or her parents are paying from three to six thousand dollars for that semester. No one would tolerate such a poor performance record when purchasing an automobile. We switch to foreign imports. Tenure may be valuable to faculty members, but it is a criminal offense, I believe, to reward faculty members who are unable to fulfill their primary reason for being in a university or a college. Tenure is too easy to come by, and thus mediocrity is protected too often.

Once upon a time, I asked a graduate student to peruse all of the university school and college catalogs to identify courses he felt would have a relationship to the field of special education. He listed many courses from the schools of law, medicine, dentistry, liberal arts, social work and, of course, from departments such as psychology and related social sciences. Once completed, I visited every faculty member on the list (it took about one year) to ascertain whether "our" students would be welcome in the professor's classes, and at the same time to make a quick appraisal of the faculty member's characteristics. This approach provided for advanced students a good library of courses as cognates with their major field of emphasis, and also provided some background on the faculty member for students and advisors. It was a successful expenditure of time.

Just as important as advising students into precandidacy courses is assisting a student in the selection of both his doctoral dissertation and oral examination committee members. The dissertation should largely represent the culmination of the student's academic performance to that date. The oral examination should provide the student the opportunity to demonstrate his understanding of his topic and research methodology, the contributions of related literature to his field of study, and his ability to respond quickly to questions asked by examination committee members.

It is dastardly when a committee is composed of some members who are angry with one another, and who use the time to air their professional barbs and problems. In these instances, the student acts as a synapse through which is funneled output appropriate to one antagonist, but inappropriate to another. The student can only be the loser in these situations. Fortunately, only once in my professional career have I experienced such an oral examination, and this was on the road to developing into a battle between two faculty members with the student caught in the middle. As the student's advisor, I suspended the examination until the dean of the graduate school could appear and assume the role of chairman, arbiter, and protector of a capable student's reputation.

I am strongly in favor of informal doctoral examinations. The student is the most knowledgeable person in the room, insofar as the topic under consideration is concerned. He should be given every opportunity to demonstrate his competence. During an ideal examination, coffee flows from pot to cup, and as it nears completion, glasses of sherry are served. The student should receive everything necessary to relax in what, in spite of precautions, can be a very tense situation. In examination situations, it is easy to see why I am very concerned not only about the professional competence exhibited by committee members, but also about their personality characteristics and the respect and cordiality they show toward a young person who is about to become a professional colleague.

I believe in standards of graduate student performance. I also believe that once a student has been accepted, the advisor has a major responsibility to see that the most and the best is siphoned out of the university to the student's benefit. There is no place in this protocol for mediocrity—only the best that can be offered.

I pride myself on being well acquainted with some students. It is, of course, nearly impossible to become close friends with all in a large class of undergraduates, and some do not wish individual attention. However, there are academic tricks available to bring the professor and student into a close working relationship. Taking one or two students to lunch on a weekly basis not only provides the opportunity for an informal social experience, but also eases the budgets of some. The swimming pool is a barrier-free climate for an informal get together. During these times, it is surprising how personal histories unfold and tales come forth that have meaning for guidance, counseling, academic advisement, and the foundation for long-term friendships. Regardless, such occasions can create a bridge between student and professor; the ancient gulf often difficult to overcome in other settings begins to fade, and often completely evaporates. The entire student-professor relationship created in the 1960s and 1970s is radically different from earlier years.

No longer are professors the hallowed beings they once were. Now the professor must prove himself, and his humaneness is measured along with his knowledge. It is by far a better arrangement. Students and professors start out as equals. When this does not happen, it is the professor who is generally the responsible party.

In a very large class of students, I often find myself lecturing to one or two persons. These young people become my focus, and whether they like or not, their attention is directed to me and what I say. During the course of the semester, I can often become well acquainted with these few students without forgetting the rest of the class. I have never apologized for having a teacher's pet; as a matter of fact, many positive results can grow from such a relationship. Lecturing to a group of nameless faces, perhaps arranged alphabetically, is depressing. It is exciting to see students respond to something that has been said, and then to spend the next sixty minutes drawing them out, making them think, causing them to reconsider their position, even if in error, and then ultimately permitting them to draw the pieces of the puzzle together in a meaningful and appropriate manner. At times, these foci students have literally left the class session with a bad case of perspiration, but they have learned. And student and professor have learned to respect one another.

Like many professors, small graduate seminars give me the greatest satisfaction. Recently, the epitome was reached when I had an advanced graduate seminar scheduled consisting of five brilliant young men and women. While each possessed extraordinary intelligence, I realized after a few weeks that one among them was extremely remarkable. Everything this young man did was perfect. His insight into human nature, human psychopathology, and human interrelationships was beyond anything I had experienced in my teaching career. This person was truly brilliant. Because of him, my own teaching improved. Because of him, the standards of the group were raised, the discussions were richer, and new standards of vocabulary were appropriately articulated. This man contributed to the lives of everyone in the class, including the professor. This is the manner in which graduate education should be experienced.

Sometimes I wonder if the overly personalized approach I take toward students is not a definite reaction to my own extraordinarily unhappy high school experiences. Some of my students who have been closest to me have heard this story, so it will not be a new piece in the mysterious mosaic known as their professor. One was a student to whom I felt very close, but with whom I apparently misjudged our relationship. I had misjudged what I thought he perceived in me. He put it this way:

Inside the Wind

it is strong at times, but gentle too;
it touches the lives of me and you.
constant in its need to flow;
it changes the course of things that grow.

it warms, it cools, to different tastes;
it never but a minute wastes.
and by its actions change is wrought;
but no one knows what it is like on the inside.

it works by will for the good of man;
it serves its nature as best it can.
despite its purpose, confusion prevails;
what is it really? what do we hail?
and no one knows what it is like on the inside.

it's like a man, a man like he;
concealed to others, his essence be.
they talk, they jest, they voice a whim;
the wind is it, and it is him,
but no one knows what it is like on the inside.

That poem is a compliment, although it illustrates to me that while the student was sharing, the professor was apparently guarding. To form a solid relationship, there must be equally significant crosscurrents of information flowing one from the other at a relatively equal pace. But let us return to the unholy situation that surrounded my early education, and which probably prompted me later to listen more carefully to my students.

I cannot remember succeeding at anything in my elementary or high school years. I learned consistency from a French teacher, but not success in French. I learned chaos in geometry and no respect for the teacher. I learned an appreciation for some English literature, but without sufficient understanding to earn a grade that brought applause from anyone. I learned gross laziness from a homeroom teacher whose weight caused him to move as slowly as he thought. Latin was a nightmare of irregular verbs, subjunctive tenses, and meaningless phrases, although in later years a professor of Greek straightened out my perspectives and gave meaning to a catastrophic earlier experience. High school years (those of elementary education form a meaningless blur of disappointments) coincided with the depth of the depression of the 1930s, and thus were marked by the coarse deprivations of loss of homes, bank accounts, automobiles, father's job, friends, and other things that should give luster to adolescent years. It is not much fun, regardless of the motivation, to come home one day and find a "Christmas Basket" on the table in the kitchen. At times, food would be plentiful, but somehow tasted poorly, and my parents facial expressions were different than in other years. The whole dinner wasn't really ours.

I left high school a month before graduation. I would have graduated with the poorest records in the class, I suspect, but I couldn't face that possibility. It would have been so artificial. I left home and began working for the Civilian Conservation Corps (CCC). Here, nobody knew me and thus I could begin the process of finding myself in a new setting that was so different from what I had become accustomed that comparisons cannot be made. Thirty years later many such young people were called flower children, which perhaps explains why it was so easy for me to understand the sixties generation of youngsters without goals. In the CCC, I grew up physically, emotionally, and socially, but not intellectually.

Up to that point, school teachers had had a disastrous effect on me. I felt as though I was destined to be a failure, and the horror of it all consisted of the small community where I lived and where everyone knew everyone else. In my mind I was certain to be voted the least likely to succeed, and I even went so far as to keep my picture out of the class yearbook. It is a tragedy when adolescents must go through life without having anyone with whom to share, discuss, and objectivize discouragements.

Time passed. The CCC was a success insofar as my morale was concerned. A friend from the CCC took me hunting, and I shot my first rifle. Prohibition was lifted, and I drank my first beer. I fought forest fires until I was certain I could never breathe again—but I accomplished something. The girls of the rural vicinity went out of their way to see that the young men of the CCC, isolated from their families, found solace and relief. Time passed, but what did the future hold?

In Henrik Ibsen's epic poem-play *Brand* (ca. 1865) (Meyer 1967, chap. 9) there is a poem excerpt and fragment that is almost autobiographical for me. It is startlingly accurate, and expresses the confusion which I felt as a youth.

When I was a boy, I remember,
Two thoughts kept occuring to me, and made me laugh.
An owl frightened by darkness, and a fish
Afraid of water. Why did I think of them?
Because I felt, dimly, the difference
Between what is and what should be; between
Having to endure and finding one's burden
Unendurable.

Every man is such an owl and such a fish, created
To work in darkness, to live in the deep;
Any yet he is afraid. He splashes
In anguish toward the shore, stares at the bright
Vault of heaven, and screams: "Give me air
And the blaze of day!"

College had always been an objective held up to me, but no college would accept one with as disastrous a record as mine. Thank goodness for the depression. Some colleges needed students and also were affordable. I was admitted to the Michigan State Normal College—on probation. It was inexpensive, and I found an elderly lady who needed a houseboy in return for a room. Thus, my life needs were met.

But then the specter of old teachers and their sadistic behavior flashed through me. Panic ensued. After all, teachers were teachers—they were all alike. I had known nothing different, or at least I had never been taught to differentiate between the good and the poor, the selfish and the helpful. I couldn't differentiate between the caring teachers and those who manipulated pupils for their own professional ends. I was afraid that I would find the same in college. From my third grade teacher, Miss Guskit, to Miss Taylor, my high school algebra teacher, they were all the same in my evaluation. Even my kindergarten teacher, Miss Brown, was the same. She never smiled, she always wore the same jumper colored after her name, she always had her charges sitting for hours each day in desks that had chairs screwed into the floor. What does a fourth grade boy tell his parents when a physical education teacher literally rips the only shirt he has off his back during an activity which was not understood by one-fifth of the class. How are children supposed to develop positive attitudes toward teachers?

During my first term in college, I registered in freshman rhetoric, because it was required. Rumors about this course abounded; a weekly theme essay was demanded, the professor was a female fury. I had barely passed my high school English courses, my spelling was lousy, and I didn't know the difference between a comma and a semicolon, and now. . . .

But on the first day of class, a beautifully dressed lady of gracious gait, wearing an absolutely magnificent piece of fine silver jewelry, moved into the room. This was no comparison with the Mildred McGinnis of high school days. The lady spoke, welcomed us to her "group," and promised us she would do her best to make this subject become significant to our lives. She would do "her best." What did she expect from me—one who had never done his best for anyone and doubted he knew the meaning of "best?"

The days passed, Mondays, Wednesdays, and Fridays at 9 A.M. No miracles took place except that I anticipated attending that class and her entrance into the room. For Maude Hagle wore a different piece of tasteful and valuable jewelry every day. She was the sister-in-law of the president of the University of Michigan, and it was obvious that she had traveled widely. I was entranced; I had never been further from home than working for the CCC in the Upper Peninsula of Michigan. I moved my seat closer to the professor to see her jewelry better. But my rhetoric papers did not improve. My morale was veering toward another low.

One day as I was leaving class, Miss Hagle called me back. We passed the time of day, and then she sprang it! "I notice you enjoy my jewelry," she said.

"Yes, but I didn't think it was so obvious. My family is 'in art' a bit, and we have always been taught to appreciate it."

"Would you like to see my collection," asked the sixty-year-old English teacher of the discouraged eighteen-year-old student, "and perhaps to have a bit of supper with me?"

"Wow, of course."

"Tonight at 7 P.M. sharp."

I left the classroom in a state of euphoria. It was the first time a teacher had even spoken to me with genuine interest.

I cannot recall what dinner consisted of that evening, for conversation was constantly directed toward me. "What do you like to read, to think, to do?" "What do you believe?" "What are you really?" "Do you have friends?" "Are you happy?" What an analytical evening, because some of the gently asked questions had never been asked of me before. The excitement of the evening, the concern for an older person of one at least thirty years a junior, was not unlike the experience that Martin Arrowsmith had on his first real visit with his mentor, Professor Max Gottleib, in the latter's laboratory at the fabled "Winnemac University" (Lewis 1924).

"We need to talk some other time," she said, "but now let's look at the jewelry." She beckoned me to follow her to another room where thin-drawered cases stood along one wall. "Open any drawer you wish." I did and gasped, for there before me was an array of beautiful pieces comparable to items found in the finest jewelry store in the land. From that point on we talked about metals, stones, designs, and beauty until the evening had long since passed. Then she said, "Go through the drawers again, and pick out two pieces—any you wish. Take them home and write a theme about them—how they were made, what the artist was thinking when he conceptualized these pieces, and your evaluation of their artistic worth."

I carefully selected two pieces and put them in my pocket, not thinking of their intrinsic worth until later when I stuck them under the pillow for the night. I dreamt that night of two things—that someone had sensed my needs and also had trusted me with valuable things. The next day I wrote a theme on the jewelry. I returned the pieces with many thanks, and I waited.

A week later in class, Miss Hagle began to read a selection of themes as was her habit. All of a sudden, I heard something familiar; she was reading my essay. She never announced the author's name, but she did give the paper a splendid critique. At the close of her remarks she said to the class that she had made some effort with this paper and had contacted the student's high school English teachers, and then had independently assigned an A grade to the paper. An A grade! The first I had ever received, but not the last. Her concern had become contagious, and I proceeded to flourish academically.

That experience taught me more than any other event in my eighteen-year-old life. I learned what real teaching meant. I learned what an interested teacher could do with a student. I gained self-confidence, and I knew what my future obligations to students would be if I ever were fortunate enough to have any. I learned to hold up my head, and to know that accomplishment was within my grasp if I wished to make the effort. In a thousand ways since, I have tried to emulate that evening I spent with Miss Hagle, which was marked by an interested professor seeking to motivate a young person who had little faith in himself. A thin thread runs between academic failure and a straight-A record. How can the former be eliminated in higher education factories which are the present academic mode? Students need the best of a college or university faculty and not a stream of teaching assistants or teaching fellows who are often too immature to sense basic needs of students and their undiscovered potentials. Every professor should teach at least one group of undergraduate students each year.

During my college years, I had some good and great professors, but they were still the minority. I learned to discriminate and generally learned to select good teachers. The great educational sociologist, Newton T. Edwards at the University of Chicago, guided me through my master's thesis. His colleagues in administration, professors Floyd Reeves and William C. Reavis, laid the foundations for my career as an administrator. Professor Franklin Bobbitt taught me the meaning of the "good life." Mandel Sherman, a psychiatrist ahead of his time, unraveled mental quirks and made them personally challenging. At Chicago's Michael Reese Hospital, Dr. Samuel A. Beck made Rorschach's *Psychodiagnostics* become more than meaningful. At Michigan Howard McClusky, Arthur Moehlman, Raleigh Schorling, William Clark Trow, Irving Anderson, Clifford Woody, each in his own way, set standards of scholarship seldom seen in today's university. The School of Education then was a respected academic entity. In the Medical School I learned about hearing from Albert Furstenburg, later the dean; from Raymond Waggoner, chairman of psychiatry; from F. Bruce Fralich in ophthalmology; Edward Kahn in neurology; and from Carl E. Badgley in orthopedics. In psychology I learned from scholars such as John F. Shepherd (and his white rats), Norman Maier, and Donald Marquis. They were among those who helped me lay a strong foundation in the broad field of human psychology. For a year, Martha Colby taught a difficult, but extraordinarily complete course in the area of human genetic psychology. While I excelled in those things that motivated me, graduate school was never an easy experience. I never learned how to study in high school. I had to learn that as I went along, and the trial and error technique was not always the most satisfactory. As I watch students in the libraries today underlining every significant word with their yellow felt pens, I wonder if that is the method that provides the key to learning. I also wonder if the author of the text would underline the same words as the students.

The negatives and positives of my educational experiences often remind me that many of my students have not always found learning an easy task. It is not their lack of ability that accounts for this. One must look deeper into their elementary and secondary school years and into relationships they had with their teachers at that time. We must also look into the nature and quality of their first years of college or university instruction. In addition, what pressures were placed on the students by their parents or relatives who perhaps demanded academic success when students lacked motivation?

The concept of "readiness to learn" is very significant, even on the graduate level. It is second only to the chronological age at which learning starts. In America, there seems to be a big hurry to enroll children in school at age five or earlier. I am impressed, not by the quality of South American education, but by the fact that for the most part school entrance takes place at the seventh chronological year. Physiologically and psychologically speaking, many, if not all children, are not ready for the confusion and trauma surrounding school at age five or earlier. How many unprepared children are pushed from kindergarten to first grade? Some of my colleagues and my children have over the years made much over the fact that I "failed" kindergarten. In view of the subsequent tragedies that marred my schooling, that was probably the best thing that ever happened to me. As I talk with university students in academic trouble, they begin their stories, as I have, with the difficulty they had in their early school years and often apologize for what to them appears as absurd, if not as inconsequential. It is not inconsequential, and I believe we would have better scholars at the university level if their educational initiation had followed the South American plan insofar as the age of entrance is concerned. Such a revolution, however, would upset thousands of afternoon bridge parties, for the players have waited seemingly forever to enroll their children in school! Perhaps better bridge players in future generations could be a product of later school entrance. There is significance in the concept of school readiness; the arbitrary selection of the fifth chronological year is not related to the significance of the issue.

The unique roles of students and teachers at whatsoever level of education are delicate and significant to a point beyond words. The United States in particular is a country of educational fads. To list them would forever be incomplete, for the number is legion: Progressive Education of the 1930s remains today; traditional education based upon textbooks and rigid unbending standards; the basics; the project method; the contract method; Education for Life and Living; return to basics, and much more. What does America stand for in terms of education? Certainly what we observe among young people since the early 1960s is not something of which to be proud. It is always surprising to me when some students escape the mediocrity of public education, educate themselves, and take significant places in society. What these few have achieved is the national birthright of every child in America, but such an achievement is far short of such a goal.

Students are the essential ingredient in my life and have been for more than four decades. They are the warp and woof of the national fabric. For national political leaders to cut back on funds aimed at insuring the legitimate development of minds and the elements allowing the intellectual expansion of our country's population, is to be politically shortsighted in the worst degree. When one sees the horrendous misappropriation of funds for what some have named "Mickey Mouse" research under the provisions of Public Law 88-164, one fears for the future of federally funded projects in the field of special education and rehabilitation. If anything can be characterized as "inconsequential," certainly the vast amount of so-called research publicized through various professional journals between 1960 and the present can be considered deficient. In the United States we do not have a national policy on either research or education. There are advantages one can list promoting the concept of local control of education, but unevenness is the result of such a policy. Variations in standards of pupil achievement, selecting and appointing teachers, in curricula and in a variety of other educational mile posts are in evidence everywhere. We give lip service to the importance of education, but when the chips are down, education loses out, and the children suffer most. Examples? The repeated failures of millage elections in local communities, federal administrative cutbacks in scholarship and student loan programs and services to the handicapped, arbitrary decisions regarding curriculum, the attempts of the Moral Majority and other interest groups to ignore the Constitution to insert "creation science" into the curricula of Arkansas and Louisiana public schools, misconceptions regarding educational testing, placement, and labeling—all of these examples are an attack on quality education and ultimately, on individuals themselves. If one ignores the fight against educationally related issues (i.e., substance abuse, alcohol, teenage sex, and related twentieth-century youth phenomena), and focuses on only the strictly educational aspects of public education, there would be years of effort that could be expended appropriately on the achievement of quality. The "nonschool" issues I have mentioned are also important. Some of these—not all—would be at least partially nullified by quality teaching staffs, a strong curriculum, and a solid teaching methodology. The end result of a program of national education is, after all, a well-prepared and educated young person. We do not need any more of the near educational tragedies that we have experienced ourselves.

References and Related Readings

Lewis, Sinclair. *Arrowsmith*. New York: Harcourt, Brace, Jovanovich, 1924.

Meyer, M. *Ibsen*. Garden City, N.Y.: Doubleday, 1967.

Chapter 14

Coda

In music the coda is a concluding section that is quite formally distinct from the main portions of the composition. Among contemporary writers, Catherine Drinker Bowen stands foremost in my opinion. Her penetrating biographies of Justice Oliver Wendell Holmes, of John Adams, and of Tchaikovsky are gems in biographical literature. Biographies of the brothers Rubinstein and Sir Edward Coke, Chief Justice of the King's Bench, are literary plums of high quality. Her volume, *Adventures of a Biographer* (Bowen 1946), is a delicate pause in the clatter of the writings of modern novelists and others whose grammar and sentences often are beyond the ability of one to diagram. Bowen has also written *The Portrait of a Family* (Bowen 1970)—her family—and therein I was surprised as I reluctantly came to the last pages to find a chapter titled "Coda." This is her idea, not mine, but I think it is a good one. It provides the author an opportunity to more or less catch his breath, and to look back over what he has written. Does the book reflect what the Preface said would happen? I think this one does. In writing I have been happy, angry, aggressive, critical, complimentary, and a variety of other emotions that hopefully helped to get my points across. I have tried to deal with issues that I feel are absolutely basic and germane to quality education and preparation for life of handicapped boys and girls, men and women.

Writing an article or a book is a pleasant experience. Some people paint in oils or watercolors; others compose music and play musical instruments. Some are professionals; others do these things for personal enjoyment. Some of my friends are choreographers or themselves participate in ballet; others are athletes. Some raise grapes and make wines; some find enjoyment in listening to music, watching plays and ballets. I like to create a book or an article. I have never painted or composed, but when the manuscript for a book or article is finished, I have a feeling that must be something akin to the artist's. It is a feeling of satisfaction that one has created something that may have a value to others. Books are not the result of an overnight decision to write. Catherine Drinker Bowen sometimes did as much as six years of research in libraries and travel to other countries before she was ready to put the first words on paper.

The essays within this cover have been on my mind for many years. The cruelty I received from a teacher when I was a child has never left my mind, although the incident was sixty some years ago. This prompted some comments in the chapter on individual differences. My experiences with a professor of English and her collection of valuable jewelry took place more than fifty years ago, but I promised myself that one day I would write about it, for to me it and other similar outreachings from a professor to a student is the essence of teaching and the essence of leadership. Better than a hundred counseling sessions, when a professor enters into the life of a student and lives are changed. Perhaps the issue that had the least amount of time to boil and bubble in my mind is that of noncategorical education. That term is recent, but from the moment I first heard it I became angry at whoever invented it, for it abrogates so much of what we really believe in special education. It constitutes a put-down.

The chapter on fear, guilt, and rejection started forming in my mind during World War II when, working in a neuropsychiatric general hospital in Europe, I was confronted with weeping teenaged soldiers who were frightened and who had deserted their units, who were confused from brain injuries received in accidents or from shrapnel, and who felt guilty that they might never be able to play the role of a man in their homes again. These men are not far removed from the teenager who suffers from a motorcycle accident, or a cerebral-palsied child who sees his mother grimace every time she picks him up. He is heavy as a ten-year-old boy. Guilt, fear, and rejection. Ideas and experiences grow, formulate, and rumble until they are released. Writing them down in book form such as happened here, stops the foment, and peace temporarily ensues. What will come next? Something will, for the creation of a single painting is usually followed by a second. Was it not Vivaldi who composed over six hundred concertos? I have no intention of composing six hundred books or even one-sixth that number. But while nothing is in sight as I bring this Coda to an end, something will develop in the near future, and start again to foment and take form as another piece of writing. There is time left for this, I hope.

I hope that this book does not leave the reader with the feeling that I am bitter. I am bitter at the mediocrity and incompetence I see in special education and rehabilitation, in psychology and medicine, indeed in all of the human services professions where a minority of persons leave a very sour taste.

A medical student told me a wonderful story that would apply to more than one professional discipline and helps minimize any bitterness I might have. Three psychiatrists were concerned about a patient who wanted to be called Jesus Christ. The student's query to the psychiatrists was "Why do you worry about him calling himself Jesus Christ, when each of you knows that you are God?"

There are many things that discourage me, but not to the point of bitterness. Professors who hold tenure, who are possessed of national reputations somehow gained, yet do no writing or research and essentially avoid students are a large part of my concern. But these and other disappointments are negated by so many remarkable experiences that bitterness regarding the topics on which I have written here is essentially minimized and controlled. When I think of Jeff and Tracy, now in their thirties, and recall because of learning disabilities the terrible hurdles they overcame to attain good social adjustment, I am excited. I remember when there were reported only eight blind teachers working with sighted children in public schools of this nation. I recall the first independent steps of an eighteen-year-old cerebral-palsied girl. I recall the marriage of two paraplegic students. I remember a cerebral-palsied woman as she received her Ph.D. degree. I am daily conscious of students who come to seek advice and in their way let me know I have a great responsibility. I think of a student from Purdue University who told his fraternity brothers that his best friend from the University of Michigan from which he had transferred was a professor. What an obligation, and how can one be bitter in these circumstances?

These are miniscule elements, however, within the midst of huge unsolved problems of special education, rehabilitation, speech pathology, medicine in all its branches, and psychology that must be faced head on and solved. Until every child who is exceptional in some way is effectively helped towards normalcy, and until every potentially disabled fetus is made normal there can be no relaxation. The contents of this book reflect too often selfishness in the minds of men in the twentieth century, and this still clings as an albatross around the necks of the disabled persons—sometimes even of the gifted. Would that by the year 2000 A.D. we could put this all behind us and replace it with the original spirit of the United Nations to eliminate the wars that create additional disabled young men and women and civilians. Let there be no more

Beiruts, Northern Irelands, Falklands, Latin Americas, Grenadas, Afghanistans, or other human-made errors on a large scale. These energies can be put to the end of salvaging hurt bodies and minds and preventing future personal catastrophies. We should be bitter toward selfishness and purposeless wars and diseases and inborn errors that maim. We have no reason to be bitter toward the problems we describe here; we have reason to be bitter toward those who ignore or perpetuate them.

References and Related Readings

Bowen, C. D. *Adventures of a Biographer*. Boston: Little, Brown, 1946.
————. *Portrait of a Family*. Boston: Atlantic, Little, Brown, 1970.

Index